To all those who have lost their lives at sea

BRIDGE RESOURCE MANAGEMENT

From the Costa Concordia
to Navigation in the Digital Age

Antonio Di Lieto

Inspired by the work of
Kari Larjo, Hans Hederström, Ravi Nijjer,
Benny Pettersson, Sven Gyldén and Peter Listrup

Editing and interviews by Roberta Giaconi

Published by Hydeas Pty Ltd
Brisbane QLD - Australia
First Edition 2015
(with minor corrections made in April 2015)

English translation by Lyndon Wilson and Antonio Di Lieto

ISBN 978-0-9942672-0-7

CONTENTS

INTRODUCTION

On 13th January 2012 at 9:45pm, the cruise ship Costa Concordia hit the rocks off the Island of Giglio at a speed of 14 knots. A tear in the hull caused the progressive flooding of five watertight compartments and irreversibly compromised the vessel's stability and survival. Within just a few hours the ship lay to rest on the seabed off the small Tuscan island in a semi-submerged state.

The accident cost the lives of 32 people and has left a legacy in its wake that may change the course of an entire industry.

How could such a modern ship complying with all main safety regulations be vulnerable to a series of "normal" human errors?

What can be learned from the events of that night?

What are the possible improvements to navigation techniques that could mitigate the risks associated with ever-increasing ship dimensions and ever-decreasing safety margins?

What are the principles that allow for an effective integration between human element and new technology on a ship's bridge?

And once possible operational solutions have been identified, what are the organisational and regulatory changes needed in order to implement them?

This book attempts to provide answers to these questions in three separate parts. The first will deal with a systemic analysis of the events and conditions regarding the Costa Concordia accident. From understanding the critical points highlighted in the systemic analysis, the second part will attempt to give an outline of concepts that will be useful in preventing navigational accidents. In particular we will propose a new concept of *"Bridge Resource Management"* (BRM) based on the potential and limitations of both human and technical resources available on a ship's bridge. For this purpose we will trace BRM history, from the reasons for its inception – the challenging conditions of the Baltic Sea – to its application, which is usually a far cry from its original intentions. In fact, considering BRM only as a series of

2

behavioural practices that improve teamwork is a myth that needs to be quashed.

Finally, in the third part we will tackle the organisational and regulatory conditions that are necessary to implement BRM.

Overall this book is meant to bridge the gap between academic knowledge and the practice of navigation. All too often theoretical concepts remain inert due to the difficulty in applying them to the constraints of operational contexts. This is why all three parts contain accounts from some of the experts that have spearheaded progress over the last few decades. Collecting these testimonies meant travelling to all four corners of the globe. In particular we went to interview the octogenarian Finnish Captain Kari Larjo to whom we are all greatly indebted.

PART I   COSTA CONCORDIA

The first part of this book aims to analyse Costa Concordia's navigation, from the port of Civitavecchia up to the moment when it hits the rocks off the Island of Giglio. The management of the emergency resulting from the flooding of five watertight compartments and the abandoning of the ship have been purposefully omitted from the analysis.

The first chapter will present and trace facts from the ship's black box data without any subsequent interpretations.

In the second chapter we will analyse the events by looking at the errors committed on the bridge together with the criticalities at organisational level (the cruise company *Costa Crociere*) and at regulatory level (the *International Maritime Organization*).

The central theme of the third chapter will concern the human condition of the accident's key players. Interviews conducted at the birthplace of the Costa Concordia's Captain during the summer of 2012, as well as the history behind the boom of the cruise industry will give us an idea of the cultural context these characters belong to.

4

13th JANUARY 2012

In Harbour at Civitavecchia

"**H**ave a look to see what speed we need to get out of here and approach Giglio... we've got to sail past this f***ing Giglio... right, let's chart the route then..."

"Is half a mile OK Captain? There's [enough] depth of water [there]."

It is 18:27 on 13th January 2012. The Captain of the Costa Concordia[1] is talking with his Second Officer. They are planning to sail past the Island of Giglio by deviating from the planned route to Savona (figure I–1).

figure I–1 : Planned route from Civitavecchia to Savona and the deviation taken on 13-01-2012

The week before, the maître d'hôtel on board had made a special request to the Captain. "Given that I'm due to sign off, I would be grateful if you could pass by Giglio for a sail past"[2], he said.

The Captain had refused due to adverse weather conditions and postponed it until the next cruise. For this reason when the maître reminds him of his promise on the afternoon of 13th January, the Captain keeps his word. He agrees to meet on the bridge after dinner and gives instructions to plan the deviation.

---

1 With its 114.000 Gross Tons, 13 decks, 290 metres length, 35 metres beam width and 8 metres of draft, the Costa Concordia was the largest Italian cruise ship ever built on its launch in 2006.

2 Court of Grosseto (2012). Captain's Interrogation Report - 17/01/2012 (p.6).

As a result, half an hour from departure, the Second Officer begins working on an alternative route using both traditional paper charts[3] and the *Electronic Chart System (ECS)*[4].

"We can't go through... we'll have to go around", he says to the Officer of the Watch referring to a nature reserve situated to the north-west of the island of Giannutri.

The intention to avoid the nature reserve can be seen clearly by the planned route which is illustrated over the next few pages from figure I–2 to figure I–6.

The original route (302°) that passed along the Promontory of Argentario is changed with a deviation that points straight at the Island of Giglio (278°). Along with this deviation, the plan includes a turn of 56 degrees to reach a course that runs parallel to the island (334°), with a minimum distance from its furthermost rocks – known as *Le Scole* – of around half a nautical mile and a Turn Radius of one nautical mile.

After about a quarter of an hour the Second Officer calls his colleague to show him the new route. This route change however is not communicated either to the Coast Guard or to *Costa Crociere*.

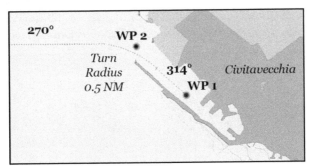

figure I–2: Planned route in Civitavecchia harbour waters

3 Chart n.6 Italian Hydrographic Office (*Istituto Idrografico della Marina* - IIM). "From Argentario Promontory to Capo Linaro", scale 1:100.000 updated to the Notice To Marines 11.7/59.

4 Sam Electronics Chartpilot 1100, with unofficial electronic vector charts (Jeppesen C-MAP Professional).

6

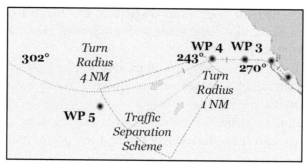

figure I–3 : Planned route through the Traffic Separation Scheme

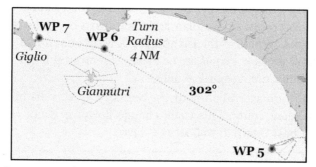

figure I–4 : Planned route around Giannutri nature reserve

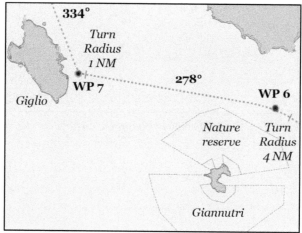

figure I–5 : Planned deviation towards the Island of Giglio

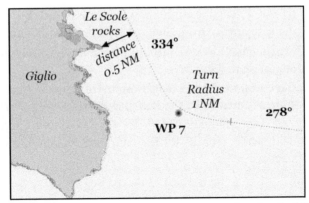

figure I–6 : Planned approach and sail past to the Island of Giglio

The planning for the final turn (figure I–7) is shown on nautical chart IIM n.6 (scale 1:100.000)[5]. Differently from the route planned on the Electronic Chart System, the Turn Radius is not plotted on this chart either as a curved track (given the chart scale) or as a waypoint note.

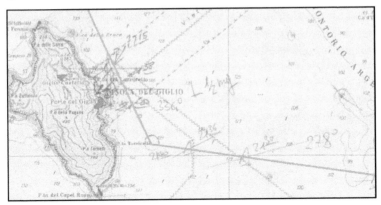

figure I–7 : Final turn planned on paper chart IIM n.6

It is now 18:45 and the departure from Civitavecchia is imminent. The pilot is already on board and weather conditions are optimum, with smooth seas, clear skies and a light south-easterly breeze.

---

[5] Image taken from the presentation of the Marine Casualties Investigative Body (Italian Ministry of Infrastructures and Transports) at the 90th meeting of IMO's Maritime Safety Committee (London, 18th May 2012).

8

According to the judicial examination commissioned by the Court of Grosseto[6], upon its departure from Civitavecchia the Costa Concordia:

- has all main certificates required by current legislation and they are all valid and up to date;
- has radio equipment and navigation instruments in line with current legislation, as certified by the *Passenger Ship Safety Certificate*;
- meets all requirements listed in the *Minimum Safe Manning Document* with regard to the number of its crew and their qualifications.

---

6 Grosseto (Tuscany) is the closest city to the Island of Giglio. The judicial examination we refer to is the Technical Report compiled by consultants appointed by the Court of Grosseto (2012). Pages 33-41.

The Voyage Towards the Island of Giglio

The Costa Concordia casts off the berth at 18:57. The Captain performs the manoeuvre and at 19:09, as soon as the ship clears the breakwaters of Civitavecchia harbour, the pilot disembarks. Two minutes later the Second Officer answers the bridge telephone. It is the officer on watch in the Engine Control Room who asks about the use of the stabilizing fins:

"Right then, the fins... At what time shall we put them out?"

"Nineteen twelve, thank you."

"OK, thank you."

In the meantime the ship approaches the Traffic Separation Scheme in hand steering, as confirmed by the judicial examination commissioned by the Court of Grosseto and from navigation data recorded by the black box, known as *Voyage Data Recorder (VDR)*. The actual turn performed by the Captain is different to the one planned, so that the distance from the original route (*Cross Track Distance* - XTD) exceeds the *Track Limit*[7] set on the *Integrated Navigation System* (INS). The Cross Track Distance reaches a maximum of 240 metres during the turn. The VDR shows that the Track Limit was set at 100 metres, however the audible off-track alarm was deactivated and would remain so for the rest of the voyage. The *Speed Over Ground (SOG)* is 11.6 knots, the *Heading (HDG)* is 268.6°, and the *Course Over Ground (COG)* is 274° (figure I–8).

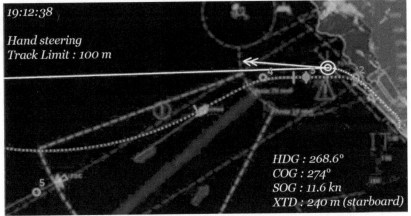

figure I–8 : Turn performed while leaving the port of Civitavecchia

7 The Track Limit is a parameter that is set as a threshold and defines the maximum Cross Track Distance a ship can deviate from the planned route before an off-track alarm is activated.

It is now 19:13.

"Two five five, Sir", says the Helmsman in English.

"Two five five, very good. Professor has the conn", replies the Captain in English as well. "Professor" is the nickname the Captain uses for the Officer of the Watch, who in this instance is the one that was consulted by the Second Officer regarding the planning of the deviation towards Giglio.

Once free from navigating, the Captain is approached by the Second Officer who wishes to show him the new routes planned before departure.

"Captain, here we are abeam of Giannutri... a nature reserve... let's go a little further... and then the course at half a mile."

"The course where?"

"Here."

"Here?"

"Here, north of Giannutri."

"Ah, OK... now I see."

Using the VHF radio, the deck Cadet calls Civitavecchia Harbour Control at 19:16. "Compamare Civitavecchia, Costa Concordia", he says.

"Go ahead."

"I would like to communicate our data: passengers aboard three thousand two hundred and eight... three thousand two hundred and eight... crew aboard one thousand and twenty three... one thousand and twenty three. Our port of arrival Savona, tomorrow at zero seven twelve... zero seven twelve."

"Yes... say again..."

"Passengers on board: three thousand two hundred and eight... three thousand two hundred and eight. Crew: one thousand and twenty three. Port of arrival: Savona. ETA[8]: tomorrow zero seven twelve, zero seven twelve."

"Roger, thank you."

At 19:18, five minutes after having taken the conn from the Captain, the Officer of the Watch engages the *Track Control System* (TCS)[9] in *Heading mode*. This system allows automatic control of Heading and Turn Radius set by the operator. Upon activation the Heading is 245.4°, Speed Over Ground is 16.1 knots and Turn Radius is set to four nautical miles (figure I–9).

---

8 ETA - Estimated Time of Arrival

9 Sam Electronics Trackpilot 1100.

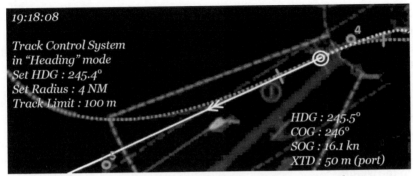

figure I–9 : Passing from manual steering to Track Control System

At 19:20, at a distance of 20 metres from the planned course, the ship reaches the *Wheel Over Point* (WOP) for the next turn. However the Officer of the Watch only initiates the turn three minutes later by gradually varying the Heading set on the *Track Control System* and maintaining the Turn Radius at four nautical miles.

As a result of the delay in turning, at 19:25 the ship again moves beyond the established 100 metre Track Limit. A few minutes later this distance reaches 150 metres and the off-track indication is still visible on the screen. The Officer of the Watch then decides to tighten the turn by inserting a final Heading of 304° and by reducing the Turn Radius to three nautical miles. The distance from the planned route reaches its maximum of 410 metres at 19:31 with a Speed Over Ground of 16.7 knots and a turning radius of 2.5 nautical miles (figure I–10). From that moment on the distance slowly reduces and the officer brings the ship towards the planned route, back within the 100 metre Track Limit.

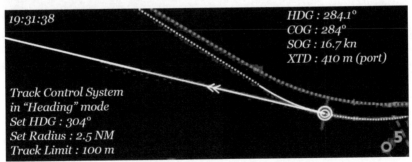

figure I–10 : Turn performed outbound from the Traffic Separation Scheme

During the final phase of the turn at 19:33, the Officer of the Watch changes the Track Control System mode from Heading to Course. This allows automatic control of the ship's heading with compensation for winds and currents in order to reach or maintain the Course Over Ground desired. At the turn's completion (figure I–11) the Officer of the Watch brings the ship back within the limits of the planned route and – at 19:45 – the off-track indication disappears from the Integrated Navigation System screens.

At 19:40, before leaving the bridge the Captain asks the Officer of the Watch the time of arrival at the Island of Giglio.

"Twenty one thirty five Captain", is the reply. Upon which the Captain requests to be informed when the ship is at "more or less five or six miles" from the island.

At 19:51 the Track Control System's mode is changed from Course to Track. In this way the ship is autonomously kept within the Track Limit by the system which controls position in relation to the planned route (turns included).

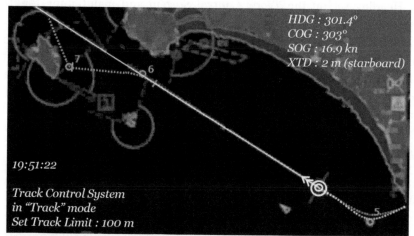

figure I–11 : Ship within the limits of the planned route off the island of Giannutri

At 20:00 the First Officer arrives on the bridge to relieve his colleague and take over duties as Officer of the Watch until midnight.

"Everything alright?"

"Everything's fine."

"You're going to do a fantastic coastal route [the Second Officer refers to the sail past along the Island of Giglio - Ed.]."

For the next few minutes the conversation moves to evaluations of staff until the First Officer begins the handover. He requests confirmation of ETA and reads the logbook notes written by the Officer of the Watch, who at this point reminds him to call the Captain six miles from Giglio.

"We should arrive at Giglio at twenty one thirty five. Apart from that you're at one hundred and three, one hundred and three [referring to shaft revolutions per minute - Ed.]."

In the meantime the other members of the incoming watch arrive on the bridge:

- the Third Officer who assumes the role of Junior Officer of the Watch;
- a seaman with the role of lookout when the Track Control System is activated and helmsman during hand steering;
- another deck officer who was scheduled to take over the First Officer's position once the ship reached Savona;
- a deck cadet.

At 20:04 the Captain returns to the bridge in search of his mobile phone. Once arrived, he jokes with the First Officer and gives another reminder to call him five miles from Giglio. Immediately after this the First Officer calls the Engineering Officer of the Watch on the telephone and they talk in Neapolitan dialect.

"...Hi, I'm taking two RPMs starboard and two RPMs port from you [referring to shaft revolutions per minute - Ed.]."

"Two RPMs? You'll put me in critical RPMs..."

"Then should I just take from starboard? ...because the Captain wants to arrive at Giglio at a quarter to ten..."

"Oh yeah? If you take from the port side you'll put me in critical RPMs... you can go with ninety eight, a hundred and three, or you can have ninety eight to port."

"Just a second... ninety eight to port..."

"You've reduced too much... ok... ninety six... increase just a little... ok... leave it like that... another little bit."

"Another little bit?"

"Increase just a touch."

"How's that?"

"...Ninety six... increase a tiny bit... ninety nine... reduce by one slowly... ok, just a sec."

"How is it (set)? ...ninety eight to port... ninety eight to starboard..."

"Starboard can remain as it is or you can reduce a little bit more..."

"Alright, that way I can regulate, for a quarter to ten... only to starboard, ok?"

"Ok."

It's now 20:20 and the ship is around 12 nautical miles from the island of Giannutri. Its Speed Over Ground is 16.4 knots, Course Over Ground is 302° and the Track Control System is set to *track mode*. Cross Track Distances remain within the Track Limits until 21:35 (when the Track Control System is switched off and the Captain assumes manual control of navigation).

At 21:00 the Costa Concordia is around four nautical miles from Giannutri and the wind blows from the North East at 15 knots.

With the Track Control System in Track mode, the route towards the Island of Giglio is controlled automatically with a Turn Radius of four nautical miles and a Speed Over Ground of 16 knots. The system follows the planned turn accurately, putting the ship right on course (278°) for Giglio. Upon the turn's completion at 21:07, the maximum Cross Track Distance reached is 37 metres (figure I–12).

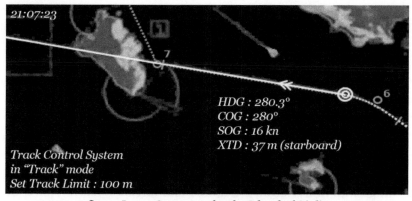

figure I–12 : On course for the Island of Giglio

At 21:10, approximately eight nautical miles from Giglio, the maître and the Hotel Director arrive on the bridge and they both greet the First Officer with a *"buonasera"*. He then asks if they have seen the Captain, to which they reply that they have not.

At 21:17 the First Officer calls the Helmsman and orders him to "standby the wheel" in English.

Officers and guests present on the bridge talk to each other exclusively in Italian, except when communicating with the Indonesian Helmsman, who can understand only conning orders in English and does not speak any Italian.

At 21:19, six nautical miles from Giglio, the First Officer calls the Captain using the bridge telephone.

"Captain... six miles."

"Six miles, six miles, ok, alright, ok."

"We are almost abeam of Giglio... at twenty one forty four."

"We are almost abeam of Giglio... fine, ok... thanks."

Immediately afterwards the First Officer calls the Engineering Officer of the Watch using the same telephone.

"...I'm reducing the engine RPMs, ok? Then we'll increase again later, only because we have to sail close to the Island of Giglio now..."

"...Ok, a moment ago you decreased to starboard, right?"

"Ah... yes, now I'm reducing..."

"I see you've evened out [the RPMs - Ed.]... right ok, right."

"Reduce to port?"

"No, now you can reduce evenly."

"Ah, ok."

"You're outside of critical RPMs, bye."

After hanging up the First Officer continues the discussion for a few moments with his relief who confirms the RPMs set:

"...Ninety to port... ninety five to starboard..."

"ninety five to starboard?"

"...and ninety to port."

"So how much now? Ninety to port?"

"Yes, ninety to port."

"How much now?" the First Officer asks again after a slight adjustment of the telegraphs' position, which is carried out by the officer at his side.

"Ninety five to starboard."

"And the port side?"

"Ninety."

"Alright."

After another adjustment of the telegraphs the other officer confirms:

"...Ninety three to starboard, ninety six to port ..."

It is 21:21 and, after the reduction requested by the First Officer, the Speed Over Ground falls slightly to 15.5 knots. At 21:23 the First Officer activates the depth data view of the electronic chart and changes the Track Control System mode from Track to Heading. As well as the set Heading, the Integrated Navigation System also displays the data regarding the next turn: Heading 333.6° and Turn Radius of one nautical mile.

These changes occur at five nautical miles from the Island of Giglio with a Speed Over Ground of 15.5 knots and a distance from the planned route of two metres (figure I–13). There is a north-easterly wind, blowing at a speed of around 10 knots.

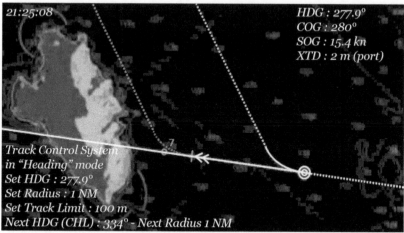

figure I–13 : Change in Track Control System's mode and speed reduction

During the next few minutes both the maître and the Hotel Director receive separate calls on their mobile telephones.

At 21:34 the Captain arrives and greets everyone on the bridge. The ship is now 2.5 nautical miles from the Island of Giglio with a Speed Over Ground of 15.5 knots, 50 metres from the planned route. The Track Control System is in Heading mode with a set Heading of 279° and a Turning Radius of 3.7 nautical miles (figure I–14).

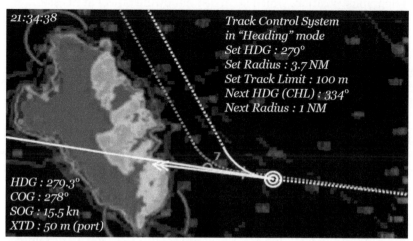

figure I–14 : Captain is on the bridge at 2.5 NM from the Island of Giglio

The Captain calls the First Officer by name and asks him:

"What's the situation? What's our current speed?"

"Fifteen and a half", is the reply.

At this moment the time is 21:35:01.

"Hand steering", orders the Captain in Italian.

"Hand steering", repeats the First Officer in Italian, who then gives a Heading order to the Helmsman in English: "Two seven eight."

"Two seven eight", replies the Helmsman.

As is normal practice once hand steering has been engaged, the Third Officer takes his place next to the Helmsman to ensure that conning orders are executed correctly.

At 21:36:02 the First Officer gives a new Heading to the Helmsman: "Two eight five", adding after only six seconds: "Two nine zero."

"Two nine zero", repeats the Helmsman.

The Captain then intervenes. "Put in a range marker of zero point five [on the radar display - Ed.]", he says to the First Officer who repeats: "Range of zero point five."

At 21:36:58 the First Officer orders the Helmsman: "Two nine zero, steady."

At 21:37:11 the Captain calls the maître by name and asks him if he has contacted a former Captain of *Costa Crociere* by telephone. According to examinations held by the Court of Grosseto this former Captain had already negotiated other sail pasts with local authorities on *Costa Crociere's* behalf.

"I'm calling right now", replies the maître and gets through to the former Captain at 21:37:36. "Good evening, we are almost abeam [of the island - Ed.] ... and I'm here with the Captain... just a second, one moment please."

At this point he passes his mobile phone to Costa Concordia's Captain.

"Captain, how are you? We are approaching Giglio right now...", he says. He listens intently, receiving information on the sail past. "Ah, I've got you, ok, so even if we pass at zero three, zero four [nautical miles - Ed.] there's enough depth of water", he replies, talking on the phone. "Right... got it, I understand... so we'll be fine then."

The two captains say goodbye to each other, and their one minute telephone conversation ends at 21:38:47.

At 21:39:12 the First Officer gains the Captain's attention saying (in Italian):

"Captain, we are on course two nine zero."

The Captain responds immediately in Italian: "two nine zero", then he adds in English: "I take the conn[10]."

The First Officer confirms: "Master has the conn."

It is now 21:39:16. The distance from the planned route begins to increase rapidly towards the limit of 100 metres.

"Three zero zero", orders the Captain at 21:39:30 and the Helmsman replies: "Three zero zero" and turns the helm to starboard.

One second later the Captain begins issuing a rudder order.

"Starboard...", he says, but is interrupted by the Hotel Directors's mobile phone ringing. He enquires as to who has called and does not finish giving the order that he began. The Captain then asks the ship speed. "Fifteen and three" replies the First Officer.

It is now 21:40:00. "Seven on both engines, go to 16 knots" orders the Captain, and the First Officer repeats: "16 knots."

At 21:40:08, Costa Concordia's Heading is 293.7° with a *Rate Of Turn* (ROT) of four degrees per minute. The Captain decides to continue the turn giving the following order to the Helmsman: "Come slowly, slowly to three one zero." It does not take long for the off-track indication to pop up on the Integrated Navigation System screens. At that moment the distance from the planned route is nearing 200 metres and rising rapidly with every passing second (figure I–15).

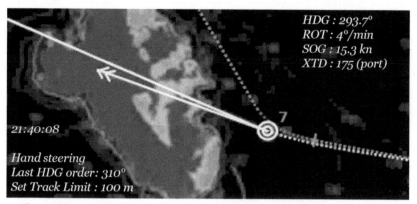

HDG : 293.7°
ROT : 4°/min
SOG : 15.3 kn
XTD : 175 (port)

21:40:08

Hand steering
Last HDG order: 310°
Set Track Limit : 100 m

figure I–15 : Turn on WP N°7 for the sail past along the Island of Giglio

---

10 The expression "I take the conn" implies only that one person can give rudder, heading and speed orders. Taking control of the ship's navigation does not mean taking charge of the watch, which remains with the highest ranking officer involved in operations.

At 21:40:11 the Helmsman acknowledges the order saying: "Three one zero."

At 21:40:13 the Captain addresses the Helmsman saying: "Easy" [probably due to listing as a result of the increased Rate Of Turn and the actual ship's speed - Ed.].

At 21:40:22 the Captain calms the atmosphere saying in Italian: "Everything's fine", followed by a light chuckle.

At 21:40:53 the ship's Heading is 300° with a Rate of Turn at four degrees per minute (figure I–16).

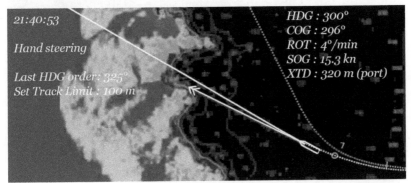

figure I–16 : Intention to reduce the minimum passing distance off Giglio

The Captain continues the approach ordering the Helmsman: "Three two five." The Helmsman misunderstands. "Three one five", he repeats.

The First Officer immediately corrects him, repeating the Captain's order with his voice raised: "Three two five."

A second later, the Captain also repeats the order louder: "Three two five."

The Helmsman then repeats the order correctly: "Three two five."

After more than a minute, at 21:42:07 the Heading is 312.5° with a Rate of Turn at 10 degrees per minute (figure I–17).

"Three three zero", orders the Captain.

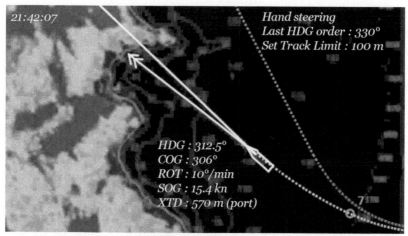

figure I–17 : Increasing the ROT from 4°/min to 10°/min

At 21:42:40 the Captain asks the First Officer's relief to go to the port bridge wing in order to visually monitor the distance off the coast.

At 21:43:08 the Heading is 322° with a Rate of Turn at 10 degrees per minute (figure I–18). The Captain continues the turn. "Three three five", he orders the Helmsman who correctly repeats: "Three three five."

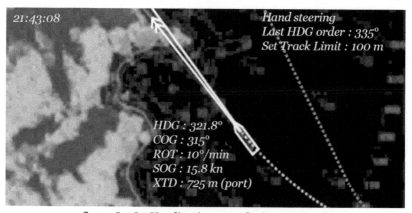

figure I–18 : Heading increase during approach

At 21:43:28 the First Officer informs the Captain of the Speed Over Ground, which is 15.9 knots. The Captain responds with a simple "thanks".

At 21:43:33 the ship's Heading is 326° with an unchanged Rate of Turn of 10 degrees per minute. The Captain orders the Helmsman: "Three four zero."

At 21:43:44, on a Heading of 327° the Captain gives another order: "Three four five."

Once again the Helmsman misunderstands and repeats: "Three three five", and again the First Officer corrects the Helmsman with his voice raised: "Three four five."

"Otherwise we go on the rocks", says the Captain ironically in English, trying to play down the error made.

At 21:44:11 the ship's heading is 331.9° which varies at a Rate of Turn of 10 degrees per minute (figure I–19).

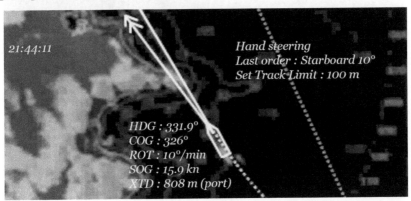

21:44:11

Hand steering
Last order : Starboard 10°
Set Track Limit : 100 m

HDG : 331.9°
COG : 326°
ROT : 10°/min
SOG : 15.9 kn
XTD : 808 m (port)

figure I–19 : Approach to the Island of Giglio with a Rate of Turn of 10°/min

The rudder angle set by the Helmsman is two and a half degrees to starboard. It is at this moment that the Captain notices rocks awash straight ahead and orders the Helmsman to steer to starboard. "Starboard ten", he says.

The Helmsman repeats: "Starboard ten."

At 21:44:18 the rudder angle has not yet reached 10 degrees when the Captain orders: "Starboard twenty" and the Helmsman repeats: "Starboard twenty."

Even though the Helmsman had immediately put the helm to 20 degrees, at 21:44:21 the actual rudder angle is only 9.5 degrees. "Hard to starboard" orders the Captain and the Helmsman repeats: "Hard to starboard."

"We are going aground!", comments the Hotel Director in Italian, disconcerted by the approach so close to the island.

At 21:44:34 the Helmsman confirms that the rudder angle now complies with the last order by repeating once more: "Hard to starboard."

Just a moment after however, the Captain becomes worried that the stern will drift towards the rocks. So he instantly decides to halt the turn. "Midship", he orders the Helmsman.

The Heading is now 342.6° with a Rate of Turn at 20 degrees per minute to starboard and a Speed Over Ground of 15.7 knots. The distance from the planned route has gone beyond 800 metres (figure I–20).

The Helmsman repeats: "Midship."

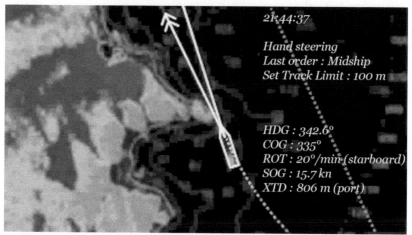

figure I–20 : Rate of Turn increase from 10°/min to 20°/min

At 21:44:44 the Captain gives a new order. "Port ten", he says to the Helmsman.

It is obvious at this point that he is attempting to avoid an impact between the ship's stern and the sighted rocks. The moment in which the order is given the actual position of the rudder is still 17 degrees starboard.

The Helmsman repeats: "Port ten", but for a couple of seconds remains undecided as to where to place the rudder which remains amidships[11].

At 21:44:46 the Captain orders "Port twenty" to the Helmsman in an effort to increase the Rate of Turn to port. But at that moment the Helmsman had still not positioned the helm to port at all.

At 21:44:48 the Helmsman turns the helm 10 degrees to starboard, the opposite direction from the orders given by the Captain. The actual position of the rudders is still amidships.

At 21:44:49 the Helmsman repeats: "Port twenty", but he turns the helm 20 degrees to starboard. The rudders begin moving from the centre to starboard.

---

11 Data regarding the settings of the helm and the actual positions of the rudders from 21:44:44 until 21:45:05 have been extracted from the judicial examination commissioned by the Court of Grosseto (2012).

At 21:44:55 the rudders reach a position of roughly 20 degrees starboard. It is only now that the Helmsman realises his mistake and immediately corrects, putting the helm to amidships (21:44:57) before applying 20 degrees to port (21:44:58).

At 21:45:05, 19 seconds after the Captain's order, the rudders reach a position of 20 degrees port. At that very moment the Captain says: "Hard to port" and the Helmsman correctly replies: "Hard to port."

When the order is given the actual position of the rudders is 20 degrees to port. However the Rate of Turn is still 20 degrees per minute to starboard. The ship's Heading is now 006° and continues to increase towards starboard. Upon which the officer stationed on the port bridge wing shouts (in Italian). "Captain, the port side is going to hit the rocks!", he says.

At 21:45:07 the port quarter hits a submerged rock that is 7.3m below the surface (figure I–21).

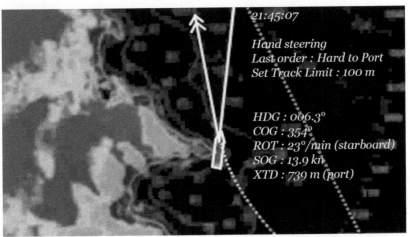

figure I–21 : The port quarter impacts with a submerged rock

It is at this point that management of the emergency starts. At 22:00:40, around 15 minutes after the impact, the ship's stability and survival are compromised due to the progressive flooding of five contiguous watertight compartments. The vessel suffers a blackout, it is adrift without engines and without steering.

In just a few hours the wind carries the Costa Concordia to rest partly submerged at the *Punta della Gabbianara*, where it is to remain for the next two and a half years.

As reported by the *Royal Institution of Naval Architects* (RINA)[12], "the flooded compartments contained a number of critical systems such as main diesel generators, ballast and bilge pumps, electrical propulsion motors. This resulted in black out of main electrical network, loss of propulsion and various high capacity sea-water service pumps. The combination of these factors effectively meant that Costa Concordia was damaged beyond any condition that it had been designed for and hence the irreversible flooding was beyond any manageable level."

---

12 www.rina.org.uk

SYSTEMIC ANALYSIS

"We cannot change the human condition, but
we can change the conditions under which humans work"
James Reason

Method

The events that took place on 13th January 2012 reveal vulnerabilities that go beyond the bridge of the Costa Concordia. In order to understand what happened we need to consider a "maritime system" that encompasses at least three distinct elements:

- the ship;
- the shipping company;
- the international regulatory body.

This analysis will therefore be conducted at the following levels:

- operational: the conduct of navigation on the bridge;
- organisational: the Safety Management System within the company;
- regulatory: international regulations concerning navigation safety.

The Costa Concordia accident is without doubt the most documented in the entire history of maritime navigation. It attracted a constant – at times invasive – international media coverage and the Italian authorities charged with investigating have rendered much information public. However it is not easy to sift through all available data and concentrate on what is meaningful to make provisions for the future. The easiest trap to fall into is to become absorbed by human errors committed on the ship's bridge without exploring the context and the conditions behind them. This chapter will look at the operational events only as a starting point – and by no means as the conclusion – of a "systemic analysis" that has two purposes: one theoretical and one practical.

The theoretical purpose – discussed throughout the first part of the book – is to understand how catastrophic navigational accidents[13] can still happen

---

13 A catastrophic accident is intended as a rare event that affects complex systems characterised by multiple interactions between humans, advanced technology and organisational structures at various levels. As opposed to accidents that involve single individuals, catastrophic accidents generate serious consequences for people, things and environments outside of the system. Lastly, a catastrophic accident is followed by the media so closely that it changes public opinion's level of acceptance, and with it the liability threshold of the company's Safety Management System. This definition is inspired by James Reason's "organisational accident" (1997) with the addition of the media element, which is more and more invasive in the digital age.

within maritime systems that are formally well defended and well organised with regards to safety management.

The practical purpose addressed in the second and third parts of the book is to formulate possible solutions at various levels of the maritime system.

The Costa Concordia was equipped with state-of-the-art navigation systems that were in working order and operated by officers holding all qualifications required by international regulations. It had a Safety Management System[14] approved by the competent authorities in navigation safety. Therefore how was it possible that such an accident occurred? The answer to this requires a multidisciplinary approach that applies the knowledge available in the field of *safety sciences* and *human factors*[15] to the maritime system.

The analysis' first step (figure I–22) will be to identify the errors committed on the bridge and the *latent conditions* that in some way induced them. With these conditions in mind we will try to find their origins at organisational and regulatory levels. The second phase of the analysis will concentrate on determining the causes of the navigational accident and on the more significant systemic conditions.

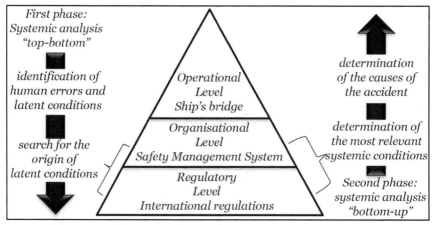

figure I–22 : Systemic analysis for understanding catastrophic accidents

14 The Safety Management System is a collection of company policies and procedures for the mitigation of risks associated with specific operational factors.

15 With the term "human factors" or "ergonomics" the International Ergonomics Association (2000) intends a scientific discipline that studies interactions between human beings and other elements of a system. The term also indicates the study of optimising man-machine interaction on the basis of theoretical principles, data and methods.

This analysis uses sources of information that have been made public over time. The main ones are:

- statements made by the officers of the Costa Concordia to the Court of Grosseto in the days following the accident (January 2012);
- navigation data from the ship's *Voyage Data Recorder* (VDR) which was published on the website of the Italian newspaper *"Il Corriere della Sera"* (4th July 2012);
- the judicial examination commissioned by the Court of Grosseto (11th September 2012);
- the accident report issued by the Marine Casualties Investigative Body of the Italian Ministry of Infrastructures and Transports together with the transcript of VDR audio recordings (22nd May 2013).

Human Error and Latent Conditions

E rror is an inevitable expression within human nature and it is impossible to create a system that is completely free from it. However many decades of studies carried out in high-risk operational contexts have strived to find solutions that not only minimise errors, but also try to block the negative consequences that may arise. It has been generally accepted that fundamentally it is important to engineer and maintain a system that tolerates and resists human error – rather than being free from it.

When an operator's performance is analysed, there are two important questions to pose:

- why were errors committed?
- why were they not corrected once committed?

In order to respond, the most important aspect is to avoid being influenced by hindsight. It is necessary to enter into the reality of the actual context and to remember that operators acted according to what they believed correct at the time. Therefore the key point is to understand why they thought the decisions and the actions taken were correct before being proved otherwise.

First of all though, it is important to define the term *human error* precisely.

Table I–1 derives from James Reason's classification[16]. According to him a human error is committed when determined actions do not obtain their desired effects.

There are different types of error:

- when the intention is correct but it is not executed as planned, the error is called a *slip*. Slips can also be divided into *attentional slips* and *memory lapses*;
- when the execution is carried out correctly but it is the intention itself that is inadequate, the error is called a *mistake*. This category includes both *incorrect improvisations* and *violations*. Incorrect improvisations occur when the operator inappropriately assesses the risk of a certain action in the absence of procedures. Whereas violations occur when a procedure exists but is not followed.

---

16 James Reason (1990). "Human Error". Cambridge University Press

After an accident, the search for violations represents the most rapid method of identifying operator responsibility. "Procedures were in place but were not followed correctly" a company could state, laying the blame on its officers. The matter however is not so simple.

Violations can have different forms according to their frequency (routine or exceptional), to the level of risk that they entail (correct or incorrect) or to their functionality to company interests (functional or non-functional).

In particular, functional violations are much more frequent than we imagine.

"If all procedures were followed to the letter, ships would never leave their ports", officers could argue.

Non-functional violations exist when operators act in order to optimise their efforts, even though it is not in the best interests of the organisation that they are part of. Reaching their objectives more easily and without any negative consequences convinces operators, violation after violation, that they are doing the right thing. Therefore this practice crystallises into attitudes that are difficult to change. For this reason, violations that are routine, incorrect and non-functional are generally the most safety critical.

Type of error	Description	Subclass
Slips	Execution inadequate, but intention was correct	Attentional Slips
		Memory Lapses
Mistakes	Execution faithful to intention, but intention was inadequate	Violations (Routine or Extraordinary) (Correct or Incorrect) (Functional or Non-Functional)
		Incorrect Improvisations

table I–1 : Types of error

To understand and evaluate human error it is useful to refer to the work of the safety scientist Jens Rasmussen[17]. His theory is that we perform in a much quicker and automated manner when faced with familiar situations, whereas in novel situations the cognitive load increases and with it the likelihood to commit errors. It is for this reason that operating procedures

---

[17] Jens Rasmussen (1982). "Human Errors: a Taxonomy for Describing Human Malfunction in Industrial Installations", Journal of Occupational Accidents, 4, 1982, p311-33.

Jens Rasmussen (1983). "Skills, Rules and Knowledge: Signals, Signs, Symbols and other Distinctions in Human Performance Models". IEEE Transactions: Systems, Man and Cybernetics, SMC-13, p.257-67.

are particularly useful in abnormal conditions, as they assist in maintaining control and in preventing being overwhelmed by events.

Let us consider the classic example of a man driving to work from home. He will operate the car's gears and steering wheel at a subconscious level, respecting traffic lights and rights of way without any problems. However, when confronted with a road never seen before the probability of committing errors increases substantially. In this case the instructions from a satnav would mitigate the risk of making an error, whilst at the same time would also free enough mental resources to hold a work-related conversation with a colleague sitting next to him.

Identifying and classifying human error is only the starting point and will not help in any way if the latent conditions that induced it are not sought out. In fact, while the sequence of human errors is different for each individual accident, the same latent conditions can be common in different ones.

Typical latent conditions at an operational level are:

- inadequate training;
- inadequate bridge procedures;
- inadequate ergonomics of navigation instruments and bridge layout.

Identifying and mitigating these conditions should be one of the main activities of those responsible for safety at an organisational level. Attempts to react to human errors made during a particular event are as unproductive as killing mosquitoes in a swamp, rather than trying to drain it.

But what exactly are these latent conditions?

We could say that they are to complex and technologically advanced systems what resident pathogens are to the human body[18]. They are always present and can remain dormant for many years before succeeding in penetrating system defences (when combined with human errors and/or external risk factors). In the maritime domain they are often caused by inadequate integration between humans, technology and the organisation. Companies attempt to eliminate them by introducing protective measures such as operating procedures, training and redundancy of both the human element and technology. Nevertheless it is very difficult to evaluate and quantify the effectiveness of these measures.

Moreover, defences widen the gap between safety managers and operators. It is this gap that contributes to creating latent conditions that leave bridge operations more vulnerable to human error and/or external threats. These

---

18 James Reason (1997). "Managing the Risks of Organizational Accidents". Ashgate.

conditions are generated not only by decisions made at an organisational level, but also from existing international regulations at a regulatory level.

From a theoretical point of view, tracing the origin of latent conditions up to regulatory level helps in understanding the patterns of a catastrophic accident, but in practice we need to remain at a level where it is possible to make changes[19]. For example, company safety managers should work solely on the origins of latent conditions at an organisational level and leave out those at a regulatory level (IMO), which they have no control over.

With the basics of human error and latent conditions defined, we are now ready to analyse the events that took place on 13th January 2012 by dividing them into the following operational functions:

- route planning;
- route monitoring and route control;
- teamwork.

Route Planning

It is 18:27, half an hour before departure from Civitavecchia. The Captain arrives on the bridge and informs the Second Officer that he intends to change the route plan to Savona in order to perform a sail past along the Island of Giglio. Change is one of the most powerful error inducing conditions and it should be managed with extreme care. However, a former Captain of *Costa Crociere* describes the concept of "touristic navigation" as common practice within the company, so much so that this practice has been included in the passenger programme on many occasions. The former Captain also explains that sail pasts are usually conducted at very low speeds (five knots) and arranged beforehand with local authorities. His words[20] give the impression that this practice is a custom controlled by the company at least at an informal level.

Therefore if it is true that sail pasts are part of cruise business, why should the decision made by the Captain be considered an error?

---

19 We will touch upon the origin of latent conditions at a regulatory level only after having gained a reasonable level of understanding of the accident, i.e. upon having reached the theoretical purpose of the systemic analysis.

20 Court of Grosseto examination (January 2012). Statement by the former Captain of Costa Crociere (p.2): "[...] between 2007 and 2011 sail pasts to Giglio at reduced speeds (approximately five knots) were agreed with the Coast Guard and the cruise company for a total of four times and always performed during summer: one with the Costa Pacifica and three with the Costa Concordia [...] The last one was performed on 14th August 2011 and I was involved in negotiating the agreement between the cruise company and the Mayor of Giglio [...]"

The aim of a sail past is to entertain passengers on board and to promote the *Costa Crociere* brand for those that watch the event from ashore. On that particular evening however, conditions were not in place: it was late (10pm), it was winter, there was no agreement with local authorities and the passengers had not been informed. Therefore the decision can be classified as a violation that is non-functional to company interests. The description of previous sail pasts seems to imply that the non-functional character on 13th January is also extraordinary. The violation can also be considered incorrect due to the increase in the level of risk associated with the close approach to the island (half a nautical mile) when compared to the one related to a coastal navigation at several nautical miles from the coastline.

Why did the Captain decide to opt for a sail past? What was his interest in modifying the original route only half an hour before departure, interrupting his dinner, going up onto the bridge and carrying out a close approach to a semi-deserted island?

In order to give answers we need to get inside the situation and distance ourselves from the tragic consequences of that decision. Conversations captured by the *Voyage Data Recorder* (VDR) can help us to understand this. When the Captain talks to the Second Officer and says "right, let's chart this route then", his tone of voice suggests that he was not at all happy about having to perform "this f***ing sail past."

Reading between the lines of the Captain's statement[21], the possibility emerges that a certain pressure could have been applied by the on-board hotel department, often known for being very influential on a cruise ship. After having already refused an evening sail past, it seems that the Captain felt obliged to go along with the request made that evening.

Management of a ship with more than 1000 crew members is based on very delicate social dynamics. Just as is the case for the mayor of a small town, the captain of a large ship cannot ignore this[22]. If present, the excessive influence of the hotel department on the ship's command can be considered a

---

21 Court of Grosseto examination (January 2012). Captain's statement (p.6): "[...] Last week [...] the maître asked (me): [...] given that I'm due to sign off, I would be grateful if you could pass by Giglio for a sail past [...]. Weather conditions were bad and I said: no I'm sorry, we'll do it next time, and he reminded me of this fact that evening, seven days after [...]"

22 Back in 1984 in his book "Normal Accidents", Charles Perrow argued that the maritime industry showed a large tendency to induce human errors. At an operational level this predisposition was attributed to two types of pressure: a commercial one from organisational level, and that coming from the social interaction and organisation on board. In this particular case aboard the Costa Concordia, given the absence of commercial pressure for a winter sail past to a semi-deserted island, it is most plausible that pressure arrived from internal factors on-board the ship.

latent condition and it is linked to cultural aspects rather than specific organisational processes.

Another latent condition consists in the absence of specific company policy on sail pasts. In this case company policy is defined by the formalisation of business objectives such as brand promotion and passenger entertainment, as well as precautionary measures concerning sail pasts.

Bearing all this in mind, imagine that we are on the bridge of the Costa Concordia at around 6:30pm. The Captain and Second Officer are working on the plan to deviate from the original route. Does the situation that we are witnessing seem strange? This is something that has been done in the past and has not presented any problems. So what harm can come from making a small concession for the sake of social equilibrium on board, given that there are no company policies that say otherwise? If we take a moment to forget what actually happened afterwards, the Captain's decision does not seem so absurd. We need rather to analyse a selection of "technical" errors that were committed during the planning itself.

Before departure the Second Officer requests confirmation of the safety margin for the close approach upon Giglio. "Captain, is half a mile ok? At the end of the day we have enough water depth."

The nautical chart used for planning was the coastal chart IIM N°6 by the *Italian Hydrographic Office*[23] with a scale of 1:100.000 (see figure I–7). Half a nautical mile on a chart scaled 1:100.000 would show up at around half a centimetre. If we consider that the width of a pencil line is 0.5 millimetres it is clear that the safety margin on such a chart would be viewed quite inaccurately. There was another nautical chart on board, the IIM N°119 with a much larger scale (1:20.000), which however was never considered during planning.

This first error to note is a violation of one of the most basic rules when planning a route – that the chart with the largest scale possible should be used. This violation can be seen as non-functional to company interests and incorrect with regards to risk assessment.

Before departure the Second Officer also transfers the route onto the Electronic Chart System[24], inserting parameters that do not figure in the official route plan on paper charts. The additional electronic parameters are the Turn Radius for each waypoint and the maximum Cross Track Distance

---

23 Istituto Idrografico della Marina (IIM).

24 The Electronic Chart System on board is not registered as a primary navigation system, but as an aid to navigation. Officially paper charts should be used as primary means of navigation on board the Costa Concordia.

(Track Limit) for each leg of the route. In particular, when planning the route for the sail past along Giglio the Second Officer chooses a Turn Radius of one nautical mile, which is far too tight at a planned speed of 16 knots. In fact company procedures[25] recommend a Turn Radius of no less than three nautical miles for this speed. This also highlights a procedural violation which is non-functional to company interests and incorrect with regards to risk assessment.

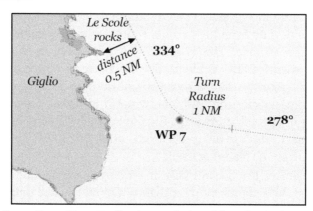

figure I–23: Turn Radius in proximity of the Island of Giglio

The decision to plan a route that heads directly towards the island is an element that represents more interest in the analysis of the planning. A route that heads straight for the island at a speed of 16 knots does not leave any margin of error during the turn, compared with a parallel route from the South.

Why did the Second Officer choose a route that heads straight for the island? It is clear from figure I–24 that the intention is to avoid the nature reserve around the nearby island of Giannutri. This is also expressed by the Second Officer with the statement: "We can't get through... we'll have to go around".

This nature reserve seems to worry him, so much so that he discusses it with the Captain. "Here we are almost abeam of Giannutri... a protected area... let's go a little higher... then the route at half a mile". The Captain nods in approval, probably not paying much attention to the fact that the proposed route heads straight towards Giglio.

---

25 Costa Crociere, "Bridge Procedures P14 Man.01 SMS par.4.1.4.2 (j)"

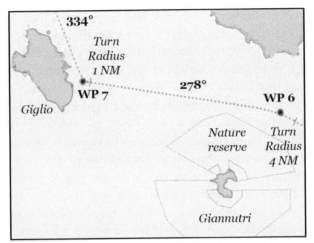

figure I–24 : Planned route to avoid Giannutri's nature reserve

The Second Officer's mistake is non-functional to company interests and incorrect with regards to risk assessment. Not checking the modified route before departure (neither on nautical charts nor on the Electronic Chart System) constitutes a violation of company procedures[26] by the Captain.

The latent condition here is inadequate training on the ship's Integrated Navigation System[27]. This condition means that the Captain probably wasn't able to check the officer's planning work, who also may have learned to use the instruments by himself, making a virtue out of a necessity.

Up until the point when these electronic systems were introduced it was the Captain of a ship that had the most expertise in route planning and charting. Nowadays however, the junior officers take care of route planning. This is because even when traditional paper charts should be formally used, the Integrated Navigation System has actually become the primary means of navigation.

And yet the only form of training considered necessary at organisational level is a *familiarisation checklist*[28] with bridge equipment. This consists of a list of functions for the various instruments, which officers must be familiar with when they step on board a ship for the first time (or when returning

---

26 Costa Crociere, "Bridge Procedures P14 Man.01 SMS par.4.1.4.1".

27 NACOS (Navigation and Command System) is produced by Sam Electronics and installed on a significant majority of cruise ships. The NACOS function dedicated to route planning on electronic charts is an integral part of the two components necessary to route control: radar with an electronic chart underlay and track control system.

28 Costa Crociere ISM P.5.03.03 MAN 01 MO09A SMS.

from a period of absence). However the Electronic Chart System is not present on this checklist, and even if it were it would not resolve the problem. Costa Concordia's Integrated Navigation System is a sophisticated tool. To understand it fully requires a training course in a simulator – something that certainly cannot be substituted by a checklist.

In short it is comparable to the Captain of a modern airliner delegating the programming of the flight computer – which he himself is not capable of operating – to his First Officer, who is self-taught in its use without any formal training. Would you feel safe getting on that plane?

Inadequate training, as a latent condition for errors committed, can be attributed to both organisational and regulatory levels. In fact, it is quite common practice to substitute formal training with *familiarisation checklists*. In particular when the primary means of navigation on board is that of using traditional nautical charts, IMO does not make training on the Integrated Navigation System and its electronic chart subsystem compulsory. The *International Code for Safety Management* (ISM) and the *International Convention on Standards of Training, Certification and Watchkeeping for Seafarers* (STCW) recommend a familiarisation for personnel with safety related duties and with specific bridge equipment. The main issue is that the word *familiarisation* is very open to interpretation and cannot satisfy the requirements of a demanding operational reality such as the Costa Concordia's. All this regardless of the fact that officially the primary means of navigation remains traditional paper charts. Given the importance of "electronic" routes for use with the Track Control System, all officers should have a proven expertise with the Electronic Chart System. Obviously this should include the Captain who is ultimately responsible for checking and approving the route plan before departure. It may seem something fairly obvious, but rarely is it ever the case. At this present time a ship can conform perfectly with all international regulations even if its Captain and its officers have never been trained in using on board Electronic Chart Systems. In this respect, those responsible for training[29] are compliant from a bureaucratic point of view, but not in its actual substance.

This analysis shows how the importance of the Integrated Navigation System – used as the actual primary means of navigation – is undervalued at organisational level.

At this point let's summarise the three main errors and their latent conditions regarding route planning that we have discussed so far.

---

29 Costa Crociere P5.03 SMS Training Management.

The Captain decides to modify the planned route to perform a sail past along the Island of Giglio that is non-functional to company interests	
Type of Error and Subclass	Mistake Extraordinary, Non-Functional and Incorrect Violation
Latent Conditions at Operational Level	Absence of operating procedures for performing a sail past
Origin of Latent Conditions at Organisational Level	Absence of a formal company policy regarding sail pasts
Origin of Latent Conditions at Regulatory Level	--

table I–2 : First error in route planning

The Second Officer plans a route that heads straight towards the Island of Giglio with a Turn Radius (1 NM) that is incompatible with the intended speed (16 kn)	
Type of Error and Subclass	Mistake Non-Functional and Incorrect Violation
Latent Conditions at an Operational Level	Inadequate training for operating the Integrated Navigation System
Origin of Latent Conditions at Organisational Level	Undervaluing of the expertise required for operating the Integrated Navigation System
Origin of Latent Conditions at Regulatory Level	Vagueness of the regulations for familiarisation with navigation instruments

table I–3 : Second error in route planning

The Captain does not check the route plan before departure	
Type of Error and Subclass	Mistake Non-Functional and Incorrect Violation
Latent Conditions at an Operational Level	Inadequate training for operating the Integrated Navigation System
Origin of Latent Conditions at Organisational Level	Undervaluing of the expertise required for operating Integrated Navigation System
Origin of Latent Conditions at Regulatory Level	Vagueness of the regulations for familiarisation with navigation instruments

table I–4 : Third error in route planning

Route Monitoring and Route Control

Route monitoring and route control errors are associated with:

- deviations from the planned route;
- improvisation of turns without regard for planned limits.

These will be analysed one by one, using VDR images from 13th January for reference.

The first error is committed by the Captain as he exceeds the Track Limit when leaving the Port of Civitavecchia (figure I–25). During the turn that was performed by hand steering, the distance from the planned route reached 240 metres, as opposed to the 100 metre Track Limit set on the Integrated Navigation System.

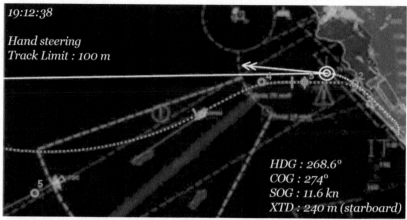

figure I–25 : Turn performed whilst leaving the Port of Civitavecchia

None of the officers present on the bridge made the Captain aware that the ship exceeded the set limit. This was not because no one had noticed it, rather that the planned route and the maximum limit under normal conditions (Track Limit) are considered by everyone as a reference and not a corridor to navigate within.

The same silent consent also occurs during the next turn when leaving Civitavecchia's Traffic Separation Scheme. This time navigation control is in the hands of the Second Officer, who the Captain ironically calls "professor". The nickname "professor" is used very commonly in the Italian Merchant Navy to identify someone who tries to study and understand the bridge's navigation instruments. It is often more experienced officers who make this joke as they are more at home with traditional methods based on hand steering and visual monitoring of position.

As soon as the *professor* takes the conn he immediately activates the Track Control System, an automated system for route control that is calibrated for the ship's specific turning ability. Amongst other things the Track Control System is able to change Heading or Course Over Ground based on the Turn Radius that is set by the operator. It is an important component of the Integrated Navigation System because it is capable of performing one of its main functions: automatic route control.

Referring to figure I–26 and figure I–27, it is possible to reconstruct how the Officer of the Watch operated the Track Control System.

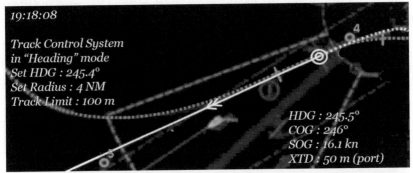

figure I–26 : Transfer from hand steering to the Track Control System

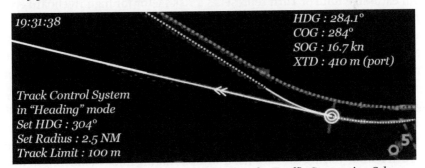

figure I–27 : Turn performed whilst leaving the Traffic Separation Scheme

At 19:20 the ship reaches the Wheel Over Point for the next course at 20 metres from the planned route and with a Speed Over Ground of 17 knots. However the officer only begins the turn three minutes later and he does it by gradually varying the setting of the heading on the Track Control System, whilst maintaining a turning radius of four nautical miles. This results in a deviation from the planned route that reaches a maximum distance of 420 metres. In an attempt to reduce this the Officer of the Watch shortens the Turn Radius to two and a half miles. Here, the minimum company recommended value of three nautical miles at speeds in excess of 15 knots is breached.

The route deviation is a result of an incorrect use of the Track Control System, which is designed to make "controlled turns" through predefined Rate of Turn values. Before each turn the Track Control System must receive its next heading (if used in Heading mode) or a new Course Over Ground (if used in Course mode) together with the desired Turn Radius. Once set, these values are used to calculate and display the Curved Heading Line (CHL), which is a projection of the next turn to perform. The moment to begin executing the turn using the values given is when the CHL and the planned route are imposed over each other (figure I–28).

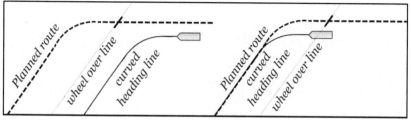

figure I–28 : Curved Heading Line (CHL) for controlled turns

An excessive Rate of Turn represents a risk factor for high freeboard cruise ships such as the Costa Concordia, so much so that a heeling of more than five degrees can be considered as a navigational incident. It is for this reason that officers must know what the Rate of Turn will be before executing the turn so that they can ensure it is within the ship's specific limits. It can also be calculated by dividing the Speed Over Ground (in knots) by the Turn Radius (in nautical miles) to get an approximate value in degrees per minute.

Going back to that evening on 13th January, the Officer of the Watch does not use the Curved Heading Line. Instead he adjusts the ship's Heading and its Turn Radius during the turn itself without taking into consideration where it will finish and without taking into account the Rate of Turn.

These initial control errors have the same consequence: that the planned Track Limit is exceeded.

The error committed by the Captain was a mistake characterised by improvisation and by the disregard of limits set within the Integrated Navigation System. For him planned routes on the Electronic Chart System are at most for reference only, as are those marked on paper charts on the chart table. The Captain monitors the ship's position visually and does not seem interested in obtaining confirmation from instruments. However, he is not the only one doing this. Improvising whilst navigating is the norm and this is the reason why the audible Off-Track alarm was deactivated and why the officers of the Costa Concordia did not inform the Captain once the Track Limit was exceeded.

The error committed afterwards by the Officer of the Watch can also be characterised as improvisation to a certain degree. This can be acknowledged by the series of variations to the Heading and the Turn Radius upon exceeding the Track Limit. Although there was no audible alarm, the Off-Track indication appeared on the Integrated Navigation System's screen and seemed to take the officer somewhat by surprise.

In both cases, the turns are:

- incorrect: because they do not take into account the risk of excessive heeling and passing outside the Track Limit;
- non-functional to company interests: because continuous variations in course and Turn Radius are less economical (in terms of fuel consumption) when compared with the controlled turn technique.

Let's imagine again that we are present on Costa Concordia's bridge while leaving the Port of Civitavecchia. What importance would we have given to these errors? Would it have seemed so strange that the Cross Track Distance exceeded the planned Track Limit by so much?

The next step is to ask ourselves why the errors were committed, or in other words to identify any eventual latent conditions.

As we have already stated previously, there are two methods for monitoring and controlling the route on Costa Concordia's bridge: *traditional* and *integrated*. Even though the paper nautical charts are formally the primary means of navigation on board, the ship is kept on track mainly by the Integrated Navigation System. These two methods however present conceptual differences that are very relevant.

The *traditional method* is based upon reporting visual bearings, radar distances and satellite positions on paper charts. Course Over Ground is determined by aligning past positions. The ship is steered manually in confined waters and by autopilot in open sea. In both cases turns are performed without paying particular attention to the turning radius and the Rate of Turn. The route is considered only as a reference at most and without any precise limits.

The integrated method is based on the use of a navigation system that links radar, the Electronic Chart System and a number of sensors such as GPS, speed logs, gyrocompasses and echosounders. The ship's position is monitored in real time with respect to the limits of a corridor displayed on the electronic chart. The Course Over Ground is also displayed in real time by the orientation of a *true vector*[30] with a magnitude equal to the Speed Over Ground. With regards to turns the planned route (track) becomes a curve according to the Turn Radius. Moreover, the Track Control System's Curved Heading Line gives the possibility of displaying a projection of the ship's turn in the near future.

The coexistence between the traditional method and the integrated method create scenarios where modern navigation systems are often used inappropriately, without taking advantage of their potential and without considering their limitations. In formal terms, it is still the traditional method that takes priority, but often in day to day situations it is a hybrid method that is used, weighted mainly towards the Integrated Navigation System.

Costa Crociere's bridge procedures do not explain "how" to manage this coexistence, rather they give only generic recommendations[31]. The resulting ambiguity can be considered as a latent condition. It comes at:

- organisational level, by the decision to maintain the traditional method as the primary means of navigation, even when there is a sophisticated Integrated Navigation System;
- regulatory level, by international regulations that allow an Integrated Navigation System to be subordinated by traditional paper charts, as well as the absence of an operational concept that defines the roles of the officers that use these systems.

The absence of formal training on the Integrated Navigation System's use also constitutes a latent condition for the errors committed. It comes at:

- organisational level, by the decision to adopt a *familiarisation checklist* in place of an official training program;
- regulatory level, by the introduction of the concept of *familiarisation* that is generic and weak in relation to the complexities of modern bridge equipment.

Yet another latent condition to consider is the more experienced officers' mistrust of navigation instruments. It is a scepticism that is deeply embedded in the professional culture of the maritime industry and based on the belief that intuition and senses are sufficient for any situation. The nickname

---

30 In all VDR images, the true vector is shown as a white line with two arrows at the end.

31 P14-102 SMS - Behavioural Standards for the Bridge Team (par.4.3): "Navigation instruments must be constantly monitored to ensure their correct functioning, whilst avoiding relying exclusively and blindly on technology."

"professor", evidently used with irony by Costa Concordia's Captain, is a clear example of this and aims to single out and put down those who have differing opinions.

Cultural aspects however cannot be easily allocated to a specific level of the maritime industry. In order to grasp it we need to put ourselves into the operational reality and comprehend who the Costa Concordia's officers are exactly and where they come from. But this is something that we will discuss later on in the final chapter of this first part.

Let us go back to that evening on 13th January 2012.

It is 21:00 (figure I–29) and the Costa Concordia is approximately four nautical miles North-East of Giannutri. The First Officer has relieved the Officer of the Watch and is now responsible for controlling the ship within the limits of the planned route. The Third Officer assists him by manually plotting the ship's position on the paper chart IIM N°6 (scale 1:100.000), where the routes to follow have been drawn.

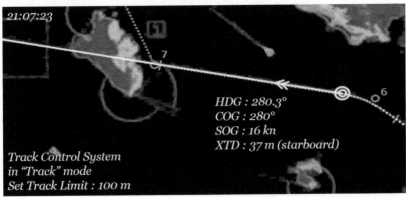

figure I–29 : Turn towards the Island of Giglio

With the Track Control System in Track mode the ship turns autonomously towards Giglio, following the planned Turn Radius (four nautical miles) accurately and remaining within the set Track Limit (100 metres). The maximum deviation from the planned route during this turn is just 37 metres.

The errors begin at 21:39 when, after five minutes on the bridge, the Captain takes control of the navigation. With hand steering the ship progressively begins to increase the distance from the planned route and by 21:40 the Track Limit has already been exceeded (figure I–30).

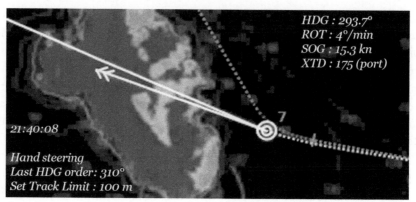

HDG : 293.7°
ROT : 4°/min
SOG : 15.3 kn
XTD : 175 (port)

21:40:08

Hand steering
Last HDG order: 310°
Set Track Limit : 100 m

figure I–30 : Approach turn along Giglio performed manually by the Captain

There is not much more to add to the analysis of the turns performed whilst leaving the Port of Civitavecchia. The planned route becomes only a rough reference and the traditional method replaces integrated navigation.

After the telephone conversation with the former Captain of *Costa Crociere*, the Captain decides to reduce the safety margin even more to around a third of a nautical mile.

The turn is performed visually by ordering the Heading to the Helmsman without contemplating any Turn Radius or Rate of Turn. The latter will soon appear to be too slow to complete the turn within the stated margins. It is the Captain himself who realises this when he says "Easy" to the Helmsman, meaning "use the rudder with care".

On passenger ships of the type of the Costa Concordia it is not difficult to cause excessive heeling with just small rudder angles, especially at a speed of 15 knots. Despite this the Captain orders the First Officer to increase speed to 16 knots. Heading and rudder orders were all given before those previously executed were completed. The result is a succession of orders that never reach the desired outcome.

The error in controlling the route during the final turn towards the Island of Giglio was ultimately the same as that committed when departing from the Port of Civitavecchia. They were both mistakes characterised by improvising and by disregarding the limits set within the Integrated Navigation System.

At this point there is another element to highlight. When approaching Giglio the Captain relied on his own senses and by the radar distance from a small group of rocks (*Le Scole*), without considering the distance from those furthermost awash. These rocks, although not detected by radar can be found using the electronic nautical charts (figure I–31).

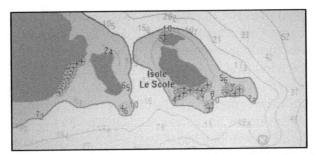

figure I–31 : Electronic Nautical Chart showing Le Scole rocks

So why did neither the Captain nor the First Officer even attempt to view them?

In order to answer this question it is important to remember what we have stated previously regarding lack of formal training and ambiguity between traditional and integrated methods. In addition, the integrated system could pose usability issues with the user interface, particularly when viewing electronic charts in vector format[32]. These charts do not guarantee the same overall view as traditional paper charts, especially when text and symbols overlap. Moreover, given that the ship's actual position must always be visible on the displayed portion of the electronic chart, an area that is too far away may not be displayed with a sufficient level of detail.

At a regulatory level, the inadequacy of the overall view and the difficulties in reading cartographic information on screen can be traced back to:

- the IHO[33] Specifications for Chart Content and Display Aspects of Electronic Chart Display and Information Systems (ECDIS);
- the IMO[34] Performance Standards for ECDIS.

The IMO Performance Standards do not contain any specific ergonomic requirements but only generic recommendations for easing the use of certain functionalities. User interface design criteria (both software and hardware) are left to equipment manufacturers, which does not always produce the best possible result.

---

32 Electronic vector charts, in contrast to those in paper format, allow selective viewing of available information. The type of charts installed on Costa Concordia's Integrated Navigation System were "CMAP Professional Plus", produced by Jeppesen in CM93-3 format. These are not recognised by the International Hydrographic Organization (IHO) as official charts, but do not present any substantial differences from the official version (CMAP-ENC), also produced by Jeppesen.

33 IHO S-52 (2010). "Specifications for Chart Content and Display Aspects of ECDIS".

34 Resolution MSC.232(82) adopted on 5 December 2006. Performance Standards for ECDIS.

Usability evaluation and the approach that regulatory bodies should take to improve it are very complex matters and have been at the centre of international debate for many years.

There is also another element that contributed to the incorrect execution of Costa Concordia's final turn – the distractions caused by hotel staff present on the bridge at the time. In fact before taking control of the ship, the Captain asked the maître if he had contacted by mobile phone a former Captain of *Costa Crociere* who had already assisted in planning previous sail pasts along Giglio with the local authorities[35].

During this telephone call[36] the First Officer leaves the ship's Heading and speed unchanged as though awaiting further orders. In fact, as the Captain is talking on the telephone, his intention to reduce the initial safety margin from half a nautical mile to one third becomes apparent.

At 21:39, about six minutes before hitting the rocks, the Captain takes control and another significant distraction occurs. It is the Hotel Director's mobile telephone that rings, just at the moment in which the Captain is giving a rudder order to the Helmsman (to increase the Rate of Turn). As a result the order "starboard…" is interrupted.

The Captain asks the Hotel Director who had called and after a few moments of silence instructs the First Officer to increase speed from 15.3 to 16 knots. The next order is not a rudder angle either, but a new Heading – three, one, zero – which leaves the Rate of Turn at the Helmsman's discretion. It is as if the Captain does not remember what he intended to do before this last distraction and continues with another strategy. Distractions and interruptions are notable for inducing errors, especially in situations where a high degree of attention is required.

Another error to consider is the Third Officer's lack of route monitoring. In fact, as soon as the Captain orders hand steering she leaves the chart table and positions herself next to the Indonesian Helmsman to assist should any misunderstandings arise. Up until that moment the Third Officer had been monitoring the route by plotting GPS position fixes on the paper chart (as can be seen in figure I–7).

---

35 Court of Grosseto examination (January 2012). Statement by the former Captain of Costa Crociere.

36 P14-102 SMS, Behavioural Standards for the bridge team (par.4.3): "All persons authorised to access the bridge must not disturb the watchkeepers. Hotel personnel must not involve the Officer of the Watch with issues that can be resolved by others [...] Use of private and on board mobile telephones is forbidden during the watch and during manoeuvres."

This time the mistake is functional as it follows an accepted practice to get over the language barrier between the Helmsman and the Captain[37]. The violation however remains incorrect with regards to the assessment of the risk deriving from the lack of route monitoring on approach to the coast.

The latent condition associated with this error is the alternation of two different languages (Italian and English) when communicating on the bridge. This condition was created by company human resource management. In fact, although Italian is the official language on board, foreign deck personnel are hired without any verification taking place of the level of their understanding[38]. It is this linguistic ambiguity that creates the condition for the Helmsman's errors on the Costa Concordia that evening. He actually misunderstands heading and rudder orders three times during the final turn between 21:40 and 21:44.

Even so, after the second misunderstanding has been immediately corrected by the First Officer, the Captain seems to remain calm. At just one minute before the impact with Le Scole he jokes with the Helmsman saying to him in English: "Otherwise we go on the rocks."

The third misunderstanding concerns the rudder angle at around 20 seconds from the accident.

The Captain notices the rocks breaking the water surface straight ahead and orders rudder to port in an attempt to avoid the stern drifting into them. The Helmsman acknowledges and repeats the order correctly, but turns the helm to starboard. This could be because he found the order to port strange (towards land) or maybe because all previous orders were to starboard. For more than ten seconds none of the crew notice this.

Obviously the Captain, the First Officer and the Third Officer were not looking at the actual rudder indicator and it is the Helmsman himself who corrects it by turning the helm 20° to port as initially ordered. The actual position of the rudders however reaches 20° port only two seconds before impact.

Would the ship have avoided the rocks if these helm orders were executed correctly? The answer to this question is not relevant in this analysis as the nature of the errors made by the Helmsman and their associated latent condition would remain unaltered.

Table I–5 and table I–6 give a summary of the route control errors and associated latent conditions.

---

37 Interrogation report by the Court of Grosseto (2012). Third Officer's statement.

38 Judicial examination commissioned by the Court of Grosseto (2012). Pg. 53.

• The Captain exceeds the Track Limit during the outbound turn from Civitavecchia's harbour	
• The Second Officer exceeds the Track Limit during the outbound turn from Civitavecchia's Traffic Separation Scheme	
• The Captain exceeds the Track Limit during the final approach to Giglio at a speed that is too high for the planned Turn Radius	

Type of Error and Subclass	Mistakes Incorrect Improvisations
Latent Conditions at Operational Level	• Ambiguity between traditional and integrated navigation methods • Inadequate training for operating the Integrated Navigation System • Usability problems on the Integrated Navigation System's user interface • Distractions and interruptions due to the presence of Hotel staff on the bridge
Origin of Latent Conditions at Organisational Level	• Underestimation of the level of expertise required for operating the Integrated Navigation System
Origin of Latent Conditions at Regulatory Level	• Vagueness in regulations for familiarisation with navigation instruments • Standards and regulations that allow the subordination of an Integrated Navigation System to traditional paper charts • Missing operational concept that defines roles of officers engaged in Integrated Navigation System • Usability requirements for certification of navigation systems too generic and weak

table I–5 : Errors and latent conditions in route control

The Helmsman misunderstands the Captain's orders on three separate occasions during the approach turn along the Island of Giglio	

Type of Error and Subclasses	Slips Attentional Slips
Latent Conditions at Operational Level	Ambiguity deriving from the use of two different languages (Italian and English) on the bridge
Origin of Latent Conditions at Organisational Level	No evaluation of language skills during the selection process of deck personnel
Origin of Latent Conditions at Regulatory Level	--

table I–6 : Helmsman's route control errors

Table I–7 summarises the route monitoring error and its associated latent conditions.

The Third Officer leaves the chart table and stops monitoring the ship's position to assist the Helmsman in receiving conning orders from the Captain	
Type of Error and Subclass	Mistake Incorrect, Functional and Routine Violation
Origin of Latent Conditions at Operational Level	Ambiguity deriving from the use of two different languages (Italian and English) on the bridge
Origin of Latent Conditions at Organisational Level	No evaluation of language skills during the selection process of deck personnel
Latent Conditions at Organisational Level	--

table I–7 : Third Officer's error in route monitoring

Teamwork

The errors committed whilst working in a group concern the interaction and coordination of all those that operate on the bridge. When compared to errors of a technical nature, these leave much more open to interpretation, especially when the fundamental principles have not been well defined. Inadequacies in teamwork procedures represent a latent condition for almost all criticalities that appear on the bridge of Costa Concordia.

So, how can it be possible to establish whether procedures are adequate? This can only be answered if controllable quality criteria are introduced.

The most common situation – not only on *Costa Crociere* ships – is that operating procedures consist of a list of "do's and don'ts" for the bridge team[39]. These are broken up by generic suggestions that use the same bureaucratic tone of international standards and regulations. The actual result is that procedures take on an encyclopaedic feel that makes consultation very difficult for bridge officers.

Captains receive memos of new procedures, often without ever being involved in the drafting process and without fully understanding their meaning and motives. As a result they see them as a shift of responsibility rather than as useful operating instructions. This together with the fact that

---

39 It is not easy to demonstrate that existing procedures are generally inadequate. The judgement on the detachment between the quality criteria mentioned and the reality on board is left to the reader with seagoing experience.

the "do's and don'ts" are often detached from real-life situations where officers need to "get the job done" to ensure navigation safety.

However the most critical element of an operating procedure consists in its failure to provide instructions on "how" to do things. This is something that is actually evident in the behavioural standards for Costa Concordia's bridge team[40].

In order to analyse and judge Costa Concordia's bridge procedures we will apply quality criteria used in civil aviation[41], which specifies for each individual task:

- when to perform it;
- who performs it (assignment of responsibilities);
- how it must be performed (including the series of actions and type of confirmation to ensure its effectiveness).

Strictly speaking the definition of principles, company policies and operating procedures for the conduct of navigation requires a lot more than the elements above. A more detailed description will be approached in the second part of this book.

Let's go back again to the evening of 13th January 2012 to look for teamwork related issues.

The first error is committed by the Captain when he fails to inform all bridge officers of his decision to perform the sail past along the Island of Giglio, thus modifying the route plan. The topic is something that is not discussed, even though there was the possibility of doing so during the pre-departure briefing that is envisaged by bridge procedures. As well as discussing variations to planned routes, limits for their monitoring and control should also have been recalled during that meeting[42]. However, none of this happened. Therefore it is an incorrect, non-functional and probably

---

40 P14-102 SMS - Behavioural Standards for the Bridge Team (par.4.8): "The Captain should ensure that, during manoeuvres and all other bridge operations, a climate of serene and effective cooperation is established between all team members (including the Helmsman), preventing hierarchical barriers that jeopardise team performance. The Captain must promote fruitful cooperation and proactivity among all team members, yet within due respect for hierarchy. Each team member should contribute in identifying and seeking to remove any barriers that obstruct effective teamwork."

41 Asaf Degani (1994). "On the Design of Flight-Deck Procedures". NASA Contractor Report 177642.

42 P14-102 SMS - Behavioural Standards for the Bridge Team (par.4.2): "The Captain assigns roles, positions and responsibilities of deck officers in a concise manner, making clear what is expected from them [...] Officers must constantly monitor the manoeuvre and inform the Captain should they realise that it does not follow the plan. If the Captain deems it necessary to modify the original plan during a manoeuvre, he must communicate this to the team."

routine violation of bridge procedures. Furthermore the Captain fails to communicate his intention to perform a much wider turn whilst leaving the Port of Civitavecchia than the one that was planned. This behaviour can also be seen as an incorrect, non-functional and routine violation of bridge procedures. None of the officers bring the deviation exceeding the planned Track Limit (100 metres) to the Captain's attention. Nevertheless, putting ourselves in the officers' shoes, the tacit consent is understandable for two reasons:

- the route and its associated Track Limit are usually considered as a reference at most, rather than as a corridor to navigate within (under normal conditions) and to monitor actively;
- the Captain improvised the turn without any confirmation or change in the limits set.

The same situation occurs when the Second Officer carries out the outbound turn from Civitavecchia's Traffic Separation Scheme (figure I–10). The final Heading and the Rate of Turn to achieve it are not communicated to the Junior Officer of the Watch before initiating the turn. Without this information the Junior Officer of the Watch cannot determine whether exceeding the Track Limit is intended or if it is the consequence of an error. Even in this case we could classify the error as a violation of bridge procedures that is incorrect, non-functional and routine.

Another critical element can be identified at around 20:00, during the change of the watch between the Second Officer and the First Officer. The handover occurs without using the standard checklist, but rather by a simple informal chat[43]. "You're going to do a fantastic coastal route" is all the Second Officer says to his colleague, referring to the sail past along Giglio. He does not however give any other detail regarding the final turn to approach the island (minimum distance off the coast, speed and Turn Radius). The conversation then glides into evaluation of staff before hurriedly turning back to the actual handover.

The Third Officer (incoming Junior Officer of the Watch) and the First Officer's relief were never involved[44] in the process. Also in this case the

---

43 P14-102 SMS - Behavioural Standards for the Bridge Team (par.4.5): "The handover must be performed as specified in the checklist P14 Man1 SMS MO3 – Watch Officer Change Checklist. The relieving officer will assume all watch responsibilities only after having viewed the aforementioned checklist and the navigation logbook."

44 P14-102 SMS - Behavioural Standards for the Bridge Team (par.4.3): "The Officer of the Watch must ensure that all team members are aware of their tasks and responsibilities, clarifying exactly what is expected of them."

mistake is a violation of bridge procedures that is incorrect, non-functional and probably routine.

Communication problems can also be identified when the First Officer talks to the Engineering Officer of the Watch in the Engine Control Room on the ship telephone. They discuss shafts revolutions (RPM) settings without sharing any of the conversation with the other two colleagues present on the bridge, leaving them in the dark regarding the ship's speed[45]. Things do not change before the approach towards Giglio when the First Officer and the Engineering Officer continue discussing the RPMs. This time the First Officer's relief is involved in setting the RPMs on the engine telegraphs. The entire operation is aimed at reducing speed and takes around a minute due to the extreme sensitivity of the telegraphs' levers.

The routine nature of informal handovers is confirmed when the Captain relieves the First Officer just a few minutes before approaching Giglio. This time though, as well as the loss of relevant information, there is also lack of clarity on who has control of navigation[46]. In fact, after only two questions addressed to the First Officer such as "how's the situation?" and "what's our current speed?", the Captain gives the order to engage hand steering without formally taking control. It takes five minutes from his arrival on the bridge before he says in English: "I take the conn".

In those five minutes the Captain changes his mind on the safety margin from the coast and reduces it from a half to a third of a nautical mile. He does not state his intentions to the First Officer who repeats the last Heading given to the Helmsman. This is his way of informing the Captain that the approach turn has already commenced without a shared plan. In the same manner as that which happened during the exit of the Port of Civitavecchia, the First Officer's tacit consent is understandable – even if contrary to operating procedures[47] – given the lack of clarity on the limits of the turn.

---

45 P14-102 SMS - Behavioural Standards for the Bridge Team (par.4.7): "Communication between the various roles involved in the manoeuvre, including engine room personnel, must be carried out in a clear and synthetic manner."

46 P14-102 SMS - Behavioural Standards for the Bridge Team (par.4.6): "The Captain formally takes command with the following phrase: "I take the conn". Up until that moment it is the Officer of the Watch who is responsible for the conduct of navigation, even if the Captain is present on the bridge. After the action of taking control has been made official, the officer must still keep a proactive attitude and monitor the navigation by plotting the ship's position, and remain available to provide any useful information to the Captain."

47 P14-102 SMS - Behavioural Standards for the Bridge Team (par. 4.6): "Officers involved in the manoeuvre must be "proactive", feeding all important information without awaiting explicit requests from the Captain. Officers must constantly monitor the manoeuvre and alert the Captain if they realise that it does not follow the plan. In the same way, the Captain must inform

The final critical element we will deal with regards communication between the Captain and the Helmsman. Captain's orders are repeated aloud by the Helmsman in accordance with a specific procedure[48], but this is not enough to avoid misunderstandings. The "closed loop" communication technique is a recognised countermeasure to avoid them. The person that gives the order is also responsible for closing the loop by saying "yes", confirming that the order was received correctly. After closing the loop the execution of the order must be checked by looking at the rudder angle indicators. However the communication technique adopted by the Captain cannot be considered as a violation of the mentioned company procedure, which recommends only the repetition of the order, not the closing of the loop.

Communication techniques such as "closed loop" and "thinking aloud" (where the intention to perform an action is verbalised before actually executing it) are part of a collection of non-technical skills inspired by the *Cockpit Resource Management (CRM)* concept, which was developed in the civil aviation domain.

The effective implementation of these skills requires a systemic effort that goes beyond writing generic behavioural procedures based on "do's and don'ts". An essential part of this systemic effort is simulator training as it allows officers to understand the importance of teamwork. Not all officers aboard the Costa Concordia had received this type of training.

Inadequate procedures and lack of training aimed at enhancing teamwork must therefore be considered latent conditions common to all errors focussed upon in this chapter. Their origins can be traced back to both organisational and regulatory levels. At the organisational level the undervaluing of the importance of procedures and training to implement effective cooperation on the bridge is evident. However, as for specific training on the Integrated Navigation System, the company is compliant with actual regulations. In fact even though some non-technical skills have been recently added to international standards for training deck officers[49], it will take some time before IMO Member States actually impose these changes.

---

the team of any changes to the existing plan that are deemed necessary during the manoeuvre itself."

48 P14-102 SMS - Behavioural Standards for the Bridge Team (par.4.6): "Orders must be given clearly and repeated aloud by those who receive them."

49 IMO (2010): "The Manila Amendments to the annex to the International Convention on Standards of Training, Certification and Watch-keeping for Seafarers (STCW), 1978.

Costa Crociere has adopted the most common approach amongst shipping companies by opting to comply with new requirements only once they enter into force. Management decisions such as this can derive either from lack of financial resources or from underestimating the competencies required to mitigate the risk of human errors not corrected in time.

At a regulatory level, even though these new competencies have been included in IMO standards, there is still the need to define an operational concept for the organisation of an integrated bridge such as Costa Concordia's.

Table I–8 summarises the teamwork errors and their associated latent conditions.

• The Captain does not inform officers on board of a change in the planned route before departing from Civitavecchia • The Captain does not state his intention to perform a turn wider than planned outbound from the Port of Civitavecchia • The Second Officer does not inform the Junior Officer of the Watch of his intentions before initiating the turn outbound from the Traffic Separation Scheme • The First Officer takes over the watch in an incomplete and informal manner, without using the standard checklist • The First Officer does not inform the Junior Officer of the Watch of his intention to change speed (discussed with the Engineering Officer of the Watch on the ship telephone) • The Captain takes over from the First Officer in an informal manner and without clarity regarding the control of navigation	

Type of Error and Subclass	Mistakes Routine, Incorrect and Non-Functional Violations
Latent conditions at an operational level	• Inadequate procedures for working as a team (behavioural standards do not state "how") • Lack of training in non-technical skills for working as a team • Ambiguity arising from the use of two languages on the bridge (Italian and English)
Origin of Latent Conditions at a Management Level	Underestimating the competencies required to mitigate the risk of human errors not corrected in time
Origin of Latent Conditions at a Regulatory Level	No clear definition of an operational concept for the organisation of an integrated bridge

table I–8 : Errors and latent conditions in working as a team

Our analysis of errors and latent conditions ends at the ship's impact with the rocks. From that moment on improvisation prevails, leading to a series of errors that depend more on the accident's context rather than systemic conditions. A detailed description of the errors committed would therefore hold no significance in understanding the navigational accident.

Hence, the first phase of the systemic analysis (figure I–32) ends with a list of errors and possible latent conditions that somehow "digitise" a complex series of "analogic" events.

The inevitable distortions need to be accepted for the purposes of the next phase: the identification of causes and conditions most relevant to the accident.

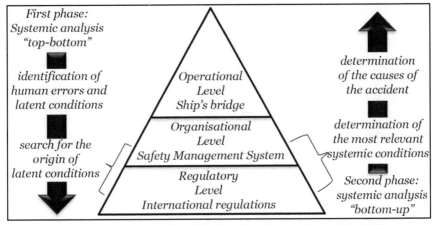

figure I–32 : Systemic analysis in understanding catastrophic accidents

Conclusions of the Investigation

F rom what has been discussed so far, it appears that possible interventions at organisational level would have been useful to defend the system from the errors committed at operational level. However it cannot be proved that the absence of organisational measures provoked the disaster.

This is why the causes of an accident should instead be looked for among the events that triggered it at an operational level. In general, the cause can be:

- human error;
- technical issues (e.g. steering and engine failures);
- external threats (e.g. restricted visibility).

Latent conditions generated at organisational and regulatory levels cannot be considered as causes but only as "conditions" that are also present during normal operations.

James Reason[50] maintains that incidents occur due to the creation of latent conditions at an operational level as a direct result of the inevitable conflict between production and protection at management level. Collectively these conditions create systemic weaknesses that allow human errors and/or other causes to penetrate all system defences until an accident occurs.

The common factors of every catastrophic accident therefore are made up of:

- conflict between production and protection;
- conditions;
- causes.

James Reason has dedicated the large part of his entire career to systemic analyses. And yet he asks if searching for causes of disasters has gone too far over the last few decades. His doubts arise from statements such as those made by the Accident Investigation Board of the 2003 Columbia space mission[51]:

"The causal roots of the accident can be traced, in part, to the turbulent post-Cold war policy environment in which NASA functioned during most

---

[50] James Reason (2008): "The Human Contribution. Unsafe Acts, Accidents and Heroic Recoveries". Ashgate.

[51] On 1st February 2003 the American space shuttle "Columbia" disintegrated during re-entry into the earth's atmosphere, causing the death of the seven astronauts on board.

of the years between the destruction of Challenger and the loss of Columbia[52]."

According to Reason, investigations should stop at the conditions which can be tackled at organisational and regulatory levels without getting lost in factors that are out of reach, such as the political and economic dynamics that affect the maritime system.

Nevertheless, the fact that latent conditions are not considered as causes does not reduce management responsibilities in identifying and removing the most critical ones (within the limits of available financial resources).

It is also fundamental that the determination of causes and conditions is weighted according to their capability in contributing to the safety of the system.

Causes

Let's look at the causes of the Costa Concordia navigational accident, while trying to avoid as far as possible the following human biases:

- *hindsight* – in retrospect all elements analysed seem to converge into a causal pattern towards the moment when the ship hits the rocks. We might think that the officers should have foreseen and anticipated the disaster. Yet this convergence would not have been so obvious if we had observed the course of events on the bridge.
- *Symmetry* – the errors committed on the bridge cannot be considered as major ones just because they generated a catastrophic accident. It is human to assume that the world around us is more ordered and regular than it really is. We always tend to simplify things by imagining a symmetry between the magnitudes of cause and effect.
- *Consequence* – our judgement of decisions made on the bridge is influenced by the knowledge of their catastrophic consequences. We should avoid convincing ourselves of a correlation between correct decisions and positive effects, and also between incorrect decisions and negative effects.

In the light of all that has been said, the causes of Costa Concordia's impact with the rocks of *Le Scole* are as follows:

---

52 Columbia Accident Investigation Board (2003). CAIB report volume 1. Washington DC: Government Printing Office (p.178).

- the Captain's incorrect decision to modify the route plan to perform a sail past along the Island of Giglio, contrary to the company's informal policies;
- the incorrect planning for the deviation towards Giglio performed by the Second Officer;
- insufficient checks by the Captain on the planning of the deviation;
- the Captain's incorrect execution of the final turn for the sail past along Giglio;
- inadequate teamwork during the final turn, with the Captain performing a one-man show on the bridge;
- distractions during the approach to Giglio from the use of mobile telephones and the presence of hotel department staff on the bridge.

It could be said that the accident was caused by common human errors and by distractions during critical moments. The "normality" of these errors highlights their routine regularity in spite of the catastrophic consequences they generated.

Therefore errors and distractions on the bridge broke down the defences *Costa Crociere* put up to prevent navigational accidents. It should also be noted that several of these defences exceed the minimum standards established by IMO, with particular reference to:

- the introduction of a Junior Officer of the Watch in addition to the Officer of the Watch;
- a modern Integrated Navigation System including radar, an Electronic Chart System and a Track Control System;
- the redundancy of sensors for positioning, speed and Heading.

The final defence to be broken down is the ship's watertight integrity, which unlike the others is designed to contain damage rather than prevent it.

In short, the errors and distractions that occurred on the evening of 13th January 2012 caused the Costa Concordia's impact with the rocks of *Le Scole*. This resulted in the flooding of five watertight compartments that irreversibly compromised the ship's stability and survival. Breaking down the last defence generated a large scale accident that cost 32 lives, left 157 crew and passengers injured, and caused the loss of a very large and technologically advanced cruise ship.

Conditions

The systemic analysis conducted in the previous chapters has identified latent conditions associated with the errors committed. Those that contributed to weakening the defences were:

- inadequate training for the specific Integrated Navigation System;
- lack of training in non-technical skills that can enhance teamwork;
- absence of a company policy and operating procedures for sail pasts;
- inadequate teamwork procedures;
- ambiguity stemming from the coexistence of traditional and integrated methods for controlling and monitoring the route;
- usability issues with the Integrated Navigation System's user interface;
- ambiguity deriving from the use of both Italian and English languages on the bridge, even though Italian is the only official one.

As already stated previously, it is impossible to establish a causal nexus between Costa Concordia's accident and the latent conditions present on the bridge. However the identification of these conditions is important in order to define which corrective actions should be implemented at organisational and regulatory levels.

Conflict between Production and Protection

The analysis conducted at an operational level identified significant interactions between the human element (those who operate on the bridge), the technological element (navigation systems and sensors) and the organisational element (procedures for effective management of all technical and human resources on the bridge).

The pace of technological progress over the last two decades has presented many challenges for its integration with the other two elements. In particular for the cruise ship sector, technological development has risen at the same exponential rate as commercial demand. As a result cruise ships have become larger and more complex, making the adaptation with the human and organisational elements more and more difficult.

The responsibility of balancing between production and protection lies with a shipping company's board of directors.

Even with due diligence and sufficient financial resources this is a very difficult equilibrium to maintain. Productive processes in the end are much easier to monitor and quantify when compared to giving a value to protective measures.

Given that production creates the resources necessary to implement safety measures, in the long term its needs will prevail and managers are usually more competent in dealing with production processes than safety ones. Moreover, the flow of information for production is direct and continuous, whereas the one necessary to assess the effectiveness of protective measures is discontinuous and difficult to interpret. This is why the success of safety initiatives cannot be evaluated solely on the basis of the absence of accidents.

Normally it is only after a significant event that safety temporarily gains priority over production. However, it would be more convenient for all parties to avoid waiting for a large scale accident before deciding to focus on safety. Each increase in production should always be balanced by further investment in protective measures. The application of this principle, known as "risk compensation", would mitigate exposure to new vulnerabilities.

In the past there have been cases where investments in safety initiatives have also contributed to advantages in production. One such case occurred during the 1990s when shipowners realised that GPS helped not only in mitigating the risk of groundings, but also in saving fuel by keeping the ships on track.

~

Even though the analysis has given us precise conclusions on the accident, the full understanding of the events on 13th January 2012 can only be reached through a description of the cultural context that the Captain and the Officers of the Costa Concordia belong to. The classification of errors and latent conditions inevitably brings about distortions of reality that is enlivened by the presence of cultural factors at all levels of the maritime system. On the bridge for example, some behaviours follow informal codes that depend on both officers background and the organisational culture of the company itself.

Hence, who are these officers? Where do they come from? How have they been educated and trained? What kind of environment do they work in?

Some answers come from reading between the lines of the interviews conducted in Meta (the birthplace and home of the Costa Concordia's Captain) during the summer of 2012. Others come from within the history of the cruise ship industry and its boom in the last few decades. Therefore the objective of the next chapter is to provide readers with the cultural context that complements the systemic analysis and brings the accident within the spectrum of the elusive human condition.

HUMAN CONDITION

"Only mad, good-for-nothings and
desperate people go to sea"
A saying from the Sorrento Peninsula

Those Who Live, Those Who Die and Those Who Go to Sea

I n Meta, the town where the Captain of the Costa Concordia was born and continues to live, seafarers make up a large part of the population.
We are on the Sorrento Peninsula, where almost 40% of the economy depends on the sea. In Meta alone it is estimated that about 400 of its 8000 inhabitants are officers in the Merchant Navy.

When talking about education here it is assumed you are referring to maritime schools, in particular the Nino Bixio Institute in the nearby town of Piano di Sorrento. This school was attended not only by Costa Concordia's Captain more than thirty years ago, but also by the shipowner Achille Lauro and by Gianluigi Aponte, founder of the *Mediterranean Shipping* Company (MSC).

When we visited in 2012 the school had around 750 students, nearly all male and for the most part sons or relatives of those who already work in the maritime industry. On average, 40% of them will pursue a life at sea and 18% will reach the qualification of Master Mariner[53].

The Dean at Nino Bixio is a woman with a degree in Architecture and a Ph.D. in Iranian Studies.

She tells us that the demand for nautical education increases during periods of economic difficulty because "it allows you to go straight into a job and begin earning good money – up to 1800 Euros per month as an Officer Cadet". This is not a small achievement in a country such as Italy, where youth unemployment in 2012 was over 35% and a newly graduated engineer earns on average around 1300 euros per month.

---

[53] Master Mariner is the professional qualification (recognised by the International Maritime Organisation) that is required to take command of a vessel – in other words to become a Captain.

Luca, Pasquale, Giovanni and Salvatore are all students at Nino Bixio[54] and all four of them have already decided that they will try to take up a career as deck officers.

"Why are you here, why do you want to become officers?", we ask.

"This is one of the few schools that gives us work", says one of them. "And also [this profession - Ed.] allows you to travel and become someone", adds another.

The Dean nods while escorting us to visit the classrooms and laboratories. It is a warm September day and the display cabinets found along the corridors are full of trophies, world maps, sextants and educational model ships.

"The ministerial curriculum cannot keep up with progresses made within the industry, so the schools try to [do it by themselves - Ed.]", explains the Dean while also pointing out that very few of Bixio's teachers are actually ex-seafarers. "The fundamental problem is quality. It is not often sufficient but there are not many inspectors responsible for monitoring and verifying it", she adds.

She is very proud of her maritime school, "the best one in Italy", yet it is unlikely that the students will find the navigational instruments used at Bixio on board a modern ship.

We ask a student recently returned from a week's work experience on a cruise ship what he thinks of the technology he found on the ship's bridge. Does he find it as something that simplifies the job or does it add problems and complications?

"It can be a little bit of both", he answers with a hint of irony, "because we still navigate using the stars rather than knowing how to use a computer."

One of the other students shrugs his shoulders. "At school we do mostly theory. The navigational instruments are different to those we found on board [during the apprenticeship - Ed.]. But then again you do learn with experience."

One of the teachers steps into the discussion and he agrees with the last statement. "Today it is much easier to manage a ship compared to twenty years ago. In the past you needed seamanship, now there's GPS", he says, adding also that a university education is useless in the maritime industry.

"Historically for us [Italians - Ed.], nautical education is provided at high school level. Attending university would just make the path too long. A cadet

---

54 All people mentioned in this chapter were met on the Sorrento Peninsula during the summer of 2012.

can be promoted to second officer or even first officer when he is only 25 years old, whereas he would be just beginning his career at that age if he were to study for a degree."

After all, here in the Sorrento Peninsula seamanship is very much anchored by tradition and stories of times gone by.

In Meta, not far from Nino Bixio, there is a local association that offers financial aid for ship captains. It is called "The Captain's Cottage"[55] and it was founded in 1890 to help seafarers in cases of accidents, diseases or financial difficulties. It is no coincidence therefore that the association's president, Michele Miccio[56] has defended the Captain of the Costa Concordia, his fellow townsman, right from the beginning.

Captain Miccio is a pleasant man. He is tall with a grey beard and speaks with the melodic cadence of Sorrento. He has been retired now for several years after 42 years at sea, 35 of which he spent with Tirrenia[57]. In the midst of display cabinets full of books and model ships we are greeted by him together with Salvatore Esposito, an instructor with 39 years of experience with Tirrenia and a younger captain who currently works for Grimaldi[58].

They are all great storytellers, as so often happens in the peninsula.

They tell us about their life on board, going back to the 1960s. About migrant transport, taking the Spanish to Venezuela or people from the Antilles to Southampton in Great Britain. They've sailed on oil tankers and cargo ships, recording with amusement their favourite – bulk carriers.

"It was like an Easter egg", says Esposito through a large grin. At that time there were no containers and the pallets were in the hold. There was all kinds of everything down there: sunglasses, shoes, typewriters, sewing machines...

"Sometimes the dock workers would drop loads on purpose so that something broke and they could take it", they say. "They even had a length of piping with one end sharpened that they used to puncture sacks and let out a stream of coffee."

At that time there was obviously no internet and people spent the evening listening to transistor radios fitted with homemade antennae.

"Whenever we managed to get a radio signal from Italy it was like winning the lottery for us", they recall.

All three graduated from Nino Bixio before beginning their careers at sea.

---

55 The original name in Italian is "Casina dei capitani".

56 In 2012 when we met him, Michele Miccio was President of the "Captain's Cottage" in Meta.

57 Tirrenia was an Italian state-owned ferry company that was privatised in 2012.

58 Grimaldi is one of the largest Italian cargo and ferry operators, based in Naples.

"I think the most important thing that has changed compared to the past are the periods at sea. I returned home from my first voyage after 22 months: I didn't even recognise my own father", says Esposito. "Now it depends on the shipowners, but usually officers remain on board for about four or five months."

The Grimaldi Captain shakes his head to show that he disagrees. He feels the biggest change is down to the progress of technology that has significantly changed the life of seafarers by taking away the freedom that they once had.

"Now the companies can monitor their ships at any time of the day", he says. "As a result, from absolute oblivion, the captain and the crew are now kept constantly under surveillance."

Esposito nods. "With AIS[59], the ship has become a snail that always leaves a trail behind it."

Miccio agrees. "Today the ship's Captain has become more of a lightning rod. He doesn't manage the ship like in the past, when he had the last word on everything. Telecommunications has changed his job."

In comparison with the past, a captain's seamanship or his experience at sea is no longer enough.

"[Today - Ed.] you need to do specific training courses to obtain the qualifications recognised by IMO. [The job - Ed.] It's becoming more and more specialised which I think is a little limiting", says the Grimaldi Captain. "In our days there wasn't any of this. The Captain more or less performed the navigation and ships didn't have any specific technologies [to be familiar with - Ed.]."

Technology has unquestionably changed the profession. In the past officers learned from experience, with seamanship being handed down on board from master to cadet, voyage after voyage. And now?

The Grimaldi Captain shrugs his shoulders.

"[All this - Ed.] is slowly being lost. Colleagues a little older than me were able to teach me something. I hand down a little less to my cadets every day, who in turn won't pass hardly anything to their subordinates regarding tradition and work in the past", he says. "In fact, in the meantime, the changes have been so great that I will soon be going on a course in electronic navigational charts at fifty years of age. We already have electronic charts on board that in theory we shouldn't use because we are not yet qualified."

---

59 AIS - Automatic Identification System, an automated system for transmitting and viewing navigational data from ship to ship and from ship to coastal monitoring stations.

The Grimaldi Captain is not the only one amongst his colleagues convinced that the ability to use new technologies is not everything.

"We are part of the old watch", he explains. "A good officer is one who knows and understands his vessel. In the end, I am happy to manoeuvre with ECDIS[60], but I come from experience and from a traditional approach to learning the trade. I encourage my officers to use whatever instrument they find on board, provided that they understand how it works. With electronics, it's enough for something small to stop and the whole show comes to a halt", he adds with an air of scepticism.

But if the captains themselves are not familiar with these new systems, who is going to teach the cadets how to use bridge equipment that are getting more and more complex?

In theory it should be the school, but that is not always the case. In Italy the majority of kids who hope to have a career at sea have only gained a diploma from a maritime school.

"When they graduate, are they ready for the job?", we ask the captains.

They shake their heads and their hands to add emphasis to their unanimous no.

"Noooo", replies Esposito. "Both when I was on board before and today when I conduct basic safety training, I see that [the standard of - Ed.] kids' education is much lower and poorer than when we were there. On navigation theory they really have problems, they don't know it. But today the way of sailing is different: you do the course, learn how an instrument works and carry on like that. Let's say they are nerds, but if you were to ask them why an instrument gives certain information, they wouldn't know how to answer."

Captain Miccio sighs. "Schools in Italy are really inadequate and there's also a lot of ignorance among the teachers. Maritime schools should change their curriculum. It's just not possible that after five years kids leave school without even being able to speak English."

The Grimaldi Captain is also of the same opinion.

"Maritime schools are not keeping up with technology", he adds. "And I often joke with young officers on board saying it's them that must be in control of the instruments, not the other way around. Their ability must lie in being able to understand if their instruments – whether it's ECDIS, AIS or GPS – are talking nonsense", he says.

---

60 ECDIS (Electronic Chart Display Information System) is a navigation system that shows the ship's position, route and speed on electronic charts in real time.

Given that the maritime schools are not able to teach students all they need on board, courses offered by privately owned institutions become fundamental to learn and use new bridge equipment. Also, even though the contents and hours of the various courses are regulated at international level, the actual quality differs from centre to centre. It happens that shipowners do not always bear the costs either, so it is the seafarers that must and as a result they look for the best bargain. Another scenario is when the company offers to pay on condition that the seafarer considers time spent on the course as vacation.

Esposito sighs.

"The problem is that seafarers are often freelance and have no form of permanent employment contract", he says. "Once a period at sea is finished they are paid off with extra time, accrued leave, etc..."

The sea freelancers are not paid for the period they spend ashore. There are those who insinuate that many pretend to be ill in order to qualify for benefits from the so-called "*cassa marittima*[61]". This was considered almost as normal practice when it was financed by the shipowners, but now that it is run by a public body called INAIL[62], not many taxpayers would agree with having to pay periods ashore for Italian seafarers in place of their shipowners.

Miccio and Esposito still remember the good old times with Tirrenia. The Trade Union Representatives were so strong that not only did they manage to ensure permanent employment, they also negotiated time at sea to a minimum. "In twenty years we passed from periods of nine months at sea to just forty days. It was like seafarer's heaven, we were very fortunate", says Esposito, while admitting that such abundance would not have been possible were Tirrenia not a state-owned company.

"Private shipowners don't even want to see trade unions from afar", he comments. "If you make any kind of trouble you don't go to sea again. If you do some research over the last thirty years, you won't ever read that a privately owned ship's crew went on strike. There's just no way in which seafarers can get together because they're scattered all over the world and don't ever get the chance to meet." Without counting on the fact that often, there is no awareness on how poor actual working conditions are.

---

61 The *Cassa marittima* is an institution which provides seafarers with financial protection in case of accidents at work and occupational diseases.

62 INAIL (Istituto Nazionale per l'Assicurazione contro gli Infortuni sul Lavoro e le malattie professionali) manages the compulsory insurance scheme against accidents at work and occupational diseases.

Captain Miccio intervenes. "The children of seafarers are aware of the fact that a 14 hour working day is the norm. But the others don't know a lot about the life they're going confront."

Working hours is one of the most sensitive points. The ship never stops and rest days during the months spent on board are not granted. Not only that. Working hours also include night shifts and upon arrival into port or in a condition of emergency, everyone is on call.

The new "Seafarers' Bill of Rights" by the International Labour Organisation (ILO)[63] states that the maximum working hours must not exceed 14 in a period of 24, and no more than 72 hours within a week.

Miccio shrugs his shoulders in resignation. "On a ship, on average you do eight hours watch and four overtime", he says.

Esposito smiles. "It's certain that you work 10 or 12 hours a day. It's impossible to avoid overtime. When ships arrive in port they need the entire crew, especially for shorter journeys. Many officers have just finished an eight hour shift but are called back anyway and that's where the extra time escalation originates", he adds. "A seafarer is on call 24 hours a day. He sleeps on the ship, so whatever happens the supervisor can call him. And obviously everyone's available during emergencies."

According to international law, seafarers' work hours must be recorded accurately on a time sheet, which makes it possible to verify that whilst on board no one works beyond ILO limits.

Seafarers refer to this jokingly as, "the book of lies."

"Filling in these time sheets is often a bit false as it's done in a watered-down way and doesn't really reflect the actual hours worked", explains Esposito.

Miccio intervenes. "The truth is that it is not convenient for the seafarer to declare his actual hours and so he signs without any problems."

But fatigue does have an influence on psychophysical performance. Four months (when things go well) without regular sleep patterns, without a single day off and doing night shifts cannot have a positive effect on attention levels and the alertness of officers.

"But how is it possible to have a day off?" asks Esposito. "When a seafarer is off-duty where can he go? It's just not feasible and whoever's on board, who's already there, wants to work."

---

63 This convention became binding law for all states that ratified it. In Italy it entered into force on 19th November 2014.

68

IMO often tackles the subject of fatigue and has issued guidelines to manage the risks derived from seafarers' excessive psychophysical stress.

Results from the project *Horizon* were published in 2012. Horizon is a joint project that gathers several European maritime universities and institutions, partly funded by the European Commission[64]. It was one of the first studies on fatigue and it used experimental data collected in simulators, observing around 90 officers working at the same rhythm and under the same conditions as those experienced when at sea. Results show clearly how much fatigue influences performance on board, especially during night watches when reaction times are much slower.

"Working day and night for four months is a question of getting used to", comments Miccio. "However fatigue is often concealed. You always think you're fine but you don't realise that [actually - Ed.] you're not. Sometimes during bad weather captains can work up to 18-20 hours. You think you're able to sustain that pace but you're not, absolutely not", he adds.

In the light of this, it seems that salaries aren't really all that high.

Esposito becomes somewhat overheated. "Everyone envies Captains because they earn 7,000 Euros [per month - Ed.], but they are on a ship 24/7 and have a huge responsibility. If I were to keep a worker in a factory for 24 hours I'd have to pay him 14,000 Euros and not 7,000. There's an old saying: you don't beg for money from seafarers, because it is hard-earned with months spent at sea", he exclaims.

Moreover, wages for freelancers who do not have a permanent employment contract are only paid when they are at sea. Once they sign off they are no longer paid and if they fall ill after disembarking they have very little protection.

At one point this instability was compensated for so much that a seafarer felt privileged. The captains discuss that maybe in the past the salary ratio between shore based jobs and those at sea was around one to ten, whereas nowadays has fallen to around one to three.

"After two years of work in the sixties I could buy a nice apartment in the centre of Meta", comments Miccio. "With today's wages it would take about 20 years."

For many officers, higher salaries also act as a sort of trap that keeps them tied to seafaring and prevents them from leaving it.

---

64 Final report of Project Horizon (2012), funded by the European Union and coordinated by the following organisations: Warsash Maritime Academy (Southampton Solent University), Chalmers Tekniska Hoegskola AB and Stress Research Institute of Stockholm University.

"I tried on at least two occasions to stay ashore for good, but I never managed it", recalls Esposito. "The problem is that you get caught up in a vicious circle, because when you're on leave for four or five months you turn into a tycoon. When I came back from stints at sea I could buy drinks for everyone, whereas the accountant couldn't. It really gets to you: you buy yourself a car, a motorbike. And then when you have to go back to sea you cry because you have to leave it all behind. Before going back to sea I would stop eating completely for about two days, I just wasn't hungry and it happened every single time. I never got used to it. After a while there were the children who cried, it was a tragedy. Why are you leaving? they'd ask."

The question of family is a very sore point indeed. For the most part of women in Meta it is quite normal to see their husbands leave for months at a time. But it is not that easy for everyone, not to mention the children...

"The terrible thing is having to stand the separation, putting up with being absent [from the family - Ed.]", Esposito points out. "It's not exactly a socially acceptable life."

The Grimaldi Captain nods: "Despite the advent of new technology this is something that has remained, the difficulty in having to manage a family as well as a ship. I like the life at sea, but the living conditions... you should really remain a bachelor."

One thing the captains do not agree on is whether they would dedicate their life to the sea if they had the chance to turn back time and start again.

"I look at those who work on land, I've got relatives addicted to their mobile phones. I wouldn't like to be in my brother-in-law's shoes", notes the Grimaldi Captain. "Look at me now: I've just done three months on board and I can stay at home for a month and a half. I enjoy my life and I like it", he says.

"And it's a job that gives you the liberty that a shore based job couldn't", adds Miccio.

Esposito thinks and shakes his head before replying.

"The beauty of being a seafarer is that you can forget everything once you get back ashore, just like a mother giving birth. Work on board is stimulating", he admits. "If there were contracts that offered forty days at sea and a month at home I'd do it today. But often we talk about four months or more away from home. If you take the profession of seafaring in itself it's brilliant, but if you include children, friends and wives... And there's also physical suffering in bad weather and the fact that you aren't really travelling. What do you see of the world? You only ever see ports."

The problem is that it is difficult to change your career in Italy, as opposed to what happens in other countries.

"In Nordic countries or in the United Kingdom, you can leave seafaring, go ashore and start over again. It doesn't happen here because there is no work. Actually, in the course that I'm teaching at the moment, there are fifty year olds doing basic beginners training. One was a goldsmith who closed down, another was a baker, but now is unemployed. They go to sea and the sea still welcomes them. But it is very difficult for a deck officer or captain to change career after all the years spent at sea. They can't find anything ashore and so they don't have any choice but to sail for the rest of their lives", exclaims Esposito.

He sighs and then looks around.

"Those who really know what a seafarer's life is like look for another profession. There's a saying in the Sorrento Peninsula: only mad, good-for-nothings and desperate people go to sea[65]."

---

[65] In Italian: "Per mare? Ci vanno i pazzi, i cazzi e i disperati."

Love Boat

They say that one of the largest contributors to the cruise ship boom was an American TV series which aired for over a decade starting from the mid-seventies. It was called *Love Boat* and was based on a book written by an ex Cruise Director, Jeraldine Saunders.

Before then people used to associate cruises with the old transatlantic liners full of poor migrants looking for a better life. But things had been changing behind the scenes. Long range flights were becoming more and more widespread and the middle class increasingly richer and more numerous. While still in its infancy the cruise industry had been looking for a way to improve its image and to understand if it had the potential to become a commercial success. On this question Love Boat made a key contribution. For the first time it showed life on board a cruise ship to the growing middle class, romanticising it and making it appealing, exotic and enjoyable. Stories of passengers, often played by celebrities, entwined with the crew in a near idyllic setting.

At the height of its success the series was watched every week by more than 50 million families and was distributed in over 40 countries. The critics slammed it mercilessly, whereas the general public adored it. It was a roaring success.

Captain David Christie, a *Carnival Corporation* Senior Manager who spent a large part of his career on board *Princess Cruises* ships, recalls that period with a chuckle. "For us Love Boat was half an hour of free advertising on prime time TV every week. People were fascinated, they used to rush home to watch the episodes."

Of course reality did not always reflect fiction, and cruise ships tried to hide it in every way possible to live up to the image being created. It has been said that people sometimes were hired to act as passengers, giving the impression that cruises were full of pretty girls searching for love rather than old age pensioners that often didn't even survive to the end of the voyage.

The youthful cruise industry tried to take full advantage of the free publicity offered by the television series. Captains and officers of *Princess Cruises* ships, for example, brandished the same uniforms as the ones worn by the actors and you could hear Love Boat's theme tune played intermittently throughout the cruise. "It was the period when the cruise industry exploded in the United States", comments Captain Christie.

Before then cruises were a hedgy bet born from the ashes of the passenger liner market. The old liners offered Atlantic crossings during the first half of the twentieth century to those who hoped for a better life in the United States. The advent of the airplane as a means of mass transport put passenger liners into crisis, backing them into a corner. People could now fly to New York or Melbourne without having to bear long voyages across the ocean. It was a safe and relatively cheap way to travel that was much, much faster.

It was a huge shock for passenger liners and as a result business crumbled. It was at this time that several shipowners saw the opportunity of the cruise market, especially in the United States.

"We started off with *P&O* taking people to Australia. We used to start cruises from Sydney, going around the islands before returning. It was a voyage that lasted six to eight months and there were clearly opportunities to seize", remembers Christie.

According to the journalist Kristoffer Garin[66], in the beginning shipowners saw cruises as an irrelevant part of their business, a small distraction compared to the serious business of passenger transport.

The first to realise the possibility of living exclusively on cruises was Frank Fraser. Frank was a ruthless businessman from 1950s Miami who suffered from seasickness. It was however a few decades later that Ted Arison, the founder of *Carnival Corporation* and Knut Kloster, the owner of *Norwegian Cruise Line* (initially *Norwegian Caribbean Line*) set up the base of today's cruise ship industry together. Hot on their heels arrived what nowadays is the second largest cruise company in the world, *Royal Caribbean Cruises*, which controls around a quarter of the entire industry.

However, it wasn't all "plain sailing".

The first ships were very old and not fit for the purpose. Shipowners used to buy rusty vessels used for the transport of migrants, or even decommissioned passenger liners put on the market in abundance due to the crisis of the sector. They were stark affairs with no frills and often full of cockroaches or lacking in basic hygiene. Even after refurbishment they still failed to live up to the expectations of new holidaymakers. There were also many things that could go wrong from an operational point of view. A good example is Carnival's first ship, the *Mardi Gras*, that went aground immediately after leaving Miami on its maiden voyage in 1972.

---

66 Kristoffer A. Garin (2005). "Devils on the Deep Blue Sea. The Dreams, Schemes and Showdowns that Built America's Cruise-Ship Empires". Most of the information in this chapter comes from this book.

The history of the cruise industry is crammed with characters that are worth a mention. One of these is Ted Arison, the founder of *Carnival Cruise Lines*. As a risk taker he made it normal practice to pick himself up and dust himself off after even the most spectacular falls. Born into an affluent family of Israeli shipowners, he found himself at the helm after inheriting the entire business. His first adventures in the shipping world were not met with success and for this reason decided to diversify and enter the airfreight sector, which turned out to be fruitful. But shortly afterwards he decided to sell everything to his business partner and look for other opportunities that could make him his fortune. This decision brought him to bet all his resources on the cruise industry. His first attempts proved disastrous, so much so that he was almost financially ruined. Yet he did not lose heart and he managed to contact Knut Kloster, a Norwegian who also came from an established shipowner family. Kloster was to become one of the key players in the birth of the cruise sector. He was very unsatisfied and bothered when Arison contacted him. In order to diversify his business he had just invested in a passenger liner named the *Sunward*, a car ferry that was bought to take British tourists on holiday to Gibraltar.

This plan was thwarted by the Spanish dictator Francisco Franco who was at odds with Great Britain. As an act of retaliation and to send a strong message to the British he completely isolated Gibraltar, leaving the Norwegian shipowner a victim of circumstances that cost him dearly. Therefore it wasn't difficult for Arison to convince Kloster to combine forces and to bring the *Sunward* to the port of Miami, officially launching what would become *Norwegian Cruise Line*. Ownership remained with Kloster, while Arison managed the booking system, marketing and on board entertainment.

It was 1966 and the pair proclaimed themselves great friends as well as business partners, but this bond didn't last very long. Kloster accused Arison of having taken too much liberty with the funds he managed for *Norwegian Cruise Line*. From his part Arison took advantage of those funds – that he claimed were his by right – to purchase decommissioned ships in Europe and build up *Carnival Cruise Lines*.

The beginnings of this new company were not exactly promising.

Not only was the maiden voyage of the first ship a disaster, but the first few years showed constant losses that resulted in a staggering debt of eight million in the first eighteen months of activity. Both Ted Arison and his son Micky never lost heart and given that the quality of their ships could not compete with those of their rivals, they tried to invent something fresh and new. They lowered their prices to tap into a different market and present themselves to a much younger audience, publicising so called "fun ships". "In the morning, in the evening, ain't we got fun? Not much money, oh but honey, ain't we got fun?", sang Kathie Lee Gifford in the publicity campaign commissioned by the company in the mid-1980s.

And it worked. Despite having been put down by its competitors, *Carnival Cruise Lines* became more and more successful. When it floated on the Stock Exchange in 1987 the Arison family fortune exceeded that of many historical American dynasties. Immediately after, a period of expansion and acquisitions began: *Holland America* in 1989, *Seabourn* in 1993, *Costa Crociere* in 1997, *Cunard* in 1998. The long shopping list culminated in April 2003 when Carnival seized, in a deal worth 5.5 billion dollars, *P&O-Princess,* a company born from the merger between the American *Princess Cruises* and the British-owned *P&O* that had origins in the early nineteenth century during the golden age of the British empire. Following these acquisitions *Carnival Corporation*, which today still controls almost a half of the entire cruise ship industry worldwide, earned the nickname "Carnivore".

In the meantime *Norwegian Cruise Line* had lost its past splendour. The only real competitor remaining was *Carnival Cruise Lines'* historical rival, *Royal Caribbean*, which the Arison family attempted, although in vain, to purchase also.

Royal Caribbean was founded in 1969 thanks to the tenacity of Edwin Stephan. Stephan was a visionary and a veteran from the Korean war. As General Manager in 1965 one of his ships, the *Yarmouth Castle*, caught fire and sank in one of the worst maritime accidents in American history. There were a total of 91 deaths. Passengers were left to themselves and it is said that the young Greek Captain had fled the ship, luring the attention of the general public. The tragedy did not succeed in ruining Stephan's reputation though, and he continued to work in the maritime industry with a dream: to build a new and revolutionary ship, unlike any other on the market. *Royal Caribbean* was born when Stephan managed to capture the attention of two rich Norwegian families, the Skaugens and the Wilhelmsens. From 1970, the first ships were amazingly beautiful, enough so to keep them continuously full without having to invest in publicity.

It was in the years that followed however that demand grew at a surprising rate for all companies within the cruise sector.

In the wake of *Love Boat*, the American middle class dived headlong into this new type of holiday. Business went so well that the 1980s was a period of expansion and exponential growth. From 1977 to 1987, in the USA the cruise ship industry grew at around 9% per year, more than doubling its number of passengers.

All major companies went on a spending spree. New ships were ordered taking emerging needs into account, whilst at the same time some existing ships were made longer. The race was on to find finances to build new vessels, also due to the fact that old passenger liners on the market were becoming fewer and further between.

The bigger a ship was, the more business it generated under the condition that it was always fully booked. After all, the personnel necessary to tend to a larger number of passengers was not a problem. In fact, hotel staff were recruited from third world countries at such a low wage it hardly showed on the balance sheet. Moreover, flying flags of convenience[67] – namely Panama, Liberia and the Bahamas – meant not only that the shipowners had to pay less taxes, but also they didn't have to worry too much about standards of job security for their crews. The increase in the number of ships also brought about an impact on those who worked on board, overturning work rhythms and habits that tradition had imposed up until that moment.

"For a large group of young officers – myself included to a certain extent – promotion was much quicker than expected. They were put in positions of considerable responsibility without having received adequate training and – worse than that – without the necessary experience", recalls Christie, who was a *Princess Cruises* deck officer in the early 1980s.

He still remembers that transformation.

"Before then, officers always relied on experience. There was no training, and once you had gained your Master License[68] that was it, no more classrooms. On the other hand, you had about 20-25 years doing watches on the bridge", he recalls. "But suddenly the industry exploded and the young guys would be promoted to senior positions and responsibilities without all that experience."

During the 1980s and the 1990s growth was even more rapid. Cruises became more widely accessible and bigger and bigger new ships continued to be built with increasing levels of technology.

---

67 The practice of flags of convenience, as told by the journalist Kristoffer Garin, was introduced during the early years of World War II when the United States searched for a way of supplying arms to Great Britain. This was needed to be done without being accused by Germany of aiding the enemy and hauling themselves into the conflict before their time. To resolve the problem, USA allowed its shipping companies to register under foreign flags and was so successful that it was adopted permanently at the end of the war more to avoid taxes rather than German hostility.

68 Here the Master License is intended as the professional qualification of "Master Mariner", which allows an officer to take command of a vessel.

This period is also remembered by Peter Listrup who today is the director of *Smartship Australia*, a simulation centre for maritime pilot training and for the development of port infrastructures.

"If we look at the actual fleets of cruise companies, many ships were built in the late 1990s", he says. "That is the period when they began growing in size. In the past the average size was 200-250 metres in length, but by 2000 onwards many began to exceed 300 metres."

At the same time the number of passengers on board also rose from an average of 2000 to 3000, with another 1000 to count for its crew. The ships had become floating cities.

"All this had a huge impact on how many people could go on a cruise each year when compared to only ten years before", adds Listrup.

This growth favoured the deck officers. All of a sudden they were much more in demand and could apply for work even if they came from different sectors of the industry. From the solitude of cargo ships and oil tankers they could enjoy the sociable atmosphere of a cruise ship. The need for deck officers became so high that companies competed against each other to hire them and, as a result, salaries increased.

"The industry has been moaning about the shortage of officers for around twenty years now. This is probably true but the scarcity is at senior positions, not at entry level. So much so that many students upon graduating find it difficult to find a job on board", continues Listrup. "You can have a quick career if you manage to get the first job. There was a question I often asked officers: how long does it take from starting college to sailing as a captain? They answered saying it depends on many factors, but if all goes well, it could be done within ten years."

David Christie gives a wry smile when he recalls the changes that took place within his *Princess Cruises*. "In the early 2000s we were building two ships every year", he says. "And there was certainly no lack of money to order new ones. The sector was exploding and business was going remarkably well – 2008 was fantastic. We had the most modern and up-to-date bridges fitted with Integrated Navigation Systems. We just needed to learn how to use the new technology made available to us."

This was not a trivial problem, considering that maritime colleges often struggle to keep up with technological progress and that training is practically delegated to each individual company. In addition to this there is the seafarer's traditional mistrust of any instruments, together with the belief that they are able to guide a ship through pure instinct, just by "looking out of the bridge's window".

"Building large ships is a big challenge from a safety point of view, and I'm not talking exclusively about the crew. Designers must meet all necessary requirements regarding both stability and passenger evacuation", explains Listrup.

"Due to the ever growing size of ships, it is also becoming more and more important to have effective operating procedures and a good training regime. In the good old days safety awareness in cruise companies wasn't that high because there weren't so many passengers and the ships themselves were relatively small. But since they have begun carrying thousands of passengers, the Port Authorities and the Flag States pay much more attention to what goes on. The outcome of this is that our industry is moving towards an approach similar to that taken by civil aviation."

One of the companies most renowned for its safety standards is *Star Cruises*. It has a shorter history than its competitors, however it has been continuously gaining ground over the last few years, particularly in Asia. When it purchased *Norwegian Cruise Line* in 2000, it became the third largest cruise operator in the world.

Nonetheless *Star Cruises* was not founded around a passion for cruise ships, rather one for gambling. It all started in 1993 when a powerful Malaysian family called Lim, owners of Genting Group, was struggling with restrictions on casinos in Asia.

"Why not buy a cruise ship and have a casino at sea?", they thought. "That way we won't need any authorisations."

The idea was deemed acceptable and Genting began moving its weight, although it had absolutely no experience within the cruise industry. It was important to move quickly, to buy the ships and start up the business as soon as possible. The two or three years it would take to build new vessels was far too long to wait. It is said that an agent of the group went to Northern Europe to examine two relatively new ships held alongside after the Swedish company that owned them went bankrupt.

They were very expensive and the broker that took them was worried about the possibility of selling them off quickly. Then the agent of the Malaysian company came along, saw the ships in good condition and immediately put down a deposit to secure them. The only problem in all this was how to get them from Scandinavia to Southeast Asia. Therefore the broker called the officers of the previous shipowner back in order to take the vessels to their destination. Upon arriving in Singapore they were made an offer to remain on board. Which is why, despite Asian ownership, *Star Cruises* still has a large number of Scandinavian officers.

The Malaysian company's great attention to safety is heavily linked to its origins in gambling. Peter Listrup smiles. Before becoming director of *Smartship Australia* he spent several years on board *Star Cruises* ships, right up to managing their training centre.

"Let's not forget that the Genting Group was involved in gambling and had casinos on their ships. As we know, gamblers can be very superstitious. The fear was that if a ship had ever had an accident, passengers would brand it unlucky and would refuse to gamble on board", he explains.

"At the very beginning a *Star Cruises* ship collided with an oil tanker. As a result the owners said that they would have done anything to prevent further accidents. And so began a period during which there were few spending limits for training and anything else that would have improved safety of navigation."

These investments seem to have worked. After that collision *Star Cruises* went on to operate for the next decade with practically no further accidents, in spite of the highly congested waters of Southeast Asia.

We Are Lord Jim

As already stated at the beginning of this first part of the book, the emergency management of the Costa Concordia has not been analysed as it does not help us in understanding the navigational accident. However the events that took place after the impact with the rocks are important to get to the bottom of the human condition of its key players: the Captain and his officers. They have all been put in the stocks by the world's media. "They ran away, they didn't help", was the charge. They didn't behave like heroes.

Is it really possible to demand that common men risk their own lives in the name of duty?

This is by no means an attempt to justify the actions of the Captain and his officers for abandoning ship with many passengers still on board. More than thirty people died in what should have been a holiday for them and it is the role of the court to ascertain where responsibility lies. But it is important to reflect upon the human condition, upon the weakness and the fragility that are experienced when faced with the fear of death.

Lord Jim, one of Joseph Conrad's greatest novels, tackles the very subject of an officer who stands trial after abandoning a ship full of passengers.

The novel is set in the latter half of the nineteenth century[69] and Jim is a young English officer, who by chance embarks as chief mate on an old vessel that is carrying pilgrims from India to the Arabian Peninsula.

On a dead calm night the ship hits a semi-submerged derelict. It doesn't seem like a serious impact and in fact the passengers do not even notice it. However the officers understand the gravity of the situation and the danger they find themselves in. The ship could sink at any moment with no way out. So they decide to abandon ship and get as far away as possible without even waking the pilgrims. According to the Captain there is not enough space on the lifeboats to save them as well. Jim looks at him indignantly with a feeling of disgust. He tells himself that he is not like the Captain, that he will stay on board and help the pilgrims.

But then, at the very last moment, something happens that he cannot explain to himself and will change his life for ever. One of the sailors who decided to leave with the Captain feels ill and falls at Jim's feet. It is at that

---

69 Coverage of the novel is taken from the critical essay by Thomas Harrison "Let Me Tell You about Lord Jim", published in the Italian magazine "Il Carabiniere", December 1997.

moment that Jim jumps into the lifeboat in the sailor's place, abandoning ship.

How could this have happened? Jim continues to think about it without finding a plausible explanation. His heroic ideals vanish with that single leap.

Contrary to all expectations the vessel does not sink and the pilgrims are rescued by a passing ship. A Court of Marine Inquiry was convened in order to establish the circumstances of the abandonment of the ship and make a judgement on the conduct of the crew. Jim is the only one to appear before the court, refusing to run away once again as the Captain and other officers do.

He admits to having been a coward and to not living up to his ideals together with the heroic image he had of himself. He says that he realised all this when he jumped into the lifeboat without any control over his fear and his natural instinct for survival.

The judges are not lenient with him and strike him off the Officers' Register. "Well, then, let him creep twenty feet underground and stay there!", says one of them during sentencing.

Absolute condemnation? No, Conrad's comment is a warning to the reader[70]:

"Nothing more awful than to watch a man who has been found out, not in a crime but in a more than criminal weakness. The commonest sort of fortitude prevents us from becoming criminals in a legal sense; it is from weakness unknown, but perhaps suspected, as in some parts of the world you suspect a deadly snake in every bush — from weakness that may lie hidden, watched or unwatched, prayed against or manfully scorned, repressed or maybe ignored more than half a lifetime, not one of us is safe..."

The author forces us to reflect before pointing the finger, to ask ourselves if we are certain to be different from Lord Jim, and if we are sure we do not hide the same weaknesses within ourselves. Ultimately, as written in an Italian introduction to Conrad's novel[71]:

"We are Lord Jim, this coward that at a certain moment leaps from the ship and abandons thousands of pilgrims to their own destiny. Then the great remorse and the sense of guilt begin. And we have all jumped off at some point in our lives".

---

70 Joseph Conrad (1900): "Lord Jim" (chapter 5).

71 Ugo Mursia, quoted by Federica Almagioni in the preface to "Lord Jim", in the Italian translation by Alessandro Gallone, Alberto Peruzzo Editore, 1989.

PART II OPERATIONAL CONCEPT

Bridge Resource Management (BRM) is a relatively new concept in the maritime industry. There are those who consider it just a set of behavioural practices that improve teamwork during navigation – however that is not the case at all. BRM's aim is actually to manage all human and technical resources on a ship's bridge by being aware of their potential and limitations.

The second part of this book will attempt to clarify the more important aspects of BRM and is divided into three main chapters. The first will analyse the potential and limitations of human resources both on a cognitive and a physiological level. In the second chapter we will concentrate on technical resources, i.e. on the accuracy and the features of navigation systems and sensors available on a modern ship's bridge.

It is only at this point that we will be able to understand the third chapter, which will explain policies, principles and procedures needed for BRM's correct implementation. As we will see, this is an operational concept with the potential to revolutionise the way we navigate in the digital age.

HUMAN RESOURCES ON THE SHIP'S BRIDGE

Know thyself
Temple of Apollo in Delphi

"Changing one's mind about human nature is hard work,
and changing one's mind for the worse about oneself is even harder"
Daniel Kahneman

Cognitive Potential and Limitations

D uring the beginning of the 1990s the civil aviation industry introduced a test for its pilots. Its aim was to assess each pilot's knowledge of human performance and limitations both physically and psychologically. Those that did not pass did not receive their pilot's licence, regardless of the level of technical skill they reached during basic training. The objective was to make pilots more aware of their psychophysical limits during flight.

The maritime industry is still some way behind on this matter and basic training for deck officers does not tackle this particular area. However it would be very useful for people who conduct ships to know what it is that influences their decisions and how the mind processes information.

With work on a ship's bridge in mind this chapter will describe cognitive potential and limitations, accompanying each topic with practical examples that help understand how to apply these notions at sea.

Let's begin with the way we express ourselves. Below are two lists of "thoughts"[1]:

I can do it!	*Why take the risk?*
It won't happen to me.	*It could also happen to me.*
What's the use?	*I won't give up.*
This is someone else's decision.	*We're all in the same boat.*
Don't tell me what to do.	*Follow the rules.*
We've always done it like this.	*Is there a better way?*
Do something, quickly!	*Not so fast, think about it.*

---

1 Tony Wilson (1993). *Aircraft Human Performance and Limitations.* Civil Aviation Safety Authority Australia.

They may seem like similar phrases, but they are not. Those on the left are known as "hazardous thoughts", whereas those on the right are their corresponding "safe thoughts". In order to understand how much they influence decisions and behaviours of a deck officer we need to have a basic knowledge of psychology, particularly cognitive psychology.

To help us out there are studies that have been conducted by psychologists such as Amos Tversky and Daniel Kahneman, a Nobel Laureate for economics. Kahneman's bestseller *"Thinking, Fast and Slow"* is a collection of three decades' work[2] and it analyses the psychological mechanisms that affect our abilities to judge and to choose. Kahneman visualises the human mind split into two parts with very different characteristics:

- intuitive – known as *"system 1"* – that operates rapidly, using our instinct;
- rational – known as *"system 2"* – that operates in a reflective and slow manner, taking time to concentrate on more complex mental activities.

With respect to our own perception, we identify ourselves with *system* 2. We think we are rational, have solid belief and that we reason and react on the basis of solid reflection. We do not realise that in reality it is *system 1* that is responsible for the majority of our choices and judgement.

Automatic, intuitive activities from *system 1* include:

- determining that a ship is further away from another simply by observing its position;
- locating a sound's origin;
- sensing hostility in a reply from the captain.

Examples of activities managed by *system 2* are:

- calculating the Course Over Ground required to maintain an established minimum distance from another ship;
- comparing a ship's GPS position to that derived from visual bearings;
- calculating the Rate of Turn necessary to perform a turn within planned limits.

When *system* 2 is being used the entire body is involved. Muscles contract, pupils dilate, blood pressure rises and heartbeat increases.

We can imagine *system 1* and *system 2* as two characters with very different personalities that are forced to work together constantly. The first is rapid and impulsive. It recognises familiar situations and so is able to make

---

2 Daniel Kahneman (2011). "Thinking, Fast and Slow". Penguin Press.

short-term predictions. It is also this system that generates the first response to new situations. The second is much more placid and thoughtful, but it is also lazy and most of the time lets the other react without much intervention, giving only its consent. When things become difficult however, it takes charge and searches the memory for pieces of knowledge that can help in resolving the problem.

The division of work into these two parts is very efficient as it minimises effort and optimises cognitive performance.

It is important to understand that *system 1*:

- is subject to numerous biases that arise in specific circumstances;
- has a limited comprehension of logic and statistics;
- cannot be switched off.

Therefore *system 1* uses minimal effort to create impressions and sensations that are at the root of opinions and choices made by *system 2*. The latter however has the ability to change how *system 1* works by reprogramming its two most important functions: *attention* and *memory*.

Attention

We are able to perform many tasks simultaneously, but only if they are easy or routine. As soon as a situation requires more concentration we have to become more selective in the activities we dedicate our mental resources to. It's when things become particularly difficult though that our attention becomes so selective it makes things that we would normally notice to disappear completely. An excellent demonstration of this phenomenon, known as *inattentional blindness,* is the experiment of the "invisible gorilla" by Christopher Chabris and Daniel Simons[3].

In a short film, the two psychologists filmed two groups of people, one in white shirts and the other in black shirts, that pass two basketballs between them. During the film they move between each other, making it difficult to follow their movements. All that is asked of those who watch the video for the first time is to count how many passes the white team makes. However, halfway through the film a man dressed in a gorilla suit comes into view on the right hand side, stops in the middle of the scene and beats his chest before slowly exiting to the left. He remains in shot for a total of nine seconds, yet not everyone actually notices him. It is estimated that around half of the thousand students that watched the video didn't see the gorilla at

---

3 "The invisible gorilla" experiment can be viewed on the website www.theinvisiblegorilla.com

all. In fact, the demanding task of counting the number of passes and ignoring the black players provokes inattentional blindness.

The most important result from the experiment though isn't the inability to notice the gorilla, but the astonishment on the faces of those who failed to see it when they are presented with the evidence. An astonishment that demonstrates not only we don't always see the obvious, but we are unaware about this possible blindness.

A classic example of this phenomenon on a ship's bridge would be to not notice a vessel overtaking us because we are too involved in evaluating the minimum distance from another ship. Being aware and accepting this limitation helps us in developing countermeasures to prevent it, such as delegating tasks and assigning a second person to check for possible ships coming from aft.

Memory

Memory is generally divided into three categories: sensorial, short-term and long-term.

Sensorial memory holds perceptions of our senses for a very short timespan. An example of this is visual stimuli that remain in our brains for just one second before being processed cognitively. Audio stimuli are held in our memory for a little longer, sometimes for up to several seconds. This is why we can respond to something we heard a few seconds before, even if we were not paying much attention at the time.

Short-term memory has a larger capacity than sensorial memory: it can retain from five to nine elements simultaneously, even for tens of seconds at a time. It is also the case that acoustically acquired information remains stored for longer periods compared to visual information. Using short-term memory efficiently whilst recognising its limits can prove crucial when we are very busy.

Long-term memory has an ability that ranges from just a few minutes to an entire lifetime. Whilst short-term memory is less prone to making mistakes, long-term memory is much more likely to return distorted information or even make it inaccessible, such as when something is on the tip of our tongue. In addition short-term memory can be improved simply through repetition, whereas long-term memory needs associations with information already present to perform better.

It should also be added however that we are able to sense a connection between elements before we begin using our long-term memory. Let's take three words: "salt", "deep" and "open". These can be immediately associated with the word "sea". Let's take into consideration other three word groups that can each be either connected via another or that have no logical association between them. If asked to only select the groups containing three connected words without giving the "binding" word, it would be much easier than we would imagine. This means that we can associate elements intuitively before even having to think about it.

Experiments of this type have been conducted to study the origin of creativity[4]. It seems that creative people are very proficient when it comes to association, however this ability is greatly influenced by their mood at the time. A good mood has a positive effect on the accuracy of intuitive association, but it is also detrimental to the vigilance of *system 2* which is even more inclined to accept sensations from *system 1*. On the contrary bad mood reduces the accuracy of intuitions but increases *system 2*'s control over *system 1*, making us more reflective and analytical as a consequence.

On discovering this it comes as no surprise that software corporations have transformed the offices of their programmers into colourful and welcoming workplaces, designed with the purpose of putting them in a good mood and hence stimulating their creativity. Something very different from the traditional grimness of offices within banks.

Back on board a ship though, what is more desirable for those who work on the bridge? Is it better to have more intuitive ability or more reflection?

Given the relative slowness of maritime operations, it's certainly preferable to encourage reflection rather than intuition. So should we stimulate a bad mood in order to increase active control of situations? Maybe this could be a little excessive. However a light yet chronic sense of unease could help operators in maintaining a fair level of reflectiveness.

Lastly, it is also helpful to know that *system 1* excels in constructing an entire situation based exclusively on ideas drawn from short-term memory. Its ability lies in creating a coherent version of reality, even in the absence of solid assumptions. The worst thing though is that *system 1* doesn't always admit to not having considered the critical elements needed to make a decision. Thus we convince ourselves that there is nothing else we need to know apart from what we can see.

Even when information is scarce, such as on a bridge with minimal equipment and/or in conditions of restricted visibility, *system 1* can still find coherence, establish causal relations between events and make decisions

---

4 Remote Association Test (RAT).

based upon them. Moreover, it is stubbornly insensitive not only to the quantity, but also to the quality of the data available.

So when rapid and intuitive thought takes over, it represents a coherent operational situation and pushes us to refuse further information that may undermine this coherence. If we also add the traditional aversion of seafarers to the use of instruments, it's not difficult to understand why captains and maritime pilots trust only visual information when manoeuvring a ship.

In conclusion, our brain stores stimuli within our memory and interprets them according to experiences from the past. It does not save us though from the misinterpretations of the outside world that are commonly known as illusions.

Illusions

The image below (figure II–1) is known as the Müller-Lyer Illusion. Let's have a look at it for a moment.

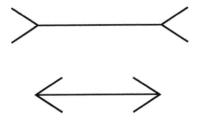

figure II–1 : Müller-Lyer Illusion

Although the two horizontal lines have the same length, they appear different. When we look at this image for the first time *system 1* prompts us to say that the line above is longer. However once we become aware of the illusion and we see the image again, *system 2* sees through the trick and corrects *system 1*'s intuition. We have in fact learned that the lines are equal in length even though we keep on perceiving them as different. In order to resist this illusion we need to mistrust how we perceive lines with opposing arrows such as the ones above. This recognition is an important process because it prevents us from making a mistake whilst easing the workload of *system 2*. The only alternative would be to question perceptions from *system 1* all the time, which would make us slow and inefficient when making routine decisions.

On a ship's bridge we are exposed to many different types of optical illusions. For example, in the presence of a current the ship's Heading might seem misaligned with the axis of a channel, whereas the Course Over Ground is correctly parallel to it. In the mind of an expert navigator, *system 2* can recognise this situation.

Optical illusions are not the only type of illusion we need to be prepared to recognise. There are also cognitive ones, such as illusions of *remembering*, *understanding* and *skill*.

The *illusion of remembering* affects our memory. When we are involved in something unusual that we have seen previously, we perceive a sense of familiarity. This makes us believe wrongly that we have already experienced what is happening and so already know how to manage it. The perception of familiarity is produced by *system 1* and sent to *system 2*, which validates the impression with its usual laziness.

Let's take the example of an alarm raised by an Integrated Navigation System. If it continuously rings we end up regarding it as a familiar sound and convince ourselves that we know what needs to be done. This happens without us even realising we are ignoring the actual reason for the alarm sounding or what the correct action is to carry out. Taken to excesses, this is a technique used by politicians during an electoral campaign: they repeat the same things until blue in the face in order to blur the difference between reality and familiarity.

Another illusion to be aware of is that of *understanding*, where our notion of people and facts is influenced by what we already know or have heard from others. We tend to use this information to create future expectations without considering bias in our judgement embedded within our very nature.

This type of illusion includes so-called "halo effect" that pushes us to judge a person's ability based on first impressions. For example, if a Captain seems just and fair in his behaviour at first sight, we tend to think positively also of his ability to manoeuvre a ship. On the other hand, if he leaves a bad first impression we are more likely to underestimate his seamanship. The halo effect helps us to keep ideas consistent and simple but it also tends to make us exaggerate in our evaluations. Heroes become invincible, whilst antiheroes – such as the Captain of the Costa Concordia – are condemned on all counts. It is easier to surrender to this illusion of understanding rather than venture into the complexity of human factors and past events. Simplifying things also helps to reduce cognitive effort and make us think much more clearly. At the same time though it does allow *system 1* to take control of the situation.

The illusion of understanding can also manifest itself when we let the judgement of others influence us. For instance, during de-briefings conducted on board at the end of a manoeuvre, listening to the views of colleagues who speak first and in an assertive manner can sway the independent opinions of those who follow. To avoid this happening, it is recommended that all operators attending de-briefings should write down their observations before the discussion starts, and that those who are less expert speak first.

The final illusion, maybe the most important to avoid on a ship's bridge, is that of *skill*. In his attempt to describe it Kahneman uses the world of finance, where in his views investors (both professional and novice) fail to pass even the most elementary proof of skill: the repeatability of their performance. After 50 years of research it has been shown that the performance of at least two out of three investment funds are lower than the market average. The traders may say that logical decisions were made during a period of great uncertainty. They cannot accept the idea that their own successes, as well as their failures, are often achieved or caused by chance and not because of their capability.

The *illusion of skill* can be much more stubborn than an optical illusion because it threatens our self-esteem. Even if we readily admit that intellectually we are not as clever as we believe, it is still difficult to take this into account and change our behaviour. This becomes more evident the higher the level of skill required. How could a ship's Captain with over 30 years experience admit to not being able to perform the same manoeuvre with the same safety margins over and over again? And even if he did accept his limits, would he be able to change the way he manoeuvres the ship? Probably not.

It is often the case that experts in the maritime industry are those who stand up for obsolete practices. They continue to believe in the so-called "art of navigation", something that is still deeply ingrained within the industry's culture. They tend to rely exclusively on instinct and traditional techniques such as monitoring positions with the naked eye or controlling routes and manoeuvres manually.

A good example of illusion of skill is when officers and/or maritime pilots order rudder angles during turns. These can be automatically determined and controlled by an Integrated Navigation System, just like the one installed on the Costa Concordia. Nevertheless those that swear by traditional techniques continue to set rudder angles manually based entirely on their intuition. Not only do they not use instruments, they feel they can do it even better by themselves, especially in confined waters.

Human beings are able to maintain a sturdy faith in shared practices within a community, with no regard as how inadequate they actually are. Maritime professionals are no exception and they have always been traditionally vulnerable to the illusion of skill. However things are gradually changing thanks to simulation centres, whose level of fidelity allows testing an officer or pilot's repeatability in performing manoeuvres within specific safety margins.

In an essay on Tolstoy[5], the philosopher Isaiah Berlin divides thinkers into two categories: hedgehogs and foxes. The hedgehogs tend to clutch to an idea or concept that seems clear and important to them. They get angry with those who do not agree and find it very difficult to admit being mistaken. On the other hand, the foxes accept that reality emerges from the complex interaction between various elements. Among these elements, good and bad luck play an important role in creating consequences that may be just as relevant as they are unexpected.

Therefore in order to be successful, Bridge Resource Management needs professionals similar to Berlin's fox, i.e. able to recognise the various types of cognitive illusions. Stubbornness and the beliefs of hedgehogs are in fact out of place in the growing complexity of the world in the digital age. A world where airline pilots, ship captains, maritime pilots and nuclear power plant operators need to be more and more aware of their cognitive potential and limitations.

Cognitive Effort

Our *system 2* is hopelessly slow and lazy. It never does more than is absolutely necessary and when active, it dilates our pupils in proportion to the amount of effort it is subjected to. Just like a speedometer shows how fast a car is going, pupil dilation shows us how much mental energy we're consuming. This effect becomes even more evident when confronted by an activity or an event that is new to us, whereas it is less relevant when dealing with more familiar situations.

Human beings tend to avoid cognitive effort. If there are different ways to reach the same objective, without a doubt the easiest path is chosen. We must accept that laziness, both physical and mental, has very deep roots in our very nature, which can be explained from different perspectives. From a physiological point of view, our blood glucose levels reduce when we are cognitively busy. From an evolutionary point of view, the intuitive ability of *system 1* has turned out to be more useful for our species: when faced with a

---

5 Isaiah Berlin (1953). "The Hedgehog and the Fox". Elephant paperback.

sabre tooth tiger in the jungle, our ancestors had a better chance of surviving by running away rather than reasoning about the best option.

However laziness does not manifest itself only during cognitive overload. In fact *system 2* shows an extraordinary tendency to confirm perceptions from *system 1* even when checking would require very little effort.

Try and respond to this brainteaser that Kahneman proposes.

A baseball bat and ball cost 1.10 dollars. The bat costs one dollar more than the ball. How much does the ball cost?

The number that probably first cross your mind was 10 cents. "Easy", you may say. But if you pay a little more attention you'll realise that if the ball cost 10 cents, then the bat would cost 1.10 dollars, making a total cost of 1.20 dollars. The correct answer is actually 5 cents, yet the question fooled over a half of the students attending the most prestigious American universities. Once again, they were tricked by their intuition.

So what do the results of this experiment actually tell us? It helps us understand that not only do we trust our intuition excessively, but also we are not designed to think rationally.

Despite its notorious laziness, *system 2* is absolutely essential when we need to:

- apply rules;
- compare different objects on the basis of their differing characteristics;
- decide from several options.

It is also *system 2* that allows us to program our memory for carrying out a task that is not familiar to us, such as *active monitoring* of navigation instruments. This is an activity that is becoming more and more important on modern ship's bridges. In fact, with the introduction of Track Control Systems – such as the one on board Costa Concordia – officers are required to select the parameters that they wish to monitor, while taking into account their own limited cognitive resources and the risk of "inattentional blindness". They must force themselves to activate *system 2* when comparing the image of the real world from the observation of external elements with the one constructed using data from navigation sensors. When faced with any discrepancies they must make decisions without succumbing to their so called "gut feeling". Lastly, they must also set out rules to make this practice of monitoring cyclical.

This is by no means a simple process. Triggering *system 2* requires a lot of discipline, especially when under pressure. If we need to simultaneously monitor a number of parameters our *system 2* struggles even more than usual as it is forced to work quickly, which is against its own nature. When the workload becomes too high, one possible solution is to delegate a part of the job to a second person. If this is not possible then the ship should be slowed down to gain time and ease the burden on *system 2*.

We can now understand how damaging distractions that are non-functional to navigation can actually be, especially when dealing with high levels of cognitive effort. Today mobile telephones are one of the most common of these distractions. The mobile phone that rang and interrupted the rudder order given by the Captain of the Costa Concordia during the final turn is a sad but unquestionable example of the potential damage that can be caused by such a simple distraction.

Anchoring Effect

Let's imagine that we are on the wing of a ship's bridge. The Captain asks us to look at the sea surface and to guess whether the current is faster or slower than two knots. How do we reply to this?

Most probably our estimate will not be too far from the two knots initially estimated by the Captain. This is because we have been cognitively influenced by that initial value. Psychology calls this effect *anchoring* and it makes it very hard for us to express judgements "outside the limits", especially when our short-term memory is already working hard. This is a concept market traders know very well. When they fix the initial price of a product, the psychological effects of anchoring will heavily influence on the negotiation that follows.

Being aware of this effect is not only useful when making bargains. For example, it can help us improve the interaction between deck officers and maritime pilots on the bridge. Let's consider a statement such as: "I feel the ship's speed is at least two knots faster than necessary". This will influence the officer with the conn, who will find it more intuitive to reduce speed rather than increase it. If however the statement were transformed into a question – such as "what is our current speed?" – the officer's opinion would remain more independent. He would probably realise that he has lost control of the ship's speed of his own accord, or he may be able to explain the reasons behind his decision.

Bridge procedures for interaction between team members should take this effect into account. Possible strategies for getting around it consist in:

- trying to limit suggestions or to express them only if the reply to the initial question was not satisfactory;
- trying to think, even if only for a moment, of the opposite of suggestions received (e.g. the officer in the previous example should ask himself if the ship's speed is actually slower than necessary).

Ego Depletion

When we find ourselves consumed by activities that require a high level of cognitive effort for long periods of time, such as the active monitoring of navigation, our own self-control diminishes. This phenomenon is known as *ego depletion* and can have a negative impact on social dynamics on a ship's bridge. Our ability to keep a positive attitude towards a colleague, especially when under pressure, can be noticeably reduced after he/she expresses doubts regarding a particular decision.

In these cases even a piece of candy can help. In fact when we are experiencing cognitive overload, blood glucose levels fall because our nervous system is consuming more than usual. Taking in sugars therefore could help our mood and make us better disposed to others.

When self-control is reduced we tend to limit our mental efforts as much as possible and rely more on *system 1*. As a result ego depletion makes us more vulnerable to errors that originate from intuitive decisions.

Intuition

Can we trust the intuitions of an expert? *Decision making* researchers have differing opinions on the answer to this question.

Two of these are the psychologists Gary Klein and Daniel Kahneman. Klein is contrary to the idea that decisions made by experts are quite so susceptible to intuitive thought's bias. His opinion is that real experts are aware of their own limits. Their perceptions can be trusted because they choose lines of action that they "recognise" as effective from past experiences, rather than assessing the many different options available. His theories seem to uphold the definition of intuition by the psychologist Herbert Simon[6]: *"the situation has provided a cue; this cue has given the expert access to information*

---

6 In Daniel Kahneman's "Thinking, Fast and Slow", reference to Herbert Simon is made on many occasions, defining him as one of the most important intellectuals of the twentieth century. Simon is considered the founder of studies in the field of artificial intelligence, as well as a pioneer in applied economics psychology.

stored in memory, and the information provides the answer. Intuition is nothing more and nothing less than recognition."

Kahneman is a little more sceptical, maybe due to the different contexts in which he has carried out his research. While Klein has concentrated his efforts on fire-fighters and nurses, Kahneman investigated the world of financial analysts, concluding that the faith they have in their intuition is generally too high and unfounded given the unpredictability of socioeconomic dynamics.

Both however agree on the fact that experts' reliance on their intuitions is not a yardstick for establishing their validity. This depends on two elements: the operational context where experts perform and the level of experience matured. If the context is stable enough to be predictable and if it has been possible to experiment with its characteristics for a long period of time, then there is a good chance that the expert's intuition is valid.

Nevertheless, a real intuitive ability depends not only on the amount of experience gained in the field, but also on how these abilities were learned. Reaching solid intuitive capability becomes difficult if the operational context is characterised by long delays between actions and their consequences. This is why it is more difficult to manoeuvre a ship correctly using intuition than it is to drive a car.

If we were to take the example of a doctor working out a general therapy for several patients suffering from a long-term illness, the delay in the various results will be so diluted over time that it is practically impossible to develop a specific intuitive ability.

When the context is unstable and unpredictable such as in the world of finance, expert intuitions have no validity at all. In this case the error is not necessarily in getting the forecast wrong, but in believing it was actually possible to do so in the first place.

In conclusion, Kahneman and Klein agree that the evaluation of experts' intuitive capabilities is conditioned by:

- the stability and the predictability of the operational context;
- the way in which the expert has gained his specific competence. Was he given the opportunity to mature enough experience? What is the typical response time generated by his/her actions?

Personality

Together with *system 1* and *system 2*, there is another factor that influences our judgements and decisions, namely our personality. But what do we mean exactly when we refer to it?

In a book on human performance and limitations written for aviation pilots[7], flight instructor Tony Wilson defines personality as a collection of behavioural traits that a person uses to adapt to the surrounding environment. For an airline pilot, just like for an officer on a ship's bridge, it is important to recognise and correct attitudes that are potentially dangerous to navigation safety, whether it be in the air or at sea.

Tony Wilson identifies six behavioural traits with as many "dangerous thoughts", which were already mentioned at the beginning of the chapter:

- *Deference*: "this is someone else's decision" – when we refuse to accept responsibility for our decisions, stating that it lies with the captain or the company.
- *Anti-authority*: "don't tell me what to do" – when we feel threatened by a suggestion and feel that the rules only apply to others.
- *Invulnerability*: "it won't happen to me" – when we refuse to accept our psychophysical limits and our vulnerability to errors.
- *Impulsiveness*: "do something, quickly" – hastily searching for a solution when confronted with difficult situations.
- *Resignation*: "what's the use" and "we've always done it like this" – when we become discouraged, convinced that we are not able to change anything.
- *Macho*: "I can do it!" – when we feel capable of doing everything on our own, having too much faith in our own abilities.

So for each of these attitudes we should always bear the corresponding "safe thoughts" in mind, which are also listed at the beginning of this chapter. It would be a simple way to recognise and challenge behaviours that may turn out to be hazardous.

Intelligence and Rationality

A minority of people excel in the typical activities of *system 2*. They are able to perform difficult calculations that require efficient memory access to find useful information for problem solving. Usually they obtain high results

---

7 Tony Wilson (1993): "Aircraft Human Performance and Limitations". Civil Aviation Safety Authority Australia.

in intelligence tests, but that does not mean that they are immune to making errors of judgement. It is actually important to make a clear distinction between *intelligence* and *rationality*. Being rational means remaining vigilant and less willing to accept intuitive answers.

Those who act with rationality are less likely to be overcome by *system 2*'s laziness, and they are rarely fooled by brainteasers such as the one about the baseball and bat. Indeed these types of brainteaser are more useful than intelligence tests in evaluating our rationality and as such, in our susceptibility to making errors of judgement.

In the digital age, instead of higher intelligence quotients, we need more and more rationality, as managing the ever increasing amount of information without giving in to deceptive intuitions has become essential. We should use our rationality to actively monitor congruence between the external world experienced through our senses and navigation instrument readings, and not just for making operational decisions.

Physiological Potential and Limitations

T he human brain is able to recreate a mental representation of the external world by putting information obtained by our senses together. In the same way it controls motor functions such as the coordination in turning our head and moving our eyes.

To be able to manage our sensory organs better it's important to be aware of their potential and their limitations. Bearing in mind that on a ship's bridge the majority of stimuli are visual and audio, seafarers need to learn certain basic notions of sight and hearing.

Sight

The human eye (figure II–2), just like a camera, is capable of:

- collecting light stimulus through photoreceptors that are found on a special film known as the *retina*;
- adjusting light intensity by varying the diameter of the *pupil* with a coloured diaphragm known as the *iris*;
- focussing by using an adjustable system of lenses, called *cornea* and *crystalline*;
- transmitting the acquired image to the brain through the *optic nerve*.

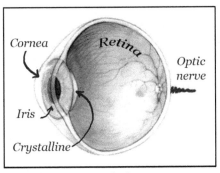

figure II–2 : The human eye

Light passes through the *cornea* and is filtered by the *pupil* inside the eye. It is then refracted by the *crystalline*, travels through the centre of the eye and arrives on the *retina*. Here there are two types of photoreceptor cells – *cones* and *rods* – that generate an electrical signal which is passed to the brain via the *optic nerve*.

The pupil's dimension depends on the amount of light present and our emotional state. It dilates both at night and when we are very concentrated or stressed.

The *crystalline* is a lens with a variable curvature that allows to focus on things that are near or far away. Visual defects such as *myopia* (short-sightedness) or *hyperopia* (long-sightedness) arise when focussing does not work perfectly. Moreover, with aging the crystalline becomes more opaque and more rigid, meaning that a sixty year old transmits around 70% less light than a child.

Cones and *rods* are nerve cells that are part of the retina. Cones are smaller in number and are found concentrated in the centre of the retina whereas rods are found around the periphery. These cells have different functions: cones deal with our *visual acuity* and the ability to distinguish colours whereas rods are responsible for our lateral vision (unfocussed) and the ability to follow moving objects. Furthermore, as they are more sensitive to light, rods activate in the dark and allow us to see at night.

Knowing the difference between cones and rods helps us understand better the three characteristics of the human eye that are relevant to bridge operations:

- *visual field*;
- *visual acuity*;
- *adaptation to night vision.*

On the horizontal plane the visual field of both eyes is around 200 degrees, whilst one eye only can cover 160 degrees. On the vertical plane they can cover up to 70 degrees downwards and up to 50 degrees upwards (figure II–3).

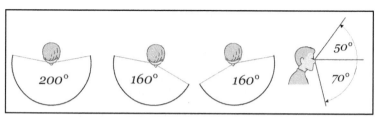

figure II–3 : Horizontal and vertical visual fields

Within the horizontal visual field we can classify other sectors that determine both the limits for reading text and in discerning symbols and colours (figure II–4).

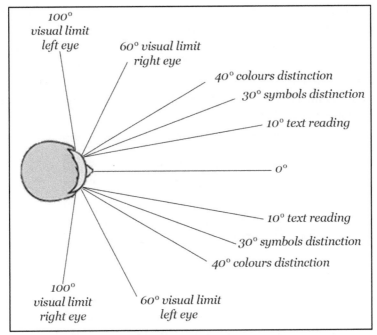

figure II–4 : Limits of our horizontal field of vision

The vertical visual field can also be divided into sectors that determine the maximum rotation angle of the eyes and the ability to discern colours (figure II–5).

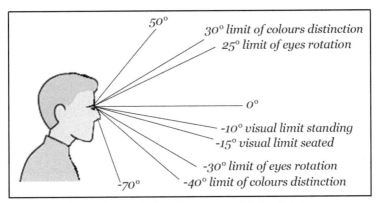

figure II–5 : Limits of our vertical field of vision

The visual field should be used as the basis of a bridge layout design. This is something that is well known in aviation. Modern cockpits are designed around the so called *eye datum,* which is a point where the pilot's eyes can see both the principal instruments and the outside world with minimal head movement. *Eye datum* also determines the positioning of indicators and displays. For example, those with moving pointers can also be placed to fall in the outer parts of the visual field, while indicators with figures to be read should be located in the centre of the visual field. In addition coloured indicators should be placed in the centre go, given the eye's inability to discern colours in its lateral vision.

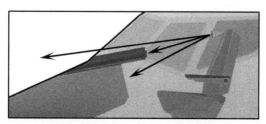

figure II–6 : A cockpit's eye datum

Both those who design instruments and those who work on a ship's bridge should also be aware of a particular part of our retina – known as the *blind spot* – that does not have any photoreceptor cells. This blind area is about seven degrees wide and can be demonstrated using figure II–7.

If we cover our left eye and slowly bring the book towards our face whilst looking at the cargo ship with our right eye, there is a point where the sailing ship disappears. Just try it and see.

Obviously this also works vice versa by covering the right eye and looking at the sailing ship.

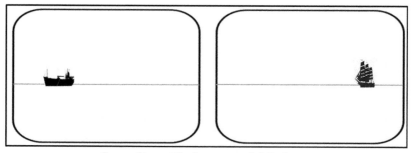

figure II–7 – The human eye's blind spot

This blind spot does not usually manifest itself thanks to the other eye's visual field. But if we find ourselves in the situation where the vision of one eye is blocked (e.g. by the frame of the bridge windows), we need to be aware of the fact that the eye we are using may not see objects that fall within its blind spot.

The second operational characteristic of the human eye is its *visual acuity*. This consists of the eye's ability to distinguish fine detail and reaches its maximum at the centre of the retina – known as the *fovea* – where the highest concentration of cones cells is found. Visual acuity decreases when moving away from the fovea so rapidly that it becomes 20% of its maximum value at just 10 degrees from the retina's centre (figure II–8).

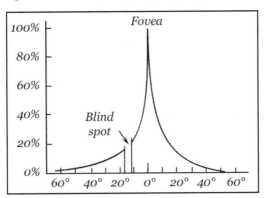

figure II–8 – Decline of visual acuity from the centre to the periphery of the retina

The last operational characteristic of the eye to consider is the *adaptation to night vision*, which slowly occurs through the work of the rod cells. When passing from a lit up environment to a dark one – such as entering into a ship's bridge at night – complete adaptation takes around 30 minutes. This could also take longer if the process is interrupted by sudden lights (e.g. a pocket torch). Given also the peripheral distribution of the rods on the retina, in the dark it is advisable to look at objects sideways on rather than directly.

Hearing and Equilibrium

The sense of hearing makes use of the ear to receive and transduce acoustic pressure waves emitted by the world around us. These vibrations (or pressure changes) are perceived as sounds when they become regular, and noise when they are irregular.

The range of frequencies audible to the human ear go from 20 to 20,000 vibrations per second (Hertz).

The acoustic intensity at which we begin to feel a light pain is 120 decibels (dB), becoming really painful at 140 dB. Normal conversation is measured at around 30 dB while a pneumatic drill can reach up to 90 dB.

The ear (figure II–9) is an organ able to:

- concentrate and amplify external acoustic vibrations through the *auricle* and the *auricular canal* (*outer ear*);
- transform changes in acoustic pressure into mechanical vibrations through a membrane (*eardrum*) and three tiny bones (*middle ear*);
- transform mechanical vibrations into electrical impulses for the brain through the *cochlea* (*inner ear*).

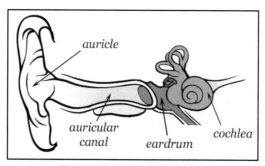

figure II–9 : The human ear

The ear is not only important for auditory purposes, it also regulates our equilibrium. This function is performed by the inner ear through a system of sensors that detect linear and rotational accelerations within the human body. Minimum detection thresholds are 10 cm/sec^2 for linear accelerations and approximately 0.5°/sec^2 for rotational ones. Moreover, given that the detection process involves a certain lag, these attitude sensors might send data to the brain that are discordant with other sense organs. So, the overall perception becomes confused and as a result provokes pallor, nausea and vomiting (seasickness).

Fatigue

A unique definition of *fatigue* does not exist, yet everyone agrees that it can impair human performance and impede alertness. According to the International Maritime Organisation fatigue is:

"A reduction in physical and/or mental capability as the result of physical, mental or emotional exertion which may impair nearly all physical abilities including strength, speed, reaction time, coordination, decision making or balance."[8]

On ships it is difficult to apply criteria for managing fatigue as adopted in other industries. On the one hand it is very difficult to distinguish between rest and work periods whilst on board. On the other, seafarers usually remain on board for months on end, without any rest days.

Within its guidelines IMO recognises that the "captivity" within the working environment is unique to the maritime industry, but it does not list long-lived periods at sea amongst the major causes of fatigue.

ILO's new Maritime Labour Convention states that a seafarer cannot remain on board continuously for more than a year. That means that a deck officer can work on board a ship for several months without any consideration of the effects of long-term fatigue. Something that certainly cannot be resolved with the daily hours of rest classed as mandatory by the convention.

The off-shore sector seems to be the only exception that guarantees four to five week periods of work on board alternated with a holiday just as long. Whereas an average seafarer spends between three to six months on board a cargo ship, with only a couple of months at home.

In the following paragraphs we will discuss the two most common causes of fatigue:

- the modification of *circadian rhythms*, paying particular attention to sleep-wake patterns;
- excessive levels of physical, psychological, social and operational stress.

Circadian Rhythms

Many human biological activities follow natural cyclic variations that last about a day, which as such are called *circadian* (from Latin *circa*:

---

8 MSC/Circ. 1014 dated June 2001. "Guidance on Fatigue Mitigation and Management".

approximately, and *dies*: day). These affect not only our muscle tone or our ability to resist fatigue, but also – to name just two – our pulse rate and blood pressure. Our body temperature for example reaches its highest peak in the evening and its lowest in the morning.

Of all circadian rhythms, the most interesting for life on board a ship is our sleep-wake pattern. Usually a person's complete cycle can vary from 24 to 27 hours. It is for this reason that some of us are more productive in the morning whilst others prefer to sleep later and are more active in the evening. To a certain extent this cycle can be influenced by external factors such as day and night (light and dark), or by social factors such as working hours and meal times.

Evidence suggests that adults are capable of shifting their sleep-wake rhythm by about an hour without any problems. However when faced with longer variations, the human body tries to reset itself to its natural patterns.

In addition it is not always the case that both maximum and minimum levels of our biological activities coincide with waking and sleeping periods. In fact, the two minimum levels of our sleep-wake circadian rhythm are between 3am and 5am, and between 3pm and 5pm. When we perceive tiredness after lunch therefore, it's not because we've eaten too much or because we didn't sleep much the night before, it's just our natural rhythm.

In the same way, the two peaks of psychophysical performance might be independent from the hours of nocturnal rest. And yet we need to consider that our body allows us to stay awake for 16 hours before requiring sleep, regardless of the actual time of the day we start a work shift. This has led international civil aviation to consider the concept of *time since awakening*. A concept that would permit fatigue risk management to be based upon physiological criteria rather than bureaucratic ones, such as establishing maximum work time from when a pilot has begun his/her work shift.

For the human body sleeping is just as important as eating and drinking. Sleep can be divided into two main types: REM and non-REM. Non-REM sleep can be divided into a further four phases that go from relaxation and light sleep – where a person can be awoken easily – to deep sleep, where awakening is difficult and can even be disorientating. *Rapid Eye Movement* (REM) sleep indicates intense cerebral activity which is similar to when we are awake and is also the period when we dream. Each night we can have four or five REM phases, lasting around 15 minutes and at intervals of two hours from one another (figure II–10).

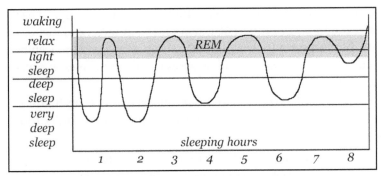

figure II–10 : The different phases of sleep

Hence we go through a series of phases whilst sleeping, with cycles each one lasting around 90-100 minutes each. This is important to be aware of because it is the correct alternating between these phases, together with the quantity of sleep, that make us feel energetic and rested upon waking. This is the reason for which alterations to our sleep/wake cycle have a negative impact on our psychophysical performance and can have dangerous consequences, as it lowers our alertness and makes us more prone to falling asleep suddenly.

Seafarers that work night shifts often experience traumatic awakenings without knowing that they are caused by the interruption of either deep or REM sleep. Being awakened during these phases actually makes us irritable, can increase stress levels or even cause a sensation of sleep inertia which is difficult to recover from in a short period of time.

Recognising and acknowledging the types of sleep and their phases can also help seafarers when trying to manage fatigue by napping. In fact, if a nap exceeds 40 minutes, it can be counterproductive as there is the risk of entering into deep sleep and thus feeling – on awakening – even more tired than before.

In industries where staff perform shift work, the effects of sleep deprivation on human performance have been studied in detail. Generally results confirm that tiredness has a negative impact on judgement, short term memory, concentration levels and on reflexes.

Moreover, with reference to the points discussed in the previous chapter, psychophysical fatigue amplifies our natural tendency to make intuitive and quick decisions, at the expense of rationality.

In the maritime industry, a recent study financed by the European Union[9] compared the impact of different watch duties on levels of fatigue. This was achieved by measuring physiological parameters (electroencephalograph, pulse rate, ocular movement) and by assessing the outcomes of psychomotor vigilance test.

Researchers used "six-six" (six hours on watch and six hours rest) and "four-eight" (four hours on watch and eight hours rest) shifts to draw the following conclusions:

- six-six shifts are more tiring than four-eight ones;
- officers on watch are more tired at night than they are late afternoon;
- levels of drowsiness are higher and reaction times are longer at the end of the night watch;
- on average it takes around 50 minutes to fall asleep at the end of the night watch, much less compared to the afternoon watch.

The study's main limitation was that it didn't take into account the effects of shift work over a long period of time. Although the impact of long-term or chronic fatigue is similar to that of everyday fatigue, the causes can be of a different nature and more difficult to identify.

Stress

Stress can be defined as the effort that the body must make in order to adapt itself to a demanding situation. Irrespective of the situation (pleasant or unpleasant), a certain amount of stress can actually have a positive effect on our alertness and, overall, on our psychophysical performance. However, if stress is too extended over a long period of time it can cause the body to break down, without any chance of quickly recovering.

In 1936 an Austrian-Hungarian doctor named Hans Selye developed a theory known as General Adaptation Syndrome (GAS), which encompasses this concept. The graph shown in figure II–11 shows how the body's response to prolonged stress is characterised by three phases:

- *alarm*: after an initial fall, the body identifies and becomes conscious of the specific source of stress and raises its resistance towards it. Physiologically this consists in contracting muscles and raising blood pressure and glucose levels.

9 Final report of the project Horizon (2012), funded by the European Union and coordinated by the following organisations: Warsash Maritime Academy (Southampton Solent University), Chalmers Tekniska Hoegskola AB and the Stress Research Institute at Stockholm University.

- *Resistance*: the body seems to be adapting to the stress, but gradually depletes available resources to combat it.
- *Exhaustion* or *recovery*: when the body is no longer able to resist the source of stress and breaks down, we are dealing with *exhaustion*. This can be preceded by psychosomatic signs such as cold sores, rashes or nervous twitches. However when the body manages to establish a balance without breaking down, the third phase is called *recovery*.

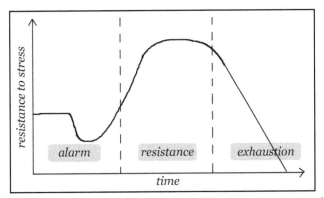

figure II–11 : General Adaptation Syndrome theory by Hans Selye

On board a ship, particularly for deck officers, sources of stress can be *physical, cognitive, emotional and social.*

A typical source of stress could well be the suboptimal ergonomics in the bridge layout, or inadequate illumination of indicators and screens during the night. Neglecting ergonomics on a ship's bridge can force officers to endure prolonged periods standing or sitting with incorrect postures.

Cognitive stress can come from excessive workloads caused by particularly demanding navigational activities and by other ancillary tasks not directly related to the conduct of navigation (compiling logs, carrying out inspections, managing cargo documentation, etc.).

Emotional stress can stem from personal issues, such as economic worries or difficulties in managing long-distance family dynamics.

Lastly, social stress sources are linked to interpersonal problems with colleagues on board and possible discontentment towards company management.

It is very important to recognise the symptoms of an excessive level of stress in order to understand the point at which we near exhaustion. If cold sores, twitches or rashes are psychosomatic onsets that are easy to detect, it gets more difficult when dealing with behavioural signs. Sudden mood swings, aggressiveness, submissiveness, even states of anxiety vary from person to person and require considerable reflective abilities in finding their true cause.

Learning to recognise the symptoms of excessive stress is not a worthless exercise. Doing so can actually help in confronting unease or in protecting oneself from it. The more drastic method of assuming medication is not recommended for a deck officer as he/she could be required to react and make critical decisions regarding navigation safety. Valid alternatives could be to delegate tasks to colleagues or to rely on standard operating procedures (if applicable to the situation) rather than improvising.

But if we really want to combat stress the first step implies identification and removal of the causes, rather than the mere mitigation of the effects. This requires a long-term strategy that includes a balanced diet, regular physical exercise and, if needed, assistance from psychologists or other trusted figures.

A different approach is required to confront acute stress coming from emergency situations. These can generate a *startling effect* which doesn't allow the body time to adapt itself. Here a certain level of improvisation is required which can increase the unease even more. In these cases, teamwork becomes an indispensable resource that eases the pressure on each single individual.

Stress can also be prevented, such as by self-imposing a heightened level of alert before engaging in the most critical parts of the voyage (departing from and arriving into a port). A good rule to follow would be to revise either mentally or together with a colleague, even for just a few seconds, possible reactions in what if scenarios.

What would happen if we lost control of the rudder when passing the breakwaters?

And what would I do if I received communication that there's a fire in the engine room immediately after having cast off the berth?

This exercise would not completely prevent stress, but without a doubt it could help in facing unexpected situations with a clear head.

Recognising Fatigue

It is certainly useful to develop our awareness regarding how circadian rhythms and stress affect fatigue, but in order to manage it we need to be able to:

- recognise its symptoms;
- adopt practical measures to reduce its negative effects.

All this however is easier said than done, given that one of the main symptoms is without doubt a reduction in the ability to judge one's own psychophysical condition. In this case the role of colleagues during the watch is therefore fundamental. Just by observing us, they should be able to recognise our status based on the following clues:

- lack of response to a radio communication;
- reddening of the eyes;
- forgetting things whilst carrying out tasks;
- symptoms of boredom;
- tendency to become obsessed by just one element;
- lack of motivation or tendency to be excessively pessimistic;
- omission of specific checks and actions.

Once a colleague has assisted in recognising these symptoms, it is important to admit a state of fatigue without hesitating and think about practical measures that we need to adopt. Examples of such methods are:

- delegating selected tasks to a colleague who is less fatigued;
- executing tasks earlier and slower than usual;
- a brief and controlled rest period – know in aviation as a *pilot nap* – during navigation in open sea.

In particular, a nap such as the one mentioned above is only possible once the following precautions have been made:

- the colleague awake must be qualified to manage eventual emergencies on the ship's bridge;
- the actual nap should not exceed 40 minutes to avoid falling into a deep sleep. Awaking from this state could cause sluggishness and a long delay in recovering full psychophysical capacity;
- the rest must terminate at least half an hour before any planned increase in alert levels on the bridge.

TECHNICAL RESOURCES ON A SHIP'S BRIDGE

"Any intelligent fool can make
things bigger and more complex.
It takes a touch of genius – and a lot of courage –
to move in the opposite direction"
Albert Einstein

Navigation Sensors

T echnical resources on the bridge of a modern ship can be divided into *sensors* and *navigation systems*. Both are essential, given that the first provides the data necessary for the other to function properly. For this reason officers must be aware of the potential and limitations not only of the navigation systems they interact with, but also of the sensors that provide data from behind the scenes.

Navigation sensors process and combine data such as:

- radar bearings and distances;
- positioning;
- orientation (*Heading, Rate of Turn* and *Course Over Ground*);
- speed (*Speed Over Ground* and *Speed Through Water*);
- wind (*relative* and *true*);
- depth (*below transducer* and *below surface*);
- attitude (*roll, pitch* and *heave*).

In this chapter we will describe these sensors in detail, but in order to fully understand their potential and limitations we need to be familiar with the concepts of integrity and accuracy first.

The *integrity* is defined as the trust that can be placed in the correctness of the information provided by the sensor. The integrity can be quantified as the probability that sensor performance is outside its nominal values. In certain cases integrity also includes the ability to alert the operator. For example, modern GPS receivers are actually able to estimate positioning integrity in real time[10] by using algorithms that guarantee a very high probability of identifying performance drops in GPS satellites.

---

10 This feature is called "Receiver Autonomous Integrity Monitoring" (RAIM).

The *accuracy* determines the sensor's ability to provide measurements that are close to a true value conventionally established. Hence accuracy can be expressed by statistical uncertainty, i.e. by the probability that a random error – in the absence of biases – does not exceed a certain distance from the true value.

Typically, random errors in navigation sensors are distributed according to a Gaussian bell curve (figure II–12). This distribution is characterised by a mean value (conventionally assumed as the true value) and by a standard deviation (abbreviated as 1 sigma or simply with 1σ) which includes 68% of cases considered. The value that corresponds to two standard deviations (2 sigma or 2σ) includes 95% of cases.

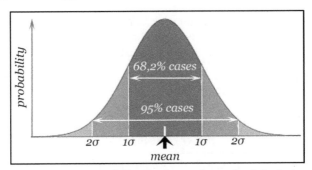

figure II–12 : Normal distribution and standard deviations

Technical documentation concerning sensor performance expresses accuracy in terms of either 1 sigma or 2 sigma. The Root Mean Square (RMS) and the Root Mean Square Deviation (dRMS) are also often used in place of 1 sigma as they are equivalent.

However, aside from the acronyms found on datasheets, we should also bear in mind the fact that a figure which expresses accuracy as 1 sigma is about half of one expressed as 2 sigma. For example, a GPS receiver's accuracy of 5 metres using 1 sigma is more or less equivalent to an accuracy of 10 metres expressed using 2 sigma.

Radar

A radar system's sensors consist of rotating antennae that emit short pulses of electromagnetic energy on two frequency bands:

- "X" or "3 cm" (from 9.2 to 9.5 GHz) which guarantees high resolution and is able to discriminate two targets close to each other from a distance;

- "S" or "10 cm" (from 2.9 to 3.1 GHz), which performs better in presence of disturbances from rain, fog and sea state.

These electromagnetic pulses are emitted and received through directional antennae that allow for the detection of a target's range and bearing when hit by the electromagnetic energy. Directional transmission is guaranteed by a relatively narrow horizontal beamwidth. Typical values of horizontal beamwidth range from 0.65° to 2°, whereas vertical beamwidths vary from 15° to 30°. The narrower the beam, the greater the distance that can be reached with the same amount of power emitted. Radar datasheets usually express the beamwidth as an angle between two points where power is half of its maximum (along the central axis of the beam).

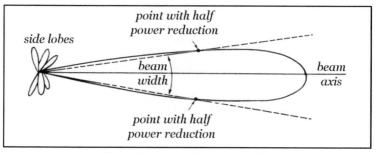

figure II–13 : Radar beamwidth

A radar's maximum detection range depends on its elevation above sea level and how the radiation bends beyond the geographical horizon. This bending depends on the *diffraction* and the *refraction* that electromagnetic waves are subject to.

Diffraction consists of the omnidirectional dispersion of electromagnetic energy upon striking an obstacle. Its effects are greater with lower emission frequencies. Therefore an X band radar has a greater possibility of finding targets in the shadow zone of an obstacle when compared to an S band radar.

Refraction consists of the bending of electromagnetic radiation caused by travelling through atmospheric layers that have different densities. Under standard atmospheric conditions[11] the bending of radar beams means they are able to travel beyond the geographical horizon and follow the curvature of the earth's surface. Under sub-standard conditions when air temperatures increase with altitude, electromagnetic radiation bends upwards, away from the sea surface. This phenomenon can be found at high latitudes when arctic

---

11 Constant atmospheric pressure (1013 mb), surface temperature at 15°C yet diminishing uniformly with altitude and constant relative humidity (60%).

winds blow along the relatively warmer surface of the sea. The difference in temperature means that the air warms upon contact with the water and so rises. An operational consequence of this could be the failure to detect small targets or ice within the geographical horizon.

Minimum range detection capabilities of X and S radar antennae specified by IMO[12] are shown in table II–1.

type of target	Height above sea level	X Band minimum range	S Band minimum range
Coast	60 m	20 NM	20 NM
Coast	6 m	8 NM	8 NM
Coast	3 m	6 NM	6 NM
Merchant ships > 5000GT	10 m	11 NM	11 NM
Merchant ships > 500GT	5 m	8 NM	8 NM
Small ships with radar reflector	4 m	5 NM	3,7 NM
Small ships without radar reflector	2 m	3,4 NM	3 NM
Navigation buoy with radar reflector	3,5 m	4,9 NM	3,6 NM
Navigation buoy without radar reflector	3,5 m	4,6 NM	3 NM
Typical signal from channel demarcation	1 m	2 NM	1 NM

table II–1 : Minimum range detection capabilities of X and S band radars

The values shown are valid under standard conditions without disturbances caused by atmospheric agents and state of the sea.

Radar technical specifications should also include drops in performance under the following conditions:

- light rain (4mm per hour) and heavy rain (16mm per hour);
- sea states 2 and 5 on the Douglas Sea Scale;
- the combination of both effects.

The accuracy in the detection of target range and bearing using radar emissions in X and S band should not exceed the following limits:

- range: within 30 metres or 1% of the distance;
- bearing: within 1 degree.

Furthermore radar antenna specifications are based on roll and pitch values that are less than 10 degrees.

---

12 Resolution MSC.192(79) adopted 6 December 2004. "Performance Standards for Radar Equipment".

Positioning

Sensors for the positioning of ships essentially rely on two different types of radio navigation systems:

- *Global Navigation Satellite System* (GNSS);
- *Terrestrial Long Range Navigation* (LORAN).

Without a doubt, GPS (Global Positioning System) is the most popular GNSS. A GPS receiver determines its position by calculating the distances from at least 4 satellites[13] with reference to the World Geodetic System 1984, known as WGS84. This consists of a three dimensional axis coordinate system (xyz) with its origin at the earth's centre of mass, and is associated to a geocentric ellipsoid, also called WGS84.

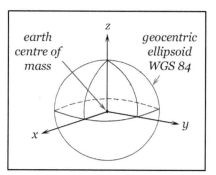

figure II–14 : World Geodetic System 1984

GPS satellites modulate different codes on three carrier waves: L1 and L2 were introduced first, and a third carrier wave called L5 has been recently devised for general transport safety, which will be available on all 24 satellites from 2021. Since 1993 (the year in which GPS reached full operational capability) these codes have been transmitted for civilian use through Coarse Acquisition (C/A) solely on L1, and for military use through Precise (P/Y) on both L1 and L2.

A project of modernisation that began in 2005 means that two military codes (L1M and L2M) and three civilian codes (L1C, L2C and L5) have been added on to the carrier waves. These new civilian codes will be fully operational on all satellites between 2018 and 2026. Dual frequency receivers will benefit from this in terms of compensation for ionospheric and tropospheric effects that the GPS signal is subject to. Triple frequency

13 The GPS space segment consists of at least 24 satellites, distributed in a way that at least four of them are visible from any point of the world in any given moment.

receivers that are able to use L1 C/A, L1C, L2C and L5 codes will reach an accuracy of less than a metre without differential corrections together with a higher level of resistance to noise and other interferences.

The distance between GPS receivers and satellites in use is calculated by using the phase either of one of the codes (*Code Phase Measurement*) or one of the carrier waves (*Carrier Phase Measurement*). Carrier Phase Measurement is much more precise than its code counterpart, but it requires the combined use of 2 distinct GPS receivers. As well as this, Carrier Phase Measurements are much more sensitive to the effects of signal reflection on surfaces next to the receiver (*multipath*) and to ionospheric and tropospheric delays.

Generally the accuracy of three-dimensional positioning varies according to the following operational modes:

- *absolute;*
- *differential;*
- *relative.*

In *absolute mode* a GPS receiver calculates distances from at least four satellites (figure II–15) using Code Phase Measurements. Since 1993 the performance of commercial GPS receivers has been continuously improved and has always exceeded the minimum standards set by the US government. Even though the actual GPS performance standard[14] states that the accuracy in the measurement of the distance between satellite and receiver does not exceed more than 7.8 metres (2 sigma), high end L1 C/A receivers can guarantee horizontal accuracy of about 3 metres (2 sigma) and a vertical accuracy of 5 metres (2 sigma).

Nevertheless, a single receiver cannot avoid intrinsic errors of GPS positioning, such as those that occur due to multipath, uncertainties in the satellites' orbit, noise from receivers and signal deviations when passing through the ionosphere and the troposphere.

In brief, GPS guarantees two types of absolute positioning accuracy for civilian use (L1 C/A):

- ≤ 9 metres (*global average);*
- ≤ 17 metres *(worst site).*

---

14 USA Department of Defence (2008). "GPS SPS Performance Standard" - 4th Edition. It is important to note that accuracy ratings do not account for anomalies in the lower layers of the earth's atmosphere (which may cause unpredictable distortions to satellite signals) and for any possible external interference that the receiver may be subject to.

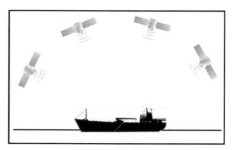

figure II–15 : Absolute mode (GPS)

In *differential mode*, a DGPS receiver improves positioning accuracy using Code Phase Measurements. This is due to the corrections obtained either from a receiver located at a point with noted geodetic coordinates or from a geostationary satellite (figure II–16). In the first case we are dealing with *coastal DGPS beacons*, whereas the latter refers to *Satellite Based Augmentation Systems* (SBAS).

The most common SBAS systems currently in use are:

- *Wide Area Augmentation System (WAAS)*;
- *European Geostationary Navigation Overlay Service (EGNOS)*;
- *Multi-functional Satellite Augmentation System (MSAS)*
- *OMNISTAR*

The first system covers North America, the second covers Europe and the third Japan, whereas the OMNISTAR system offers differential corrections at various levels of accuracy with a global coverage.

The transmission of differential corrections – both from coastal beacons and from SBAS satellites – aims to correct the effect of errors due to variations in ionospheric layers and GPS satellite orbit.

When corrections are received by coastal beacons, the positioning accuracy of a DGPS receiver decreases as the distance from the base station increases (i.e. the coastal station which calculates them).

With SBAS corrections, DGPS positioning accuracy depends on the various technologies made available by its system providers. For example, WAAS and EGNOS positioning accuracy is about 2 meters, whereas OMNISTAR can guarantee sub-metric accuracies. However, the latter can only be used by paying a subscription, as opposed to WAAS and EGNOS that are open to anyone within their respective coverage.

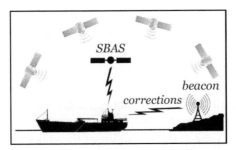

figure II–16 : Differential mode (DGPS)

In *relative mode*, a mobile GPS receiver, called a *rover*, compares its carrier phase measurements with those made by another GPS receiver, called a *base*, which is in a fixed position at known geodetic coordinates (figure II–17).

To use it for navigational purposes, this processing technique is performed in real time and is called *Real Time Kinematic* (RTK). Data exchange can be accomplished via radio (UHF or VHF) or also through GSM-UTMS cellular networks. Cellular networks are generally used in ports that offer RTK corrections for pilots' portable navigation systems.

RTK positioning can be accurate down to centimetres. The expression *relative mode* derives from the fact that the result is not the rover's position, but the difference in the coordinates with the base. The actual accuracy depends mostly on the distance between the two receivers, known as the *baseline*. The shorter the baseline, the more accurate the difference in coordinates, which as a result means better accuracy in the rover's position.

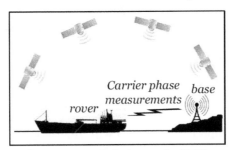

figure II–17 : Relative mode (RTK)

With the passing of time the integrity guaranteed by the three GPS segments (satellites, ground control stations and receivers) has significantly improved. Nowadays the probability that minimum performance standards established by the US government are not met is very small indeed.

This integrity however can be compromised most commonly by radio jamming, and also (but less likely) by intentional spoofing. In fact spoofing is generally found in military contexts and aims to remotely take over control of GPS receivers by transmitting signals that simulate those received from satellites.

So-called electronic warfare techniques have been known for decades, but remain something that is still relatively unheard of in the civilian world, just as computer viruses were at the beginning of the 1990s.

Spoofing can produce more serious consequences than jamming, simply because the operator might take more time to realise the anomaly. In fact, GPS receivers that are not equipped with autonomous integrity monitoring capabilities could accept any signal similar to those transmitted by GPS satellites and use it to produce navigational data without any further internal verification.

Multi-PNT (Position, Navigation and Timing) positioning systems would constitute a first line of defence against spoofing, given the low correlation between the vulnerabilities of each individual sensor. Such systems would be able to identify and manage inconsistencies between positional data given by:

- two different GNSS receivers such as a GPS and a GLONASS, both with RAIM functionality;
- a terrestrial radio navigation receiver such as E-LORAN.

GLONASS is a global satellite positioning system managed by the Russian government with an accuracy that is equivalent to that of GPS in absolute mode.

The geodetic reference used by GLONASS is called PZ90 and was updated in 2007 to reduce the differences with WGS84 to 40 centimetres in all three dimensions. For navigational purposes though, both geodetic reference systems can be considered as equivalent.

Unlike GPS, each of the 24 GLONASS satellites transmits navigation signals (C/A and P) on their own carrier frequency (derived from the two main frequency bands L1 and L2). Transmission of the navigation signals uses a different technique[15] compared with that of GPS codes, which makes GLONASS receivers incompatible with GPS ones (and vice versa).

However, the modernisation programme undertaken by the Russian government includes a third frequency band (L3) and a transition towards

---

15 The channel access technique adopted by GLONASS is called FDMA (Frequency Division Multiple Access). It consists of a subdivision of the available frequency bands (L1 and L2) in a number of slightly different frequency channels. Each one of these channels is assigned to a satellite which will use it to transmit its navigation signal.

the same access technique[16] to GPS navigation signals. The aim is to enhance the interoperability between the two systems and to reduce the complexity of GLONASS receivers.

At present, multi-receivers that are able to process both GPS and GLONASS signals can only guarantee an improved positioning continuity, especially in the presence of obstacles which make one of the two GNSS temporary unavailable. This is why many modern mobile telephones – designed to work in built up areas – are equipped with GPS-GLONASS receivers.

These improvements in terms of continuity could be particularly useful in harbour waters, where the proximity of dockside structures or other large ships can compromise the performance of a single GPS receiver.

GPS-GLONASS combination however is not the only one available given the development of two more GNSSs: *BeiDou-Compass* by the People's Republic of China and *Galileo* by the European Union.

Unlike GLONASS, Galileo and BeiDou receivers will be compatible with GPS ones.

As of today (2015), the Chinese regional system *BeiDou* already covers most of the Asian Pacific area (figure II–18), and will evolve into the global system *Compass* in 2020.

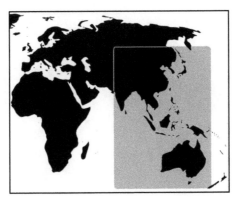

figure II–18 : BeiDou system coverage (2015)

The *Galileo* system has only just entered into its *Initial Operational Capability* (IOC) phase, which foresees the launch of 18 satellites and the

---

16 The technique to access GPS transmission channels (L1 and L2) is called CDMA (Code Division Multiple Access) and presents a few advantages when compared to FDMA, such as faster transmissions and reduced complexity for front end receivers.

activation of land-based control centres. The *Full Operational Capability* (FOC) phase will include a total of 30 satellites in orbit by 2020.

In addition to these European and Chinese GNSSs, there are also two regional satellite positioning systems under development:

- the Japanese QZSS (*Quasi Zenith Satellite System*) which covers the Pacific area down to Australia (figure I–18);
- IRNSS (*Indian Regional Navigation Satellite System*) that covers both the Indian subcontinent and the Indian Ocean (figure II–20).

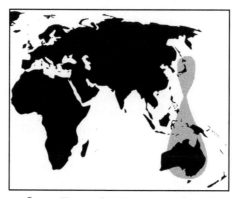

figure II–19 : QZSS coverage (2015)

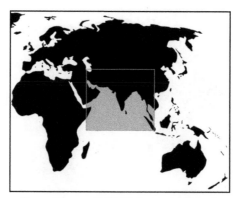

figure II–20 : IRNSS coverage (2015)

The presence and interoperability of both global and regional satellite positioning systems is paving the way to the development of multi-PNT receivers.

As mentioned previously, these multi-PNT receivers can guarantee higher levels of performance than single system receivers, especially in terms of continuity of positioning and reduction of vulnerability to jamming and spoofing.

Now let's switch the discussion to long-range terrestrial radio navigation systems.

E-LORAN is the only system in this category that is actually capable of reaching an accuracy on a par with GNSSs. The acronym E-LORAN stands for *Enhanced LOng RAnge Navigation*, which emphasises the evolution of the old LORAN system that was designed immediately after the Second World War. At that time the low frequency of coastal stations allowed a range of 1600 nautical miles, an accuracy of less than a quarter of a nautical mile and a solid resistance to intentional jamming.

In order to calculate its position every LORAN receiver had to process signals from at least three stations, which were used to create a spatial intersection between two sets of hyperbolic curves.

From the 1990s onwards, despite modernisation of the system LORAN-C that performed at an accuracy of less than 100 metres, the number of its users decreased rapidly. The decrease correlated with the widespread adoption of global satellite positioning systems, so much so that in 2010 the US government decided to dismiss LORAN-C.

Just three years earlier though, the *International Loran Association (ILA)* published its first document[17] defining the evolution from LORAN-C to E-LORAN. The main difference between the two systems consisted of an additional data channel on the transmitted signal. This channel supplies both differential corrections and information on signal integrity to receivers.

E-LORAN's positioning accuracy varies from 8 to 20 metres and so can be compared to that of GNSS in absolute mode. This accuracy conforms to international maritime standards for navigation in harbour waters and for non-precision instrumental approaches.

With regards to navigation within harbour waters, IMO has established a minimum standard of 10 metres on positioning accuracy. However an E-LORAN receiver can only meet this requirement if:

- it has the errors derived from radio-electric propagation for the specific port stored in its internal memory;
- it receives (in real time on data channels) differential corrections needed to compensate for signal fluctuations due to both atmospheric conditions and the UTC time transmitted.

---

17 International Loran Association (2007). "Enhanced Loran Definition Document", report version 1.0.

Atmospheric electrical effects represent the main limitation of the E-LORAN system. Accuracy improves when a receiver detects a signal that follows a direct path (*ground wave*), but can degrade when a signal refracted by the ionosphere (*sky wave*) interferes with it, especially at night. At sunrise and sunset in particular, variations of the ionospheric layers can cause interference that is not easy to predict.

The illustration below (figure II–21) shows a functional diagram of the E-LORAN system's components. It demonstrates clearly the role played by the differential station managed by the Maritime Service Provider, which supports the heart of the system known as *Core E-LORAN Service Provider*.

In 2007 the UK Department of Transport financed an E-LORAN development plan that includes the installation of many differential stations along the Eastern and Southern coasts of Great Britain, due to be completed in 2022.

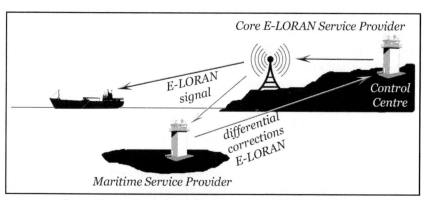

figure II–21 : Functional diagram of the E-LORAN system

E-LORAN's strength lies not so much in its positioning accuracy, but rather in its independence from GNSS. This characteristic allows it to be proposed not so much as an alternative to GNSS but as an interoperable system that ensures redundancy in the case of problems with GNSS, particularly in the presence of jamming or spoofing.

To the eyes of an operator using a GNSS/E-LORAN multi-receiver, geographical coordinates do not show any difference whatsoever.

Moreover, E-LORAN positioning is synchronised with a UTC time that comes from certified coastal sources, which are also GNSS independent.

Lastly, E-LORAN is potentially interoperable, just like GNSS, with other navigation systems such as:

- ECDIS (*Electronic Chart Display Information System*);

- ARPA (*Automatic Radar Plotting Aid*);
- AIS (*Automatic Identification System*);
- TCS (Track Control Systems);
- DP (Dynamic Positioning Systems).

Table II–2 summarises the accuracy of GPS, GLONASS and E-LORAN, according to the operational mode and the processing technique of the radio signals received.

System	Operational mode	Signal processing technique	Positioning accuracy
GPS	Absolute	Code Phase Measurement "global average"	≤ 9 m (2 sigma)
		Code Phase Measurement "worst sites"	≤ 17 m (2 sigma)
	Differential	Coastal beacon correction applied on Code Phase	~ 2 m
		SBAS corrections applied on Carrier Phase	~ 0.5 m
	Relative	Comparison of Carrier Phase Measurements from two static receivers	Up to 10^{-6} of the baseline
		Real-time comparison of Carrier Phase Measurements by one static and one mobile receiver (RTK)	Order of cm
GLONASS	Absolute	Code Phase Measurement on all frequency channels	~ 10 m
E-LORAN	Differential	Spatial intersection between sets of hyperbolic curves with differential corrections	from 8 to 20 m

table II–2 : Accuracy of positioning sensors

Table II–3 shows the minimum standards required by IMO for positioning accuracy during navigation[18]. These standards have been established according to various operational conditions and are expressed as 2 sigma (95%).

Even though the regulation clearly states the possibility of adopting a combination of positioning systems to achieve minimum standards, IMO

---

18 Resolution A.953(23) adopted 5 December 2003. Revoked by Resolution A.1046(27) adopted 30 November 2011. "World Wide Radio Navigation Systems".

does not impose the redundancy of positioning systems to mitigate the risk of intrinsic anomalies, jamming and spoofing.

Operational context	Minimum positioning accuracy	Update rate of computed and displayed position data
Navigation in harbour entrances, harbour approaches and coastal waters with a high volume of traffic and/or significant degree of risk	10 metres (2 sigma)	Not less than once every 2 seconds
Navigation in ocean waters	100 metres (2 sigma)	

table II–3 : IMO Minimum Standards for positioning accuracy

When comparing table II-2 with table II-3, it is evident that existing technology notably exceeds minimum standards established at international level for maritime navigation. In particular the minimum update rate required for position fixing is much lower than the commercial options available. An update rate of 5 Hz (or five times per second) has more or less become the norm for consumer grade GPSs too. We should not forget either that the update rate plays an important role not only for GNSS positioning accuracy, but also for determining Speed Over Ground and Course Over Ground.

Orientation

The gyrocompass is the most common instrument for measuring the true Heading (HDG). The first to be used for navigation was made in 1906 by the German *Anschütz-Kaempfe*[19]. The instrument was originally adopted by the German Navy for ships and submarines. Two years later the American *Elmer Ambrose Sperry* designed a gyrocompass that was adopted by the US Navy during World War I. It was not until 1913 that the gyrocompass appeared on merchant ships.

Before the advent of the gyrocompass, several attempts were made in Europe to measure the Heading by means of gyroscopes. These instruments only actually represented the sensing element of a gyrocompass. Both the Royal Navy and the French Navy conducted trials, but the performance of their gyroscopes were no match for German gyrocompasses.

---

19 In reality the first experiments that demonstrated the effect of the Earth's rotation on moving rotors were conducted by the French physicist Leon Foucault in the latter half of the nineteenth century. Foucault first used a pendulum before adopting a gyroscope.

Nowadays the accuracy of a gyrocompass with a rotating gyroscope is expressed on the basis of three types of error:

- *settle point error;*
- *steady state error;*
- *dynamic error.*

With regard to the first type of error, a gyrocompass is considered "settled" (after start-up) when at least three Heading readings at half-hour intervals lie within the limit of 0.7°.

The *settle point heading* is the average of ten readings taken at twenty-minute intervals. The *settle point error* is the difference between a heading reading in a certain moment and that which has been stabilised. For the more modern mechanical gyrocompasses a typical value for this error lies around 0.2° multiplied by the secant latitude (1 sigma). This means that at 45° latitude, 68% of *settle point errors* measured are less than 0.14°.

The second type of error, i.e. the *steady state error*, must be evaluated during navigation with a steady route and speed. Usually it is also contained within 0.2° multiplied by the secant latitude (1 sigma). In transients caused by alterations of a vessel's attitude not greater than 20° roll, 10° pitch and 5° yaw, the heading error is around 0.3° multiplied by the secant latitude (1 sigma).

Finally, the *dynamic error* of a mechanical gyrocompass during significant turns is typically contained within 0.5° multiplied by the secant latitude (1 sigma).

Gyrocompasses that use fibre optic gyroscopes are known as *Fibre Optic Gyros* (FOG) and can reach higher dynamic accuracy compared to those with mechanical gyroscopes. However a fibre optic gyroscope measures only angular variations to the Heading by interpreting interference produced by two laser rays travelling through a fibre optic spiral.

In figure II–22, a laser source emits two rays (A and B). These travel along the fibre optic spiral in opposite directions until they meet at a detection device that measures the interference between them. If the entire system (source, spiral and detection device) remains immobile, the rays reach the detector at exactly the same time. But if the system rotates in space, the two rays must travel different distances before meeting each other again. It is possible to calculate the rotation angle of the entire system by the type of interference produced.

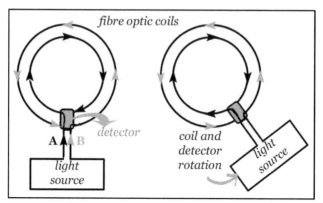

figure II–22 : Theory behind the functionality of a Fibre Optic Gyroscope (FOG)

This technology began being used in navigation in the 1970s, taking advantage of progress made in fibre optics for telecommunications. Given the absence of moving mechanical elements, fibre optic gyroscopes have a high reliability and it is for this reason they were mainly used for aerospace missions or as sensitive elements of inertial missile navigation.

Ring Laser Gyrocompasses (RLG) use the same principle as Fibre Optic Gyros except that the laser rays travel through a cavity filled with a special mixture of inert gases. Both the Fibre Optic Gyro and the Ring Laser Gyro measure the Rate of Turn in instruments called *Rate Gyros*. To set the heading with reference to true North, both gyros must be associated to a magnetic sensor or to a GNSS receiver.

Their reduced dimensions (compared to a mechanical gyrocompass) make it possible to integrate them with Inertial Measurement Units (IMU) and GNSS receivers. In this way it is possible to measure movement and rotations using a three dimensional axis coordinate system directed along the main directions of a ship. This integration with tactical level IMUs[20] means that normal heading accuracy can be as slight as 0.01° (1 sigma) and Rate of Turn 0.1°/min (1 sigma).

Developments in the field of microelectronics allow us to make Fibre Optic Gyros and Ring Laser Gyros on microchips. This technology is known as MEMS (Micro-Electro-Mechanical Systems) and ensures dimensions that become ever smaller, even though performance is slightly inferior.

---

20 See section dedicated to attitude sensors.

In order to compare the three types of gyrocompass (mechanical, fibre optic and ring laser, both traditional and MEMS) an analysis of three gyroscope error types is needed:

- *scale factor;*
- *drift or gyro bias;*
- *gyro bias stability.*

Scale factor indicates how the accuracy in the Rate of Turn measurement is dependent upon the values measured. It is generally expressed as parts per million (ppm).

Drift, or *gyro bias*, characterises a gyroscope's ability to measure Rate of Turn null values when there aren't any real variations.

The *gyro bias stability* defines how the gyro bias varies through time. It is generally expressed in either degrees per hour (°/hr) or degrees per minute (°/min).

Figure II–23 shows how mechanical gyrocompasses give better performance both in terms of scale factor and gyro bias stability.

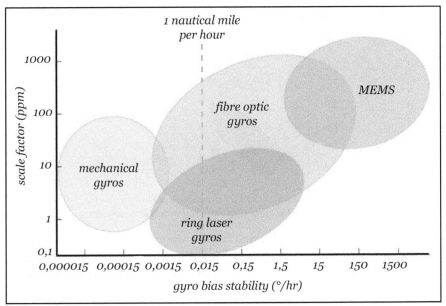

figure II–23 : Comparison of different gyroscope performance

As well as with mechanical gyrocompasses, a ship's Heading can be measured with the combined use of electronic sensors, which IMO defines as a *Transmitting Heading Device* (THD). Satellite compasses are part of this group and are made up of a GPS receiver capable of measuring the instantaneous phase of a carrier wave at two antennae associated to it and placed in fore-and-aft direction. This is why such systems are also known as Dual Antenna.

In order to solve the ambiguity of all possible orientations of the segment that joins the two antennae, the receiver needs to be told the actual distance between them (*baseline*). If the baseline between the two antennae (A and B) in figure II–24 is aligned with the ship's centreline, the angle formed with the direction of the geographic North is the ship's Heading. If the two antennae are installed athwartships on the bridge wings, simply offsetting the reading by 90 degrees will also provide the ship's Heading.

The Heading accuracy calculated by a GPS satellite compass does not depend much on the positioning accuracy. It depends mainly on the length of the baseline (the longer the better) and on an installation that minimises multipath effects. In fact, the receiver is unable to distinguish between signals received either directly or from a reflected path due to ship's structures adjacent to the antennae. Overall a typical GPS satellite compass can provide an accuracy in the order of 0.1°, whereas the high end ones can reach accuracies in the order of 0.01°.

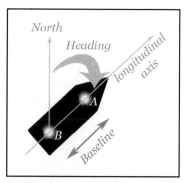

figure II–24 : Working principle of a satellite compass

All of the instruments mentioned in this section are much more accurate than the minimum standards set by IMO as long ago as 1979[21] (for gyrocompasses), 2000[22] (for Transmitting Heading Devices) and 1983 (for Rate of Turn indicators)[23].

---

21 Resolution A.424(XI) adopted 15 November 1979. "Performance Standards for Gyrocompasses".

22 Resolution MSC.116(73) adopted 1 December 2000. "Performance Standards for Transmitting Heading Devices".

23 Resolution A.526(13) adopted 17 November 1983. "Performance Standards for Rate of Turn Indicators".

Table II–4 shows the typical accuracy of orientation compared to minimum standards set by IMO.

Instruments for measuring Heading	Type of Error	Typical Accuracy[24]	IMO minimum accuracy
Gyroscope with mechanical rotating gyroscope	Settle point	0.2° per sec lat	0.75° per sec lat
	Steady state	0.2° per sec lat	0.25° per sec lat
	Transients at steady state	0.3° per sec lat	1° per sec lat
	Dynamic	0.5° per sec lat	3° per sec lat
Transmitting Heading Device based on fibre optic gyroscope (non MEMS) integrated in IMU-GNSS systems	Dynamic	0.01°	1.5°
	Rate of Turn	0.1°/min	0.5°/min + 5% of reading
Transmitting Heading Device based on Dual Antenna Satellite Compass with short baseline	Dynamic	0.1°	1.5°
Transmitting Heading Device based on Dual Antenna Satellite Compass with long baseline	Dynamic	0.01°	1.5°
	Rate of Turn	0.1°/min	0.5°/min + 5% of reading

table II–4 : Heading sensor accuracy

Measuring the magnetic heading is done by traditional magnetic compasses and the more modern *flux-gate* compasses. A traditional magnetic compass uses a magnetised needle that aligns itself with the Earth's magnetic field. Once it has been compensated for the presence of ferromagnetic materials aboard, its accuracy reaches 0.5° (1 sigma).

Fluxgate compasses measure the direction of the horizontal component of the Earth's magnetic field directly using a coil of wire wound around a permanent magnet. Magnetic headings arrive at an accuracy along the lines of a magnetic mechanical compass (0.5°), but only when there are no significant variations to a ship's attitude (roll and pitch). As a result fluxgate compasses dynamically perform less well than mechanical ones, especially during turns when roll-induced errors can occur. It is for this reason that they are often integrated with a three-axis gyroscope, which comes into play during these turns, thus minimising any rolling or pitching effects.

---

24 Typical accuracy is based on an indicative average of the more modern models available on the market and it is stated here as 1 sigma.

However these compasses do have a great advantage in being able to electronically transmit magnetic headings to other instruments such as autopilots and Electronic Chart Systems. When used in this manner there isn't even the need to install it in a place where it needs to be viewed, and so can be fitted in an area where there is minimal magnetic interference. Both types of magnetic compass satisfy the minimum standards (0.5°) set by IMO[25].

The Course Over Ground value can derive from:

- a GNSS receiver using recursive algorithms[26] based on the last position received and the last Course Over Ground estimate;
- a navigation system by summing the drift angle (calculated by a dual axis Doppler speed log) and the heading (measured by a gyrocompass or by a Transmitting Heading Device).

In the first case, the accuracy of the so-called *true vector* estimate depends exclusively on GNSS, and particularly on the positioning accuracy and the update frequency of satellite position. So, even though a sub-metric positioning may seem uselessly accurate for a ship 300 metres long and 50 metres wide, in terms of Course Over Ground it gives a substantial improvement (compared to positioning accuracies in the order of 10 metres).

The update rate of position fixes given by the GNSS receiver also has an important role. The greater this frequency, the less delay there is during changes in course. Currently GNSS receivers with a frequency of 5 Hz (5 fixes per second) are relatively economical and also allow an instantaneous update of the true vector for sudden changes in Course Over Ground. However the limitation in courses computation at low speeds remains, which is when the distance between two successive fixes falls below the positioning error. Also here, the greater the positioning accuracy the less the speed threshold becomes for calculating an acceptable Course Over Ground.

As already mentioned, Course Over Ground can be calculated without the aid of GNSS. To do it we need the drift angle calculated by an instrument such as a dual axis Doppler speed log, and the Heading measured by a gyrocompass or a Transmitting Heading Device. In this way, Course Over

---

25 Resolution A.382(XI) adopted 14 November 1977. "Performance Standards for Magnetic Compasses".

26 These algorithms use the so-called "Kálmán Filter", after the Hungarian engineer that in 1960 conceived a new filtering technique for signals affected by random errors, especially in electronic systems and gyroscopes. Initially his ideas were opposed, so much so that the first article written ("A new approach to linear filtering and prediction problems") was only published in a mechanical engineering magazine. During the next few years the Filter was used on the Apollo space missions before being adopted in GPS receivers for estimating speed and course.

Ground will depend on the accuracy of both the speed log and the gyrocompass. As we will see in the next section, a dual axis Doppler speed log can calculate the drift angle by comparing longitudinal and transversal speed values, with respect to both the seabed and the mass of water moving underneath the vessel. Here the restriction lies in the log's minimum and maximum operative depths.

Speed

Speed on board ships can be measured:

- with respect to the seabed (*Speed Over Ground* - SOG) when calculated by GNSS, inertial navigation systems or speed logs in *Bottom Track* mode;
- through the mass of water underneath the ship (*Speed Through Water* – STW) when calculated by using speed logs in *Water Track* (WT) mode.

Similarly to what happens with Course Over Ground, Speed Over Ground is "estimated" by the GNSS receiver by means of recursive algorithms using last position received and the last speed prediction calculated. These two parameters allow the algorithms to make successive predictions of Speed Over Ground (and its accuracy) before verifying them with the next positioning reading. Obviously the prediction relies heavily on the accuracy of GNSS positioning (therefore on its mode), together with the update rate and the filtering algorithm used by the receiver. Speed Over Ground accuracy is not commonly included in a receiver's datasheets.

We could generalise here and say that a standard GPS receiver (L1-C/A) in absolute mode is able to estimate speed with an accuracy of 0.5 knots. In differential mode (SBAS) a GPS receiver's accuracy is usually contained to within 0.2 knots. With the accuracy of RTK positioning being down to a matter of centimetres, the speed can be accurate to as much as 0.1 knots. In all cases Speed Over Ground estimate errors are greater during turns, especially sudden ones. Moreover, the limit for low speed remains when the distance between two fixes falls under the positioning error. The higher the positioning accuracy, the lower the ship's speed threshold becomes for an acceptable estimate.

In order to be within 0.1 knot accuracy when using GPS in absolute mode, the use of carrier waves' Doppler effect (*Speed Doppler* - SDOP) is required. This is why the more modern receivers (*Phase Lock Loop* - PLL) are able to measure carrier wave frequency variations of a large number of satellites.

When this method is used along with a high frequency of Doppler measurements (at least four per second), it guarantees a significant improvement in the Speed Over Ground calculation when compared to the estimate derived solely from successive fixes[27]. In addition, this improvement can also potentially reflect on the calculation of a ship's position. However, even if four Doppler measurements per second with 0.1 knot accuracy correspond to a potential positioning accuracy of five centimetres. GPS chip producers do not supply elements to establish how much Doppler measurements actually influence improvements in positioning.

Speed Over Ground can also be calculated via instruments called *speed logs*. There are many different types but the most common are acoustic and electromagnetic ones.

Acoustic logs use the Doppler effect of acoustic pulses sent by a transducer that is installed under the ship's keel. The change in frequency between transmitted and reflected impulses is proportional to the relative speed between the source (vessel) and the reflecting surface (seabed)[28]. The indirect calculation of this relative speed is the actual *speed over ground*. There are two different types of Doppler logs: single axis and dual axis. Single axis speed logs can only calculate the longitudinal component of the Speed Over Ground, whilst dual axis logs also measure its transversal component. The two measurements are made possible by four acoustic beams orientated in a *Janus configuration* (figure II–25), devised to compensate for the effects of rolling and pitching.

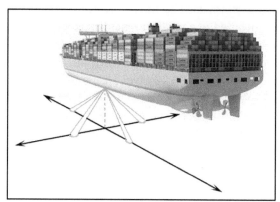

---

27 Tom J. Chalko (2007). "High Accuracy Speed Measurement by Using GPS".

28 $\Delta f = (\Delta v/c) \times f_0$ where "Δf" is the change in frequency, "Δv" is the relative velocity between ship and seabed, "c" is the velocity of propagation of the acoustic pulse underwater and "f_0" is the frequency of the acoustic pulse transmitted.

figure II–25 : Dual axis Doppler speed log in Janus configuration

As well as Speed Over Ground, a dual axis Doppler speed log can also calculate the drift angle, which is the angular difference between Heading and Course Over Ground. The calculation is made by processing the longitudinal and transversal components of both the true vector and the surface vector.

Speed Through Water can only be obtained from the acoustic backscatter of the water layers closest to the ship's hull.

Figure II–26 shows the geometric breakdown of components that are used to calculate the drift angle and to estimate the intensity and the direction of the current.

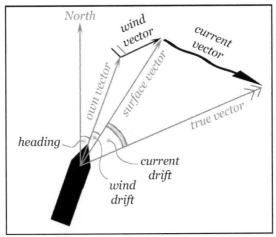

figure II–26 : Calculation of drift angle and sea current values

The vector components are listed in table II–5:

Vector	Direction	Magnitude
Own	Heading	Speed set on telegraphs
Surface	Heading ± leeway	Speed Through Water
True	Heading ± leeway and drift	Speed Over Ground

table II–5 : Ship vector components under the effect of the wind and current

The result is that the direction of the surface vector is only corrected by the wind's leeway effect. The true vector though is also corrected by the drift from currents. IMO standards on navigation displays symbology envisages a single-headed arrow for the surface vector and a double-headed arrow for the true vector. Generally navigation systems display the *set* and *drift* values[29] that represent the combined effect of wind and current (figure II–27).

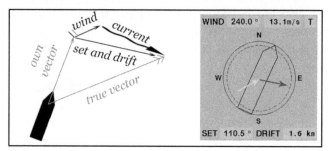

figure II–27 : Set and drift values on navigation systems

Figure II–26 shows the origin of all vectors in the forward part of a ship consistent to the Doppler log transducer's position and the *pivot point*[30]. If the vector's origin were astern of the pivot point the true vector would point, outside the trajectory described by a ship during a turn (figure II–28).

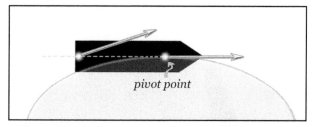

figure II–28 : True vector orientation during a turn

Irrespective of the point of measurement, if the Doppler speed log also has Rate of Turn available (supplied by an external gyrocompass), then it is possible to calculate transversal speed components for all points along the centreline of the ship and so represent a true vector at any point.

---

29 The difference between drift angle and intensity of the current should be noted. The term "drift" is commonly used interchangeably.

30 The pivot point is a position along a ship's longitudinal axis that does not register any transversal speed during a turn. Generally we can confirm that for a ship with headway, the pivot point is situated approximately one third of the ship's length from the bow. Whereas with sternway, the pivot point is situated at about one quarter of the ship's length from the stern. In reality this generalisation does not take into account any eventual effects of strong lateral forces applied to any of the two extremities of the ship's hull. When this happens, the pivot point moves away from the extremity to which the force is being applied, towards its opposite. When these forces play a part, the traditional concept of the pivot point risks simplifying the actual complexity of a ship's movement by too much.

The most common installations include a fore transducer (the most convenient point from an acoustic point of view) and a processor capable of calculating the transversal speed aft from Rate of Turn data given by an external gyrocompass.

The *pivot point* is the only point along the centreline of a ship where the transversal speed (i.e. the drift angle) is zero. Performing turns with a strong current abeam can mean that the pivot point is actually found outside the ship along its extended fore-and-aft direction.

The accuracy of longitudinal and transversal speeds measured with high end Doppler logs is in the order of 0.01 knots or 0.2% of the measured value. The maximum depth for Speed Over Ground measurements depends upon the frequency and power used by the acoustic transducer. At 100 KHz and with a transmission power of 100Watts the acoustic pulse can reflect off the seabed up to a depth of about 500 metres.

The log can only measure Speed Through Water when depths exceed this. At around 200 KHz, measurements in Bottom Track mode are possible up to around 100 metres depth. The minimum depth for calculating Speed Through Water also depends on the transducer's frequency. At 100 KHz the transducer requires tens of metres of water, whilst a higher frequency – in the order of 200 KHz – means that just a few metres are sufficient. The biggest limitation of acoustic speed logs comes from turbulence and the presence of air bubbles around the transducer. This is something that particularly occurs in shallow waters with an Under-Keel Clearance of around a metre or less. In any case the minimum Under-Keel Clearance established by IMO for measuring Speed Over Ground is two metres and three metres for Speed Through Water. It should also be mentioned that rough seas do not favour the correct functioning of speed logs, especially when the vessel is not fully loaded.

Contrary to acoustic speed logs, electromagnetic logs are only able to measure Speed Through Water. Their working principles are based on Faraday's law of induction, where a conductor fluid that flows through a magnetic field induces an electromotive force that depends on the speed of the fluid itself. Typical accuracy is around 0.2 knots or 2% of the value measured. According to the minimum standards set by IMO[31] the systems that calculate speed must also be able to measure the distance that a ship travels during the voyage (not less than 999.9 NM).

---

31 Resolution MSC.96(72) adopted 22 May 2000 as amended by Resolution MSC.334(90) adopted 22 May 2012. "Performance Standards for Speed and Distance Measuring Devices".

Table II–6 gives a summary of the accuracy of speeds measured using GNSS and speed logs (acoustic and electromagnetic).

Speed Sensor Types	Technique	Typical accuracy	IMO minimum required accuracy
GNSS absolute mode	Speed over ground estimate from recursive processing of past fixes	~ 0.5 kn	0.2kn or 2% of measured value if digital display
GNSS SBAS differential mode		~ 0.2 kn	
GNSS RTK relative mode		~ 0.1 kn	
GNSS absolute mode	Measures Speed Over Ground through Doppler effect of carrier waves	~ 0.1 kn	0.25 kn or 2.5% of measured value if analogue display
Dual axis Doppler speed logs	Measures Speed Over Ground and Speed Through Water using the Doppler effect	~ 0.01 kn or 0.2% of measurement	
Electromagnetic speed logs	Direct measurements of Speed Through Water	~ 0.2 kn or 2% of measurement	

table II–6 : Accuracy of speed sensors

Wind

Measuring the direction and intensity of wind plays a particularly important role for algorithms used by Track Control Systems and Dynamic Positioning Systems. It is only possible to take relative wind measurements on board a moving ship. True wind direction and intensity can be calculated by correcting relative ones with the ship's motion data.

The accuracy in determining true wind measurements depends mostly on the turbulence that the flow of wind can generate when coming into contact with the ship's superstructure. Because of this factor, wind speed measured by an on board anemometer can vary significantly from measurements taken some distance away from the vessel. In order to minimise this effect anemometers are generally installed on the highest part of a ship, which is higher than the "meteorological" level (10 metres above sea level). We shouldn't forget however that an anemometer installed tens of metres up can actually measure wind magnitudes up to 20% higher than those at 10 metres above the sea level.

Another factor to consider are wind gusts. Traditional anemometers with rotating elements present delays in viewing a gust of wind. Unfortunately even the most modern anemometers without moving parts cannot establish the extent of air mass associated with a gust, and as a consequence are unable to determine where it applies its force to the side of a ship. It is still only a point measurement after all, which is why on very long ships with large windage at least four anemometers should be installed – one forward, one amidships on the port side, one amidships on the starboard side and one aft.

Modern anemometers, as opposed to traditional ones, measure the intensity and direction of the wind with ultrasound technology. The sensing element consists of a series of small transducers that measure the amount of time it takes for acoustic waves to travel between them (just a few centimetres). The accuracy of the intensity measured is generally contained to within 2% of the reading obtained (e.g. 0.5 knots with a 25 knot wind) and two degrees for its direction. High temporal resolution (up to 20 Hz) makes acoustic anemometers ideal for measuring turbulent flows. A disadvantage when compared to traditional rotor anemometers is their limited performance in the rain.

Acoustic anemometers are usually used to provide wind direction and intensity data to Dynamic Positioning Systems installed on offshore vessels.

Depth

Depth is measured on board merchant ships by ultrasonic echosounders (from 20 KHz and upwards). Differently from Doppler speed logs, an echosounder measures the time it takes between the emission of an acoustic pulse and the return of its reflection off the seabed. By estimating the propagation of sound velocity in water, it is possible to measure the distance between the transducer and the bottom of the sea. This value is known as the *Under-Keel Clearance* (UKC) or the *Depth Below Transducer* (DBT). It is worth mentioning that the Under-Keel Clearance is different from the surface depth, which is calculated by adding the vessel's draught to the measured value.

In order to give the minimum Under-Keel Clearance value during manoeuvres in confined waters, long ships are equipped with two transducers (forward and aft).

Echosounders for navigation emit acoustic pulses contained within a single beam, which is directed downwards and perpendicularly to the ship's keel. Generally the accuracy of depth measurements varies according to:

- the frequency of the acoustic pulse;

138

- the acoustic beamwidth;
- the correctness of the underwater sound velocity estimate.

The acoustic pulse's frequency is directly proportional to the instrument's resolution and inversely proportional to the maximum depth that can be measured. The most common frequency is 200 KHz, which is considered "high" when compared to the more typical "low" 50 KHz frequency. When used with a transmission power of hundreds of Watts, a 200 KHz pulse's range is around 200 metres, whereas a 50 KHz pulse can reach to about 1000 metres.

Datasheets of echosounders express accuracy in terms of a percentage of the measured value. Typical values vary from 1% (high frequency) to 2% (low frequency), i.e. within the 2.5% set by IMO's minimum standard[32]. If we take the example of an echosounder with a 200 KHz transducer, it has the ability of measuring an Under-Keel Clearance of 10 metres with an accuracy in the order of a decimetre. The minimum range requirement however is fixed within an interval from 2 to 200 metres. This is why low frequency transducers are not as common as high frequency ones, due to the latter being more accurate in shallow waters and also for having lower costs and dimensions. The acoustic beamwidth influences its resolving power. The narrower the beam, the higher the resolving power in depth and in its associated position. The range of transducers used for navigation have beamwidths that vary from a few degrees to tens of degrees. Figure II–29 illustrates the concept of an echosounder's resolving power. In order to guarantee the minimum under-keel measurement within the beam, the returning echo that is processed by the receiver is the one reflected by the nearest obstacle. As a consequence, seabed depressions appear "filled in" on the echogram, while peaks are "flattened".

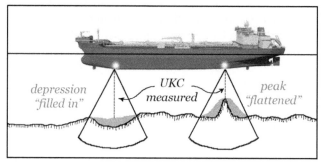

figure II–29 : Effects of an echosounder's resolving power

32 Resolution MSC.74(69) adopted 12 May 1998. "Performance Standards for Echosounders".

These effects are linked directly with the horizontal resolving power, which is represented by the width of the beam's acoustic footprint on the seabed[33]. On the other hand the vertical resolving power depends on the bottom detection algorithm acting upon the acoustic energy received, given the condition that sound velocity is constant at 1500 metres per second.

Variations in sound velocity (tens of metres at the most) are mainly caused by temperature variations within the more superficial layers of the water column. An acoustic pulse that travels perpendicular (or almost) to these layers does not suffer significant alterations for the purpose of measuring the Under-Keel Clearance. Things change when we need to direct the acoustic beam parallel to the sea surface to look for any submerged obstacles ahead of the ship. Here the sound velocity estimate becomes important for a correct interpretation of the acoustic echoes that are transmitted, reflected and refracted through the water columns layers with greatest variability. These instruments are called *forward-looking sonars* (figure II–30) and their range covers a few thousand metres on a horizontal plane with a beamwidth that goes from a few tens of degrees (which can be set by the operator) to omnidirectional (e.g. for the purpose of anchorage monitoring).

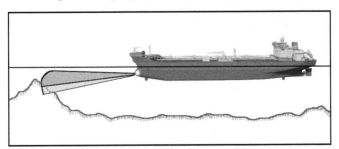

figure II–30 : Forward looking sonar

Measuring sound velocity is also important for multibeam echosounders that emit hundreds of lobes with a growing incline in a transversal direction, which creates an acoustic swath with a typical width of 120° (figure II–31). Lateral lobes are more influenced by propagation errors and so are less accurate. The effects of roll also become significant in calculating the correct positioning associated to each depth measured by the lateral lobes. This is why multibeam echosounders usually require attitude data (roll, pitch, heading and vertical movement) to correct seabed measurements in real-time. Only Inertial Motion Units (IMU) can supply these data at the accuracies required.

---

33 The most common directional transducers show beamwidths within 10 degrees.

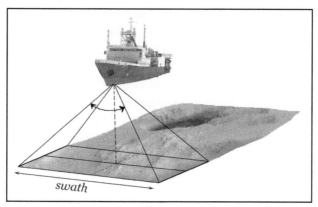

figure II–31 : Multibeam echosounders

Over the last few decades these systems have been used for hydrographic surveying, but in the future they could be used on merchant ships to acquire valuable bathymetric data for updating and/or improving existing nautical charts. This approach has already been explored by producers of land cartography through so-called *crowd sourcing* strategies. However it does present some technical and legal issues that derive mostly from the lack of quality control in place during data collection.

Attitude

The frontier in the field of navigation sensors is made up of systems that integrate GNSS receivers with Inertial Measurement Units (IMU). An IMU contains accelerometers and gyroscopes that are capable of measuring the linear accelerations and rotational angular velocities of a moving object, respectively, within a three-dimensional Cartesian coordinate system (figure II–32).

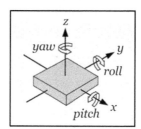

figure II–32 : An IMU's reference system

The processing of IMU linear accelerations in real-time also allows an autonomous estimate of the ship's position (with respect to the three axes *xyz*) in the event of a GNSS outage. Movement along the *z* vertical axis is known as *heave*, whilst movements along the *x* and *y* axes represent longitudinal and transversal components of the ship's Speed Over Ground.

The processing of angular velocities provides variations in *roll, pitch* and *yaw* (Heading) angles. All these parameters are normally used for Dynamic Positioning Systems that are widespread in the offshore industry. Nevertheless, inertial navigation techniques were developed well before the advent of GPS. In fact it was an inertial navigation system that was used to put man on the moon in the Apollo space missions. At that time IMU sensors were composed of high precision mechanical accelerometers and gyroscopes that were only used on space missions due to their prohibitive costs.

Today, MEMS (Micro-Electrical-Mechanical Systems) technology means that sensors are put on microchips with dimensions that are increasingly smaller and with an accuracy that becomes ever more competitive. It is these small dimensions that allow IMUs to be integrated with GNSS receivers.

When precise navigation is required, a system that integrates IMU and GNSS can guarantee:

- improved accuracy in positioning and speed compared to a GNSS receiver without IMU;
- positioning continuity even during loss, disturbance or jamming of a satellite signal due to the inertial sensors' autonomous estimates;
- improved accuracy in the Heading by at least one order of magnitude (0.01° - 1 sigma) compared to the more common mechanical gyrocompasses found on merchant ships;
- improved Rate of Turn accuracy of one order of magnitude compared to that calculated using Heading data from a normal mechanical gyrocompass;
- accurate roll and pitch measurements (0.01° - 1 sigma), well over the minimum standard set by IMO for electronic inclinometers (1° or 5% of reading)[34]. Such accuracy could also improve the dynamic calculation of the Under-Keel Clearance, correcting the value measured by the echosounder in real-time according to roll and pitch angles;
- accuracy in vertical movement (heave) equal to 5 cm (1 sigma).

From the six listed points, the most neglected one for precise navigation is positioning continuity in the event of GNSS outages, jamming or spoofing.

---

34 Resolution MSC.363(92) adopted 14 June 2013. "Performance Standards for Electronic Inclinometers".

However, the level of accuracy for this "inertial" dead-reckoning varies greatly on the type of IMU used, whose performance levels can be grouped into five grades:

- *marine;*
- *navigation;*
- *tactical;*
- *industrial;*
- *automotive/consumer.*

Apart from the custom inertial navigation systems used on Intercontinental ballistic missiles, the *marine* grade IMUs are the highest grade of sensors that are commercially available. These units are typically used on submarines and space crafts, however an inertial navigation system based on these type of sensors would not be cost effective for the actual needs of shipping. The accuracy in the autonomous positioning estimate is usually contained to within 1.8 km after a day of autonomous navigation.

Navigation grade IMUs are slightly less accurate than marine grade ones and are generally used in civil and military aviation. Positioning drift in this case is typically contained to within 1.6 km after an hour of autonomous navigation. Their price range is far lower than marine grade IMUs, yet their dimensions are also smaller, which makes integration with GPS receivers in confined spaces possible. It is this grade of IMUs that merchant ships may look at in order to mitigate risks arising from an overreliance on GPS.

A *tactical* grade IMU can offer autonomous positioning for only a few minutes. Its cost is less due to the use of accelerometers realised on integrated circuit boards (MEMS) and Fibre Optic Gyros (FOG). Its cost-performance ratio makes it suitable for *Portable Pilot Units* (PPU), which are used by maritime pilots for independent positioning from that provided by a ship's sensors.

An *industrial* grade IMU has slightly lower performance values than tactical ones because they use MEMS gyroscopes and not fibre optic ones. Another important difference when compared with tactical grade IMUs is that autonomous positioning is limited to just a few seconds rather than a few minutes. Its limited cost makes this type attractive for integration with GNSS to counter brief losses in satellite signal integrity.

Finally, automotive and consumer grade IMUs are typically used in *Advanced Braking System* (ABS) and airbags, as well as in videogames and smartphones. Their accuracy is not sufficient for autonomous navigation, even when integrated with GNSS. Table II–7 summarises the accuracy in autonomous positioning carried out by Inertial Navigation Systems. These accuracies are defined according to IMU performance grades and the time passed since the last valid position fix. It is important to note that for a rough evaluation of an Inertial Navigation System's accuracy based on an IMU, we can assume that autonomous positioning errors depend exclusively on acceleration biases.

IMU Performance Grade	Acceleration Bias	Error in autonomous positioning of Inertial Navigation Systems			
		after 1 sec	after 10 sec	after 60 sec	after 1 hr
Navigation	0.025 mg	0.13 mm	12 mm	0.44 m	1.6 km
Tactical	0.3 mg	1.5 mm	150 mm	5.3 m	19 km
Industrial	3 mg	15 mm	1.5 m	53 m	190 km
Automotive/Consumer	125 mg	620 mm	60 m	2.2 km	7900 km

table II–7 : IMU performance grades

The values shown in table II–7 are valid when an IMU's accelerometer axes and the platform's orthogonal axes are perfectly aligned. This alignment is done by means of a calibration procedure during installation. Portable systems should therefore be calibrated before each use. Any misalignments could in fact have a significant impact on the performance of the Inertial Navigation System. Table II–8 shows errors in autonomous positioning depending on the accelerometer's misalignment angle.

Accelerometer Misalignment	Error in autonomous horizontal positioning of Inertial Navigation Systems			
	after 1 sec	after 10 sec	after 60 sec	after 1 hr
0.05°	4.3 mm	0.43 m	15 m	57 km
0.1°	8.6 mm	0.86 m	31 m	110 km
0.5°	43 mm	4.3 m	150 m	570 km
1°	86 mm	8.6 m	310 m	1100 km

table II–8 : Inertial positioning errors caused by IMU misalignment

In the absence of GNSS (or other external reference), an IMU would not be able to steadily measure a ship's orientation in space (Heading). However, tactical level (non MEMS) IMU gyroscopes can guarantee Heading variation measurements (Rate of Turn) with better accuracy compared to processing Heading data from a mechanical gyrocompass.

Nonetheless, we need to consider the fact that the accuracy of these direct Rate of Turn measurements is conditioned by:

- a gyroscopes' *scale factor*;
- *drift* or *gyro bias*;
- *gyro bias stability*.

As already mentioned with regards to gyroscopes, the scale factor expresses how Rate of Turn accuracy depends on the range of values measured. For example, if we were to lift up the IMU and rotate it 360° on one of its axes before putting it back in its original position, the final value of its orientation would be different from the initial one. This error is usually expressed in parts per million (PPM) of the measurement range and is known as the scale factor. Table II–9 shows orientation errors that correspond to different IMU performance grades (with different scale factors) after a rotation of 360°.

IMU Performance Grade	IMU Gyroscope Scale Factor	Angular Error after a 360° Rotation of IMU upon its Axes
Navigation	5 ppm	0.0018°
Tactical	100 ppm	0.036°
Industrial	500 ppm	0.18°
Automotive	60,000 ppm	22°

table II–9 : IMU orientation errors depending upon scale factor

The drift or gyro bias characterises a gyroscope's ability to measure Rate of Turn null values when the IMU is immobile. The error can be calculated by using the average of a long series of Rate of Turn measurements taken when the instrument is still. Once calculated, this error can be subtracted from the actual Rate of Turn measurements. Temperature variations are the main cause of drift, which is why an IMU may include temperature sensors to perform drift calibration alone.

Gyro bias stability is maybe the most important parameter for determining orientation accuracy in the absence of GNSS. This defines how much the gyro bias varies over time due to random oscillations of the IMU's electrical components. Gyro bias stability is usually given either in degrees per hour (°/hr) or in degrees per minute (°/min). The lower this value, the more accurate the autonomous positioning in the absence of GNSS (table II–10).

IMU Performance Level	Gyro Bias Stability of IMU Gyroscopes	Error in autonomous horizontal positioning of an Inertial Navigation System			
		after 1 sec	after 10 sec	after 60 sec	after 1 hr
Navigation	0.002°/hr	0.01 mm	0.1 mm	1.3 mm	620 m
Tactical	0.07°/hr	0.1 mm	3.2 mm	46 mm	22 km
Industrial	3°/hr	10 mm	0.23 m	3.3 m	1,500 km
Automotive	5°/hr	20 mm	0.45 m	6.6 m	3,100 km

table II–10 : Inertial positioning error depending upon IMU gyro bias stability

Table II–11 summarises the accuracy of integrated GNSS-IMU sensors, assuming the IMU used is a tactical grade one.

Navigation Type	Navigation Parameters	Accuracy	Application
Combined Inertial-GNSS	GNSS Positioning Speed Over Ground Course Over Ground	3 times greater than GNSS (for the same mode)	• Track Control System (TCS) • Dynamic Positioning System (DP)
	Heading	0.01°	• Electronic Chart Display Information System (ECDIS) • Automatic Identification System (AIS) • Automatic Radar Plotting Aid (ARPA)
	Rate of Turn	0.1°/min	
	Roll Pitch Heave	0.01°	• Track Control System (TCS) • Dynamic Positioning System (DP) • Electronic Chart Display Information System (ECDIS) • Echosounder
Inertial (autonomous) in the absence of GNSS	Autonomous inertial positioning	~ 5 m after 60 sec	Dead-Reckoning in absence of GNSS caused by intentional jamming/spoofing
	Orientation (Heading)	~ 0.1°/hr	Estimated orientation (Heading) in absence of geographical reference caused by intentional GNSS jamming/spoofing

table II–11 : Accuracy of GNSS-IMU integrated sensors

Up to now we have discussed the "sensors" that measure and calculate data of radar bearing and distance, positioning, orientation, speed, wind, depth and attitude. Strictly speaking in some of these cases, as with GNSS-IMU integration, it would be more correct to refer to them as "systems of sensors".

With this chapter concluded we can now turn our attention to navigation and communication systems that use data from sensors and/or systems of sensors to ensure the operational functionality of a modern ship's bridge.

Navigation and Communication Systems

T he following sections will look at the potential and limitations of the navigation and communication systems that are listed below in table II–12. Each one is associated with one or more operational functions on a modern ship's bridge.

Navigation and Communication System	Acronym	Associated Operational Function
Automatic Radar Plotting Aid	ARPA	Route monitoring and collision avoidance control
Automatic Identification System	AIS	Collision avoidance control
Electronic Chart Display Information System	ECDIS	Route planning and route monitoring
Track Control System	TCS	Route control
Dynamic Positioning System	DP	Manoeuvre control
Steering Control System	SC	Route and manoeuvre control
Main Engine / Thruster Control System	MEC THC	Route and manoeuvre control
Bridge Alert Management System	BAMS	Centralised monitoring of alert signals
Global Maritime Distress Safety System	GMDSS	Ship external radio communication

table II–12 : Operational functions of navigation and communication systems

Automatic Radar Plotting Aid (ARPA)

Radar began to be used on merchant ships during the 1950s. Before then route monitoring was carried out by angular measurements (sights) between celestial bodies and the visible horizon, as well as coastal bearings. Collision avoidance manoeuvres were performed exclusively using visual bearings and by evaluating the aspect of other ships. All officers actively participated – even when the pilot was on board – in the conduct of a purely visual navigation.

The balance between operators upon a ship's bridge and the roles they carried out were profoundly changed by the advent of radar. Initially it was very expensive and so ships were equipped with just one that was only used in the event of reduced visibility. Its screen (*Plan Position Indicator* – PPI) was so small that it could only be used by one person at a time (either the Captain or Pilot).

The absence of gyroscopic stabilisation allowed for only a fixed orientation in the direction of the ship's bow (*Head-up*). So the radar image corresponded to what could be seen from the bridge windows: conspicuous landmarks during the day and navigational aids at night.

Using radar bearings and distances for route monitoring, as well as the Rate of Turn to control Turn Radii, was something that came much later. In particular, controlling the Turn Radius was dependent upon the availability of radar reference points at the centre of curvature of a turn's arc. As a result, the only way of monitoring a ship's curved trajectory was to follow targets' trails on the radar screen.

This type of visual navigation with Head-up radar displays needed conning orders such as "steady as she goes", rather than ones using Headings.

In the 1970s, radar image stabilisation with the geographic North indicated by gyrocompasses made the North-up representation popular. With a fixed North, turns could be monitored with a clearer radar image without the trails left by fixed targets. Not everyone welcomed this new feature and, as a result, two schools of thought were formed: those who wanted to maintain Head-up and those who preferred to move to North-up. Both types have their advantages and disadvantages, which are summarised in table II–13.

Radar Representation	Advantages	Disadvantages
Head-up	Immediate correspondence between what can be seen out of the bridge windows and radar images	Difficulty in monitoring turns by using the trails of targets - Limitation of "steady as she goes" orders for controlling Headings at the end of a turn
North-up	Alignment with the chart North-up presentation	Easier monitoring of turns for the clarity of a radar image without trails - Possibility of giving Heading orders to the Helmsman rather than generic ones such as "steady as she goes"

table II–13 : Comparison table of the two types of radar representation

The first international resolution on radar was made by what was then known as IMCO[35] (*Inter-governmental Maritime Consultative Organization*) in 1971. This established the minimum diameter of a radar screen (9 inches), the stabilisation of the gyrocompass and the presence of Variable Range Markers (VRM). Two years later, IMCO also recommended the use of standardised symbols on radar screens instead of buttons with text[36]. Only one manufacturer actually followed this recommendation and it ended in failure. From that moment onwards IMCO abstained from regulating navigation system ergonomics, limiting itself to a generic recommendation – in 1981 – regarding the user-friendliness of radar features. This is why radars have such different user interfaces from each other still today. However, there is some movement in this area, given IMO's recent interest in reconsidering the issue of ergonomics with *e-navigation*, which we will discuss in the third part of this book.

There have been substantial regulatory delays throughout the history of radar. Just think that its use as a collision avoidance device was only made official in 1972 with the *International Regulations for Preventing Collisions at Sea* (COLREGS), which came into force in 1977. This convention posed an end to an era where there hadn't been any policies and standards for almost thirty years since radar first appeared on board merchant ships. Because of this delay different schools of thought originated together with differing procedures through time. So much so that even today, the act of implementing legislation for navigation systems is still an arduous task.

Finally in 1996 and again in 2004, IMO[37] established minimum characteristics of radar systems for ships larger than 10,000 Gross Tonnage. These features include:

- PPI dimensions of at least 320 mm;
- 2 *Electronic Bearing Lines* (EBL);
- 2 *Variable Range Markers* (VRM);
- 4 *Parallel Indexes* (PI);
- the possibility of offsetting the ship on the radar screen;
- automatic acquisition and tracking of at least 40 targets, with the ability to supply a target's first movement tendency within a minute and a definitive estimate within three minutes;

---

35 Resolution A.222(VII) adopted 12 October 1971. The name IMCO – which was used since the organisation's foundation in 1948 – was changed to IMO in 1982.

36 Resolution A.278(VIII) adopted 20 November 1973.

37 Resolution MSC.192(79) adopted 6 December 2004. "Performance Standards for Radar Equipment".

- the possibility of changing radar data reference to one point of the ship, known as the *Consistent Common Reference Point* (CCRP);

With regards to CCRP it is important to know which point of the ship is chosen as a reference for radar distances, as well as for CPA (*Closest Point of Approach*) and TCPA (*Time to Closest Point of Approach*) values. The CCRP can usually be selected by the operator in positions where radar antennae are and also at the centre of the ship's bridge (conning position). Figure II–33 shows these two different CCRP cases, with the bridge aft and a radar antenna installed in the forward part of the ship (*bow scanner*).

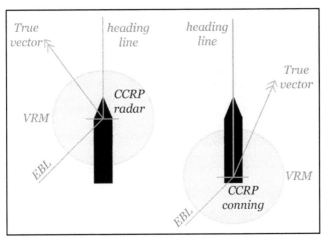

figure II–33 : Consistent Common Reference Point (CCRP)

The ability to automatically acquire and track targets was introduced to radar systems as early as the 1970s under the name ARPA (*Automatic Radar Plotting Aid*). Minimum performance of automatic tracking is summarised in table II–14 as a function of time passed since target acquisition (one minute or three minutes).

Relative Route	Relative Speed	CPA	TCPA	Course Over Ground	Speed Over Ground
Target tracking accuracy after 1 minute					
11°	1.5 knots or 10% of relative speed	1 NM	-	-	-
Target tracking accuracy after 3 minutes					
3°	0.8 knots or 1% of relative speed	0.3 NM	0.5 min	5°	0.5 knots or 1% of relative speed

table II–14 : Minimum performance standards of ARPA automatic tracking

150

The accuracy of bearings and distances must not exceed 2 degrees and either 50 metres or ±1% of target distance.

As well as signals received by the antennae in X and S bands, every radar system receives navigation data from the following sensors (figure II–34):

- Heading from a gyrocompass or Transmitting Heading Device;
- Speed Over Ground and Speed Through Water;
- geographic position from an electronic positioning system.

In addition to sensors, more modern radars also integrate an Automatic Identification System (AIS).

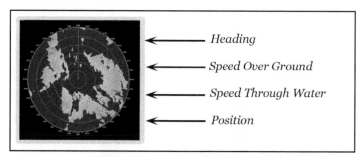

figure II–34 : The ARPA system and the sensors connected to it

At this point it's also worth tackling the age-old question of the choice between Speed Over Ground and Speed Through Water.

Many still think that radar "must" use Speed Through Water, but this is not the case. The misunderstanding arises from previous IMO specifications that required the use of Speed Through Water to maintain consistency between the radar image and a target's visual aspect. This requirement was born from the idea that in situations where routes cross each other[38] in the presence of currents, the true vectors could appear to be inconsistent with the aspect of the other ship.

In the example used in figure II–35, the aspect can be misleading and a decision based on water-stabilised vectors could increase the risk of collision, especially in reduced visibility.

Resolving this ambiguity could be done by visualising relative vectors, irrespective of the type of stabilisation.

---

38 Rule 15 of the International Regulations for Preventing Collisions at Sea states that when two power-driven vessels are crossing so as to involve risk of a collision, the vessel which has the other on her own starboard side shall keep out of the way and shall, if the circumstances of the case admit, avoid crossing ahead of the other vessel.

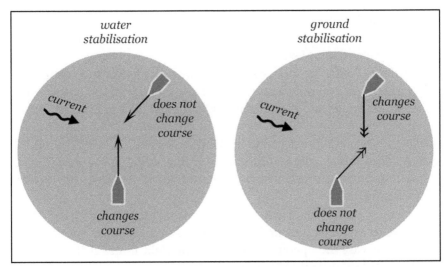

figure II–35 : Different types of radar stabilisation

The fact is that using Speed Through Water conforms with COLREGS (based on the visual aspect of targets), but is not effective for another important use of radar systems: route monitoring. For this purpose Speed Over Ground and Course Over Ground – represented as length and direction of the true vector – offer many more advantages, especially when using a planned route and electronic charts as a background for the radar image.

In short, we can say that when using a radar PPI stabilised with Speed Through Water:

- fixed targets move together with the current;
- the appearance of moving targets is consistent with true vectors;
- the danger of collision is clear but the collision point is incorrect;
- the true vector of the own ship does not show the actual direction in which it is moving (Course Over Ground).

Whereas on PPI stabilised with Speed Over Ground:

- fixed targets remain still;
- the aspect of targets might not correspond with its true vectors. However in reduced visibility, collision avoidance decisions cannot be based on aspect[39], contrary to that which occurs in good visibility conditions. The radar operator must therefore understand that true vectors do not represent a target's Heading;

---

[39] Rule 19 of the International Regulations for Preventing Collisions at Sea does not foresee course alterations based on aspect when visibility is restricted.

152

- the collision point is correct;
- the own ship's true vector shows the actual direction in which it is moving (Course Over Ground).

According to what has been said above, we can confirm that stabilisation with Speed Over Ground offers a more realistic image to the operator both for collision avoidance decisions and for route monitoring. This has become even more evident since the 1990s with the diffusion of GPS receivers able to calculate more and more accurate Speed Over Ground values. In 2004 IMO acknowledged this change by removing the obligation to use Speed Through Water from its most recent version of performance standards for on board radar systems.

The year 2004 also marked IMO's decision[40] to give priority to AIS targets over those tracked by ARPA in the absence of significant differences between them. In any case the operator is left with the right to invert this condition and show ARPA targets if AIS malfunctions.

In reality the possibility to choose the type of radar stabilisation can create confusion, as is the case with the coexistence of a number of other display options on modern PPIs. These actually allow the selection of several combinations using the following modes:

- *Head-up*: the ship's Heading is fixed to the PPI's longitudinal direction;
- *Course-up*: the Course Over Ground value fixes the PPI's longitudinal direction;
- *North-up*: geographical north is fixed to the PPI's longitudinal direction;
- *Relative Motion*: target vectors are orientated in the direction of their relative motion on the PPI;
- *True Motion*: target vectors are orientated in the direction of their actual motion on the PPI;
- *Relative Trails*: the trails left by targets follow their relative course on the PPI;
- *True Trails*: the trails left by targets follow their actual course on the PPI.

A modern radar also offers the option of adding electronic vector charts to the PPI's background. The corresponding alignment between background chart objects and their radar echoes becomes a tool for checking the integrity

40 Resolution MSC.191(79) adopted 6 December 2004. "Performance Standards for the Presentation of Navigation-Related Information on Shipborne Navigational Displays".

of the navigation sensors that are connected to the radar. With this in mind, minimum radar performance standards include the ability to manage the following failure modes:

- unavailability of Heading input: radar automatically switches to Head-up and Relative Motion after no more than one minute after the last valid Heading value received;
- unavailability of Speed Through Water: radar allows manual speed input by the operator;
- unavailability of Speed Over Ground: radar continues to work using Speed Through Water or manual speed inputs;
- unavailability of positioning: radar allows the removal of the background chart in one swift action;
- unavailability of data from X and S band scanners: the frozen radar image disappears from the PPI and only AIS targets remain visible.

Automatic Identification System (AIS)

AIS is a system that allows the automatic exchange of information between ships, coastal *Base Stations, Aids to Navigation* (AtoN*), Airborne Search And Rescue* (SAR) and *Search and Rescue Transmitters* (SART).

Shipborne AIS can transmit and receive information from other ships and from coastal stations known as *Vessel Traffic Systems* (VTS). These transmissions use two FM channels on the VHF band: AIS1 (Channel 87B) and AIS2 (Channel 88B). In areas where these are not available, a shipborne AIS can automatically switch to alternative VHF channels that allow for the reception of specific messages from available base stations.

There are two types of shipborne AIS: class A and class B. Class A shipborne AISs are mandatory on all SOLAS ships that are:

- greater than 300 Gross Tonnage and engaged in international voyages;
- greater than 500 Gross Tonnage, whether they are engaged in international voyages or not;
- that carry passengers, regardless of their Gross Tonnage.

Class B AIS are not mandatory for either non-SOLAS ships or for leisure crafts.

Both types of shipborne AIS are restricted by VHF radio propagation but are different with regards to their operational range. Class A AIS can operate up to 30 nautical miles, while Class B from 5 to 10 nautical miles. This difference is mainly due to the limits of their transmission power: 12 Watts for Class A and 2 Watts for Class B.

A Class A shipborne AIS includes:

- a VHF transmitter;
- two VHF receivers that use SOTDMA (*Self Organized Time Division Multiple Access*)[41] technology;
- a VHF channel 70 DSC (*Digital Selective Call*)[42] receiver;
- a two-way VHF antenna;
- an internal GNSS receiver used for the synchronisation of transmission time, as well as a redundant system to an external GNSS receiver which provides positioning, Course Over Ground and Speed Over Ground data;
- a dedicated screen for the visualisation of AIS data received (*Minimum Keyboard Display* – MKD).

A complete Class A AIS must be connected to the following sensors (figure II–36):

- an external GNSS receiver for positioning (WGS84), Course Over Ground and Speed Over Ground;
- a gyrocompass or other Transmitting Heading Device (THD) for Heading data.

And as an option, it can also be connected to:

- a speed log for Speed Over Ground;
- a gyrocompass or a rate gyro for Rate of Turn data.

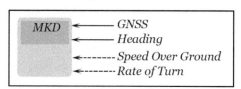

figure II–36 : Sensors connected to AIS

---

41 SOTDMA technology allows users to share one unique transmission channel through the synchronisation and time distribution of transmissions. Users transmit in rapid succession, each using his own automatically assigned time slot. This allows simultaneous transmission of many users on the same transmission channel.

42 DSC technology allows the sending and receiving of radio messages (VHF, MF and HF) selectively and with the automatic compilation of the ship's position and Maritime Mobile Service Identity (MMSI). Two-way DSCs were introduced to allow for the reception of eventual distress signals without having to remain tuned to traditional distress frequencies (VHF channel 16 and 2182 KHz).

Information transmitted by AIS can be divided into three categories: *static, dynamic* and *voyage related*[43] (table II–15).

Type of information	Parameters	Class A	Class B
Static	Ship name	√	√
	Call sign	√	√
	Maritime Mobile Service Identity (MMSI)	√	√
	IMO Number	√	Absent
	Length and beam of ship	√	√
	Type of ship	√	√
	Location of AIS transmitting antenna	√	√
Dynamic	GNSS position with indication of differential corrections, and accuracy[44]	√	√
	UTC time associated to GNSS positioning connected to the AIS	√	√
	Course Over Ground from GNSS	Optional	Optional
	Speed Over Ground from GNSS	Optional	Optional
	Heading from a gyrocompass or THD	√	Optional
	Navigational status according to COLREGS	√	Absent
	Rate of Turn from a specific sensor or from gyrocompass data	Optional	Absent
	Pitch and roll angles	Optional	Absent
Voyage Related	Ship's draught	√	Absent
	Type of cargo (dangerous cargo, harmful substances, marine pollutant)	√	Absent
	Destination and Estimated Time of Arrival	√	Absent
	Route plan (waypoints)	Optional	Absent

table II–15 : Type of information transmitted by Class A and Class B AIS

The frequency at which AIS information is updated and transmitted depends on the category. Both static and voyage related information is transmitted either every six minutes or the moment in which they change. Dynamic information intervals however depend upon:

- navigational status;
- Speed Over Ground;
- Rate of Turn.

---

43 Resolution 74(69) adopted 12 May 1998. "Performance Standards for a Universal Automatic Identification System".

44 Accuracy control is based upon the estimated error from GNSS receivers using RAIM (Receiver Autonomous Integrity Monitoring) technology. The estimated RAIM error is equal to the square root of the sum of estimated latitudinal and longitudinal errors squared. RAIM estimated error values of 10 metres are encoded in AIS transmission.

Table II–16 lists reporting intervals for AIS class A dynamic information. These intervals aim to avoid any worthless overloading of VHF transmission channels.

Class A Shipborne AIS Dynamic Condition	Reporting Interval
Ship at anchor with Speed Over Ground less than 3 knots	3 min
Ship at anchor with Speed Over Ground greater than 3 knots	10 sec
Speed Over Ground from 0 to 14 knots	10 sec
Speed Over Ground from 0 to 14 knots and ROT greater than 10°/min	3 sec
Speed Over Ground from 14 to 23 knots	6 sec
Speed Over Ground from 14 to 23 knots and ROT greater than 10°/min	2 sec
Speed over ground greater than 23 knots	2 sec
Speed Over Ground greater than 23 knots and ROT greater than 10°/min	2 sec

table II–16 : Reporting intervals for Class A AIS

Reporting intervals for all other AIS types are summarised in table II–17 as a function of various dynamic conditions relating to Class B shipborne targets.

AIS Type	Dynamic Condition	Reporting Interval
Shipborne class B	Speed over ground less than 2 knots	3 min
	Speed over ground from 2 to 14 knots	30 sec
	Speed over ground from 14 to 23 knots	15 sec
	Speed over ground greater than 23 knots	5 sec
Airborne SAR	--	10 sec
AtoN	--	3 min
Base Station	--	10 sec

table II–17 : Reporting intervals for non-class A AIS

As already mentioned in the section dedicated to ARPA, as of 2008 all new radars must be able to represent data received from AIS with a standardised symbology[45], and prioritised over those tracked by ARPA.

As a result the Minimum Keyboard Displays – which are only able to show AIS information in text format – are destined to disappear from bridges over the next few years.

---

45 SN.1/Circ.243/Rev.1 dated 23 May 2014. "Amended Guidelines for the Presentation of Navigational-Related Symbols, Terms and Abbreviations".

MSC.1/Circ.1473 dated 23 May 2014. "Policy on Use of AIS Aids to Navigation".

The most acknowledged AIS international symbolism mainly regards collision avoidance with a representation of sleeping and active targets that are shown in table II–18.

Type of AIS Target	Symbol	Meaning
Sleeping		Indicates only the presence of a ship fitted with AIS in a certain position
Active		Upon acquiring the sleeping AIS target, the symbol above is displayed with an added true vector (dotted line) derived from COG GNSS, a graphical indication of its Heading (solid line) and also an indication of its Rate of Turn (small hook) if more than 10°/min

table II–18 : AIS symbology

If queried, both sleeping and active AIS targets show static, dynamic (including CPA and TCPA values) and voyage related information in text form. If an AIS target (both sleeping and active) then enters within the CPA and TCPA limits set by the user, its symbol flashes red until the operator accepts the alert.

Activation of an AIS target has priority over the acquisition of an ARPA target relating to the same radar echo. This default feature, which is mandatory for all radar systems produced since 2008, is justified by the fact that the active AIS target is more accurate than its ARPA counterpart during the initial tracking phase. The difference also becomes evident later on during changes in course, which is when the AIS target can follow target movements on the PPI more accurately.

Nevertheless the risk is that the operator puts too much trust in AIS target tracking, thus totally neglecting the ARPA target acquisition. This goes against IMO guidelines[46], which remind us that even though AIS plays an important role in collision avoidance, it cannot entirely replace ARPA.

It is for this reason that more modern radars are able to compare AIS and ARPA data for the same target in real-time, showing one unique symbol if differences between Course Over Ground, Speed Over Ground and distance

---

46 Resolution A.917(22) adopted 29 November 2001. Amended by Resolution A.956(23) adopted 5 December 2003. "Guidelines for the On Board Operational Use of Shipborne Automatic Identification Systems (AIS)". See also MSC.1/Circ.1473 dated 23 May 2014.

fall within limits set by the operator. The operator can also choose which type of target (ARPA or AIS) to display as a result of their fusion.

The main limitation of AIS is the risk of receiving misleading information from other ships. Since 2007 IMO publishes a quarterly report[47], which lists all of the anomalies communicated by its member States and by other organisations. Those less critical consist of missing or incorrect static information such as a ship's name or the offset of GNSS positioning associated with AIS. More critical anomalies include erroneous dynamic information such as Heading and position.

The anomalies mentioned are identifiable by using the cues listed in table II–19.

Type of AIS Target anomaly	Cues
Incorrect position of AIS target	A unique AIS target (active or sleeping) appears out of position with respect to the radar echo and/or the tracked ARPA target. All other AIS targets match with radar echoes and/or associated ARPA targets.
Incorrect Heading of AIS target	The heading of an active AIS target moves away from its true vector (COG) in a significant way. The significance of this difference must be evaluated taking into account the current in the area and the actual target's speed.
Incorrect offset of GNSS position associated with AIS	The visible AIS target symbol on the PPI moves away from its associated radar echo at a reduced range. An incorrect offset can result in a difference of around a ship's length.

table II–19 : Identification of AIS target anomalies

On the other hand, AIS information allows the identification of anomalies on own ship's navigation sensors. Table II–20 lists cues for identifying anomalies in positioning and orientation.

Type of anomaly on own ship's navigation sensors	Cues
Incorrect GNSS positioning	All AIS targets (active and sleeping) are out of position (with respect to radar echoes and/or tracked ARPA targets) by the same amount.
Incorrect heading	All AIS targets (active an sleeping) are out of position (with respect to radar echoes and/or tracked ARPA targets) by an amount that is proportional to the distance from the ship itself.

table II–20 : Identification of navigation sensor anomalies by means of AIS

---

47 MSC 83/28 dated 26 October 2007. "Report of the Maritime Safety Committee on its Eighty-Third Session". See par. 4.34.

Following the diffusion of the so-called *AtoN* (*Aids to Navigation*) AIS, IMO has introduced a new series of symbols to standardise information shown on PPIs in radars manufactured from 2008 onwards. As well as AtoN AIS, symbols have also been devised for SAR (*Search And Rescue*) both for aircraft and for SART transmitters. An example of these symbols (which is not complete) is shown in table II–21.

AIS Type	Symbol if AtoN is physical	Symbol if AtoN is virtual
AtoN - generic *(also used for fixed structures)*	◇	⟨+⟩
AtoN - Beacon Cardinal Mark North	◈	◈ ⟨+⟩
AtoN – SART	⊗	

table II–21 : Examples of AIS AtoN and SAR symbology

Generally physical AtoN AISs are designed to transmit the following information:

- AtoN type and name;
- AtoN actual position in real-time, particularly important for non-fixed AtoNs;
- as an option, also AtoN status (e.g. the error in light characteristic or the offset of drifting buoys).

Virtual AtoN AISs are designed to signal navigational information either permanently or temporarily.

Permanent AtoNs are located where it is difficult or is not economically viable to deploy physical ones. They can also be used to signal seabed features that vary through time under the influence of tidal streams or other atmospheric agents. This type of virtual AtoN may be encoded onto Electronic Navigational Charts (ENC). In this way temporary virtual AtoNs can be used to compensate for the absence of temporary or preliminary Notices To Mariners (*NTM T&Ps*) in Electronic Navigational Charts (ENC).

In both virtual AtoN cases, ARPA and ECDIS navigation systems should not duplicate information already present on electronic charts.

Electronic Display Information System (ECDIS)

ECDIS is designed to assist deck officers in route planning and route monitoring. According to IMO performance standards[48], an ECDIS must:

- allow for the installation and update of vector electronic navigational charts in a format established by the International Hydrographic Organization (IHO), and distributed by or on behalf of governmental Hydrographic Offices. Electronic charts that respond to these requirements are called *Electronic Navigational Charts* (ENC);
- represent own ship and the abovementioned ENCs using IMO and IHO standard symbology respectively;
- continuously receive the position (from an electronic positioning system), the Heading (from a gyrocompass or a transmitting heading device) and the Speed Over Ground (from a Doppler log or from GNSS);
- allow automatic verification of planned routes, aimed at alerting the operator to the presence of dangers or elements of interest on the ENC within a certain distance from the route;
- allow automatic route monitoring via specific operator alarms and indicators;
- record significant navigational elements over the last 12 hours – at least once every minute – and for the entire duration of the voyage – at least once every four hours;
- be equipped with an adequate backup navigation system, which allows completion of the voyage if the primary one fails. The backup system must be connected to an independent power supply source from the primary system;
- as an option, guarantee the visualisation not only of ARPA and AIS targets, but also of AIS AtoNs (physical and/or virtual) that are not yet present on ENCs.

By 2018 all SOLAS ships engaged in international voyages must carry ECDIS on board.

Electronic navigation systems that do not comply with IMO performance standards are called Electronic Chart Systems (ECS). Typical examples of these include:

---

48 Resolution 232(82) adopted 5 December 2006. "ECDIS Performance Standards".

- Portable Pilot Units (PPU), irrespective of whether they use ENCs or not. In fact both their screen dimensions and electro-technical requirements are not usually compliant with minimum standards;
- radar systems equipped with vector chart underlays, also irrespective of whether they use ENC or not. This is due to the PPI not being square, but also because the chart underlay does not comply with ECDIS colour palette standards;
- on board navigation systems that meet ECDIS hardware standards but use unofficial electronic vector charts.

Let's now go through some additional considerations regarding the most common potentials and limitations of ECDIS used on ships at present (2015).

We'll begin with electronic vector charts that presents both advantages and disadvantages when compared to paper charts. In order to understand them we need to distinguish between the contents of an ENC and its visualisation. For its contents, the IHO reference standard is S-57 whereas its visualisation is covered by S-52. S-57 regulates the way in which chart data must be encoded while S-52 standardises symbols and their presentation methods on an ECDIS's screen[49].

So far electronic vector charts were created by an out-and-out translation of symbols into objects and attributes in compliance with the S-57 standard. A little like attempting to transcribe all the elements of a nautical chart onto an electronic worksheet under the form of:

- points (e.g. buoys, soundings, isolated dangers, etc.);
- lines (e.g. bathymetric contours, coastlines, etc.);
- areas (e.g. traffic separation schemes, dredged channels, etc.);
- information (e.g. scale, edition, update status, etc.);

This process is known as *compilation* and every ENC has its associated *compilation scale*. In turn, each compilation scale is associated to a visualisation scale expressed in nautical miles that corresponds to certain radar ranges on PPIs[50]. The aim is to use a common reference for ECDIS and radar visualisation.

Table II–22 shows the various types of ENCs of which their *navigational purpose* matches specific intervals for both compilation and visualisation scales.

---

49 IHO S-57 "Transfer Standard for Digital Hydrographic Data" Ed.3.1 (2000) and IHO S-52 "Specifications for Chart Content and Display Aspects of ECDIS" Ed.6.1.0 (2014).

50 The visualisation scale of a radar screen corresponds to PPI radius, whilst ECDIS is equal to half of one side of the screen. Both are measured in nautical miles.

ENC Navigational Purpose	Compilation Scale 1:	Radar Range (NM)
Overview	3,000,000	200
	1,500,000	96
General	700,000	48
	350,000	24
Coastal	180,000	12
	90,000	6
Approach	45,000	3
	22,000	1.5
Harbour	12,000	0.75
	8,000	0.5
	4,000	0.25
Berthing	< 4,000	< 0.25

table II–22 : ENC navigational purposes and compilation scales

Changing the visualisation scale of ECDIS also means that the ENC is probably changing, the same as opening a drawer on the chart table and taking out another nautical chart. If a chart is viewed beyond its compilation scale it means that there are no ENCs with greater detail present within the system. In this case ECDIS gives an *overscale* indication which is shown via vertical lines known as *prison bars* or *jail bars* (figure II–37), together with a descriptive indication in a dedicated area of the ECDIS interface.

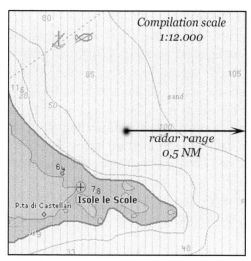

figure II–37 : Overscale indication

Viewing an overscaled ENC is like using an enlarged photocopy of a section of a traditional nautical chart. In both cases there is no greater detail.

However, whilst with a photocopy the symbols are also enlarged, with ECDIS the ENC symbols remain the same size, irrespective of the scale of visualisation[51]. This could induce us to overestimate the accuracy of an overscaled ENC's.

As with any nautical chart, an ENC is as accurate as the hydrographic surveys used to produce it. In fact it is possible to extract horizontal and vertical accuracy values of bathymetric data from each ENC. Each pair of these values is connected to a Zone Of Confidence (ZOC) as shown in table II–23.

If we consider that at best (ZOC A1), uncertainty of the actual depth is around half a metre, we can understand why the minimum Under-Keel Clearance established by port authorities is generally greater than this value.

As well as for horizontal and vertical accuracy levels, ZOC also reveals whether the sea floor has been fully searched (ZOC A1 and A2) or only partially (ZOC B, C and D). In the latter case the possibility that significant seabed features were not found during surveying can't be excluded, which means they will not appear on the ENC.

Zone of Confidence	Horizontal Accuracy	Vertical Accuracy	Notes on Hydrographic Surveying
A1	±5 m + 5% depth	0,5 m + 1% depth	Full area search undertaken. Significant seabed features detected and depths measured.
A2	±20 m	1 m + 2% depth	
B	±50 m	1 m + 2% depth	Full area search not achieved; uncharted features, hazardous to surface navigation are not expected but may exist.
C	±500 m	2 m + 5% depth	Full area search not achieved, depth anomalies may be expected.
D	Worse than ZOC C		Full area search not achieved, large depth anomalies may be expected.
U	The quality of the bathymetric data has yet to be assessed.		

table II–23 : Zones of Confidence (ZOCs)

51 The ECDIS visualisation standard (IHO S52) actually envisages fixed dimensions in terms of pixels for each individual symbol.

As already mentioned, each single symbol and its presentation rules must comply with IHO Standard S-52. The symbols are physically stored in a *presentation library* within ECDIS's software. Therefore each new edition of this library must correspond to an ECDIS software update.

Even though ECDIS symbology is similar to that used on traditional nautical charts, it is worth noting the fact that there are new additional symbols and different presentation rules.

An example of this using ECDIS is that it is possible to establish the extension of the non-navigable waters from the coastline to a bathymetric contour selected by the operator, which is known as *safety contour*.

The safety contour must not be confused with the *safety depth*, which simply determines the colouring of spot soundings: those that are deeper than the safety depth are grey, whereas those that are shallower are black (figure II–38).

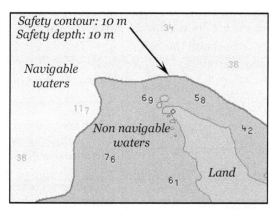

figure II–38 : Safety contour and safety depth

Another novelty is the symbol associated with a *generic isolated danger* (figure II–39), meaning the presence (in navigable waters) of either rocks, obstructions or wrecks with a depth that is:

- shallower than the set safety contour;
- or unknown.

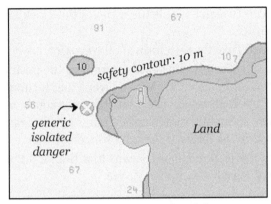

figure II–39 : Generic isolated danger

One of the main limitations of many ECDISs is that they do not offer visualisation of depth data that varies with the tide. The static depths referenced to the *Lowest Astronomical Tide* (LAT) are not operationally useful in places where tidal ranges guarantee (during high water) the passage of ships with a deeper draft than the charted depth.

All of which should be overcome with the new standard for hydrographic data, IHO S-100. At the moment this is still in its trial phase, but with a new data architecture, – which is no longer restricted to 5 megabytes for each individual S-57 ENC – it will be possible to display:

- ENC with depth contours and spot sounding that vary dynamically with the tide;
- three-dimensional bathymetric surfaces in high definition;
- nautical publications in electronic format.

Next generation ECDISs will therefore be able to view all cartographic information and products compliant with IHO S-100.

In the future, high definition bathymetric surfaces might even make it possible to select safety contours within a decimetre. A clear improvement compared to actual ENCs that contain only the bathymetric contours (2-5-10-20-50-100-200 etc.) present on the traditional charts they derive from.

Let's leave the potential and limitations of electronic charts for a moment, and concentrate on the two ECDIS operational functions: route planning and route monitoring.

Routes planned using ECDIS (figure II–40) require the definition of:

- a corridor[52] (usually double the width of the Track Limit) for each leg of the voyage;
- a Radius of Turn for each individual waypoint.

The insertion of a Turn Radius also determines the position of the Wheel Over Point, and in some cases the Wheel Over Line. It should be mentioned that once the Turn Radius has been set, the waypoint's position becomes irrelevant because automatic route verification is performed along the curved trajectory and within the limits of the established corridor.

Lastly, setting the planned speed means that the ECDIS can calculate the maximum Rate of Turn for each manoeuvre.

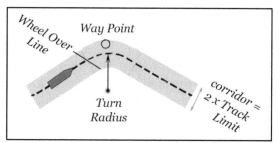

figure II–40 : Planned route parameters using ECDIS

One of ECDIS's main limits consists in the lack of features for planning docking and anchoring manoeuvres. In this phase the idea of waypoints, Turn Radii and Wheel Over Points is no longer meaningful. Here we require swinging circles, minimum distances from established points, transversal speeds, orientation during manoeuvre and last but by no means least, balance between forces under control (e.g. propulsion and tugboats) and environmental ones (e.g. wind and current).

In the light of this, the concept of voyage planning should be redefined, differentiating route planning from manoeuvre planning (docking or anchoring).

To this end route planning would simply constitute the basis for route control and route monitoring, whilst manoeuvre planning would be a reference for manoeuvre control and manoeuvre monitoring.

In contrast to this ideal distinction, table II–24 summarises various uses of the terms *voyage*, *passage* and *route* within the context of IMO documents.

---

52 Many ECDISs now have the option of defining the width of the corridor asymmetrically, with right and left track limits.

Term	Utilisation by IMO
Voyage	Used in the STCW Convention and in IMO Guidelines for the planning of a voyage (Resolution A.893(21)), meant as the path from berth to berth. However throughout the guidelines "passage" and "voyage" are used as synonyms for the same concept.
Short international voyage	Used in the SOLAS Convention to identify a voyage that includes stopovers in various ports before beginning its return voyage (Chap. III Part A Regulation 3.22), or a voyage that does not exceed 20 nautical miles from the coast (Chap. III Part A Regulation 2.1). In this case the concept of voyage that includes many ports is in contrast with that of berth to berth used within IMO guidelines mentioned above.
Passage	Used in IMO guidelines for the planning of a voyage (Resolution A.893), meant as the path from berth to berth. However, "passage" and "voyage" are used as synonyms throughout the guideline. In fact, the expression "entire voyage or passage from berth to berth" is also used, suggesting that a voyage is composed of a number of passages.
Route	The expression "route planning" is used in the IMO ECDIS performance standard (Resolution MSC 232-82) to identify one of its operational functions.

table II–24 : IMO terminology for the planning of a voyage

Route monitoring takes place through the activation of two alarms:

- *off-track*, when the ship exits the planned corridor
- *look-ahead*, as the ship draws close to the safety contour.

The off-track alarm activates when a ship's specific point finds itself at a Cross Track Distance that is greater than the planned Track Limit. This point, known as the *System Position*, is usually set in the forward part of the ship, so that it is likely to be close to its pivot point. The advantage of this solution is that during turns ECDIS provides Cross Track Distances that are consistent with those taken into account by the Track Control System (TCS).

The disadvantage is that with long ships and large drift angles, a Cross Track Distance equal to zero may not correspond to the ideal condition. It is also worth considering that the system position could be different from the radar's CCRP (*Consistent Common Reference Point*), which is the reference for VRM, EBL, CPA, TCPA and the true vector (figure II–41).

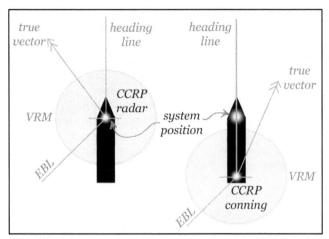

figure II–41 : System position and Consistent Common Reference Point

The *look ahead* alarm consists of a guard zone that stretches in the direction of the true vector at a range set by the operator (figure II–42).

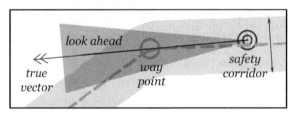

figure II–42 : Guard zone (look ahead)

Track control system (TCS)

A *track control system* allows a route to be automatically controlled in three operational modes:

- *Heading*: the system controls the Heading set by the operator;
- *Course*: the system controls the Course Over Ground set by the operator;
- *Track*: the system follows the route planned by ECDIS within the Track Limit established for each leg.

It also allows for automatic speed control by using another three modes:

- *RPM/pitch*: The operator sets the shaft revolutions (*Revolutions Per Minute* - RPM) or the propellers' pitch. The system controls them independently from the resulting Speed Through Water or Speed Over Ground.

- *Speed over ground*: the operator sets a target Speed Over Ground and the system controls it by varying the RPMs or pitch.
- *Arrival speed*: the operator sets an arrival time to the destination waypoint of the ECDIS route plan, and the system adjusts the Speed Over Ground to respect it.

Both in Heading mode and in Course mode it is the operator that decides when to initiate turns after having set both the next Heading (or Course Over Ground) to follow and the next Turn Radius. These set values are displayed on radar PPI and ECDIS as Curved Heading (or Course) Lines (figure II–43).

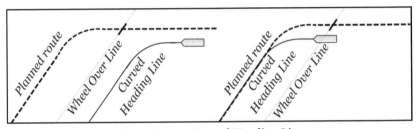

figure II–43 : Curved Heading Line

This type of line is known as a *Curved Heading Line* (CHL) even when in Course mode, where it would be more correct to call it *Curved Course Line*. The substantial difference is that in Heading mode the curve does not take into consideration the effect of wind and current. Whereas in Course mode the curved line represents the desired turn with respect to the seabed, which means that the system constantly compensates for *set* and *drift* caused by current and wind.

In Track mode there is no need for the operator to set the Heading (or Course Over Ground) and the radius for the next turn. The system is capable of initiating and controlling turns by itself on the basis of the ECDIS route plan. In this case planned Turn Radii are equivalent to Curved Course Lines.

In all three modes described, the Track Control System makes its calculations with reference to a specific point of the ship called the System Position (figure II–41). As mentioned previously, this point should ideally be set in the forward part of the ship, as close as possible to the pivot point with headway. The Cross Track Distance is measured beginning from this point.

The main difference between a Track Control System and a regular autopilot goes further than its interaction with ECDIS and the possibility of controlling Turn Radii. A Track Control System is actually "adapted" to specific characteristics of the ship that it is installed on.

170

The parameters necessary for this adaptation are the *rudder accuracy, the rudder rate, the turning ability and the turning lag.*

Turning ability and turning lag are determined empirically by sea trials conducted in deep waters, at a nominal speed (cruising speed) and under various loading conditions (fully laden, half-loaded and in ballast). The turning ability (KR) is the Rate of Turn reached with a specific rudder angle at a nominal speed. The turning lag (KT) is approximately a quarter of the time interval required to reach a constant Rate of Turn.

Figure II−44 shows the abovementioned parameters with:

- *Δr*: specific rudder angle used for sea trials;
- *Δh*: Heading variation;
- *Δh/Δt*: Variation of Heading over time (*Rate of Turn*);
- *t1*: time to reach the set rudder angle from its neutral state;
- *t3*: time required to reach a constant Rate of Turn.
- $KR = (Δh/Δt)/Δr$
- $KT = (t2 − t1) \cong (t3 − t1)/4$

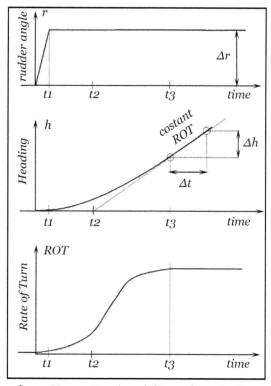

figure II−44 : Turning ability and turning lag

The accuracy of the parameters KR and KT affects the Track Control System's behaviour during turns. In particular KT influences the beginning and ending of turns more. KR has more influence during the central part of the turn where the Rate of Turn is constant (figure II–45).

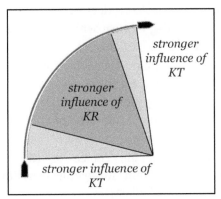

figure II–45 : Influence of KR and KT during a turn

In Heading mode, if KR is higher than the ship's actual turning ability, the rudder angle chosen by the Track Control System is smaller than that which is necessary for a specific turn. But if KR is too low, the rudder angle will be too high to accomplish this same turn. Finally if KT is smaller than necessary, the Track Control System will apply counter rudder later than required.

Based on what has been said above, we are now able to comprehend the Track Control System's controlling mechanism. It is a PID (*Proportional, Integrative, Derivative*) control that aims to minimise – moment by moment – the difference between the desired value and the actual value measured by the sensors.

For example, when a ship initiates a turn in Heading mode, the control of the actual Rate of Turn is directly proportional (P) to the difference with the new Heading and inversely proportional to the desired Turn Radius. Once the Rate of Turn reaches a constant value, controlling is mainly of an integrative (I) nature. That is, the small differences in the Rate of Turn are corrected at predefined time intervals. At the end of the turn controlling becomes mostly derivative (D) and the new Heading is obtained without exceeding the desired value. This is eventually maintained by integrating Heading values through time and correcting any eventual deviations.

A Track Control System must always be adapted to the ship on which it has been installed. This is done by calibrating its proportional, integrative and derivative components.

The adaptation can be considered correct if whilst in Heading mode:

- in a straight direction, desired Heading deviations do not exceed ±1 degree;
- at the end of a 10 degree turn with a 0.5 nautical mile radius, the Heading does not exceed ±1.5 degrees;
- at the end of a 90 degree turn with a 0.5 nautical mile radius, the Heading does not exceed ±3 degrees.

If deviations go over these limits, the adaptation of installation parameters must be repeated with additional sea trials.

Even though installation parameters are important for the Track Control System's correct functioning, they cannot be modified by the operator, who can however manage the following operational settings:

- *Loading*: determines the choice of KR and KT parameters (memorised by the system) for loading conditions of the ship (fully laden, half-loaded, in ballast).
- *Rudder economy*: affects the frequency with which the rudder is used to reach headings and courses set by the operator. Low rudder economy values mean more frequent adjustments to the rudder angle that results in greater reactivity of the Track Control System, but also a lower fuel efficiency.
- *Rudder Limit*: represents the maximum rudder angle that can be used by the Track Control System. For *Det Norske Veritas* (DNV) classified ships, the Rudder Limit is merely a threshold that generates an alarm for the operator.
- *Track Limit*: influences the accuracy of the automatic control in Track mode, as well as representing half the width of the corridor planned using ECDIS. The Track Limit also determines the limit for the activation of Track mode.
- *Course Limit*: represents the threshold for the *off-course* alarm, that is when the Course Over Ground value diverges from the route planned using ECDIS by an angle greater than the limit set. Its second function is related to the way the ship steers towards the planned route once Track mode is activated. The higher the Course Limit, the wider the turn towards the planned route, as well as the risk of undesired heeling.
- *Drift limit*: represents the drift angle's value beyond which the Track Control System does not compensate for wind and current in Course or Track mode. If the drift angle reaches the Drift Limit, the system notifies the operator through an alert.

As well as the Curved Heading Line (or Curved Course Line), a Track Control System also makes the so-called *predictor* available (figure II–46). This represents a projection of the ship's position in the immediate future[53] by using instantaneous values of Heading, Speed Over Ground and Rate of Turn.

The predictor is a feature that is becoming ever more popular on Portable Pilot Units (PPU). Its main limitation is that the prediction does not take into account differing wind and current effects upon the ship's hull during a turn.

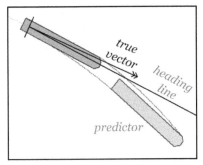

figure II–46 : Predictor

This limitation is linked to the intrinsic inability of Track Control Systems to anticipate the effects of the current and the interaction with the seabed. These are aspects that can be very significant for shiphandling, especially with reduced Under-Keel Clearances and in the proximity of river and canal banks. In order to be able to anticipate these effects, a Track Control System would require:

- a model of surface currents (either according to a model or supplied in real-time by external current meters);
- a three-dimensional model of the seabed based on high definition bathymetric surveys.

New generation Track Control Systems will include this ability to anticipate thanks to *fast time simulation*[54] technology, which at present is still in its experimental phase.

Overall, the actual technical potential of a Track Control System consists in:

---

53 Generally selectable at up to three minutes by the operator.

54 Knud Benedict et al. (2014). "Use of simulation-augmented manoeuvring in shiphandling simulator training". University of Applied Sciences - Technology, Business and Design, Dept. of Maritime Studies Warnemuende & Maritime Simulation Centre Warnemuende, Institute ISSIMS / Germany.

- high precision of automatic control for desired Headings and Course Over Ground on straight routes;
- high precision of control during turns with constant Rate of Turn;
- enhanced efficiency in the use of rudders and/or azimuth thrusters;
- enhanced fuel efficiency derived from automatic speed control.

These last two aspects are of particular importance for shipping companies, whose profit margins can be significantly improved by reducing fuel consumption.

With regards to *man-machine interaction*, a Track Control System removes the possibility of misunderstandings in communication between who controls navigation and the helmsman. However it does introduce new problems such as:

- the operator becoming accustomed to the high precision of automatically controlled navigation, thus gradually losing the ability to control the ship manually;
- the operator's passiveness in monitoring navigation, which makes switching from automatic to manual control difficult (*out-of-the-loop syndrome*).

To contrast operator passiveness, in the next chapter we will propose the application of an *active monitoring* technique that envisages a visual scanning pattern of critical navigational parameters at regular intervals.

The history in the development of modern Track Control Systems can help to understand their operational philosophy. The definition of the first operational concept goes back to 1980, when a Finnish Captain named Kari Larjo proposed his idea to the company *Atlas Elektronic* for the project *"The ship of the future"*. Captain Larjo sensed the potential of the integration of bridge equipment. He was the man who conceived the integration between radar and an autopilot that was not only able to control the desired Heading, but also to perform turns at a constant radius. In "his" system the visualisation of the Curved Heading Line allowed the operator to focus on the point where the turn ends and not just where it begins. This concept represented a paradigm shift for navigation within the archipelagos of the Baltic Sea. As a result Wheel Over Points turned into Wheel Over Lines.

In 1982 a booklet[55] called *"Navigation in Fog"* began circulating between Swedish pilots. The authors Sven Gyldén and Benny Pettersson, in the wake of Captain Larjo, felt the need to put a set of instrumental navigation techniques in writing. They devised these techniques to face the challenging

---

55 Sven Gyldén and Benny Pettersson (1982). "Navigation in Fog" (second edition 1991).

conditions in the Baltic Sea, which are often characterised by reduced visibility. In particular they described radar operating procedures designed to:

- monitor the ship's position with reference to the planned route by using the *parallel index* technique;
- perform turns with a constant Turn Radius.

They also emphasised the concept of active monitoring on radars and gyrocompasses, knowing full well that pilots had often experienced problems in the accuracy of sensors and navigation systems.

Gyldén and Pettersson asserted the superiority of *controlled turns* using Rate of Turn compared to those performed with a constant rudder angle. In particular, they backed the advantage of a smaller drift angle towards the end of the turn and of a minor loss in speed.

The relationship between Turn Radius (R), Speed Over Ground (SOG) and Rate of Turn (ROT) is expressed by the following formula:

$$ROT_{°/min} = (SOG_{kn} \times 3)/(R_{NM} \times \pi) \cong SOG_{kn}/R_{NM}$$

As soon as the rudder angle is applied though, the ship's pivot point does not immediately follow the circular trajectory corresponding to the Turn Radius. The distance that a ship travels before beginning to turn depends on several factors such as its size, its loading condition and its speed. This distance can be obtained either from the diagram in figure II–44 by calculating the space travelled in time equal to t_2, or empirically by measuring how much the ship overshoots the new course if the rudder is applied at the beginning of the turning arc.

In the 1980s the biggest technical challenge was in measuring the Rate of Turn, given that the dynamic accuracy of mechanical gyrocompasses was only just under the three degrees required by IMO. For this Captain Larjo pushed his shipping company (*Silja Line*) to adopt Fibre Optic Gyros able to measure the Rate of Turn more accurately than mechanical gyrocompasses. He believed that instrumental navigation could be made possible by the combined use of mechanical gyrocompasses for straight courses and Fibre Optic Gyros during turns. This is how the first autopilots were conceived. They were not only designed for constant radius turns but also to reduce fuel costs thanks to a more efficient use of rudders.

Nevertheless a Track Control System's PID control mechanism does not provide the same accuracy of systems based on mathematical models such as those used for Dynamic Positioning (DP).

Dynamic Positioning Systems (DP)

The most modern Dynamic Positioning Systems are mainly found on off-shore supply vessels, but over the last few years their use on passenger ships has increased too. In fact, even though its main objective is to maintain orientation and positioning at low speeds, a DP system also has the ability to control the Heading at cruise speed.

In both cases, control takes place on three different movements of the ship (figure II–47):

- longitudinal (*surge*);
- transversal (*sway*);
- rotational (*yaw*).

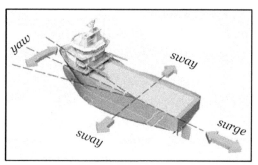

figure II–47 : Ship movements that are controlled by a DP system

As already mentioned, DP systems use mathematical models that define hydrodynamic and aerodynamic ship behaviours subject to internal and external forces. With this model a DP can estimate the propulsion power to allocate in order to maintain the desired position, Heading and Speed Over Ground. From feedback received by specific sensors (orientation, positioning, speed, attitude and wind) a DP constantly corrects – moment by moment – the mathematical model's estimations.

Figure II–48 shows the functional diagram of a complete DP system, composed of:

- thrusters, both azimuth and transversal;
- a control system for allocating propulsion power based on the position, Heading and Speed Over Ground set by the operator;
- an extended *Kálmán filter* for estimating position, orientation and speed values based on both the ship's mathematical model and on real time data from on board sensors.

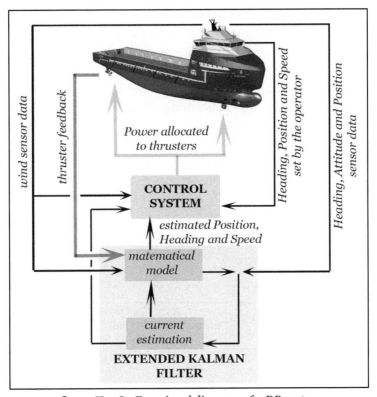

figure II–48 : Functional diagram of a DP system

Unlike bow and stern thrusters, azimuth thrusters are installed outside the hull. A vertical shaft allows them to rotate 360 degrees, thus directing the thrust in any direction without the use of traditional rudders.

Compared to conventional shaft-propeller-rudder propulsion, azimuth thrusters have the following advantages:

- greater manoeuvrability, especially at low speeds;
- higher hydrodynamic efficiency and lower fuel consumption.

However, azimuth thrusters involve higher initial costs as well as additional training to develop an operators' ability to handle them. When steering the thrusters by means of a joystick in particular, operators must fully comprehend the way DP drives them. This is because manual control may be needed in the case of malfunctioning or if the thruster orientation is not set by DP as desired. The allocation of power to the thrusters is guaranteed by a control system that continuously calculates the longitudinal, transversal and rotational force to apply. This force is then translated into signals of orientation (azimuth) and propeller revolutions (and/or pitch) for each thruster. The extended Kálmán filter estimates the ship's motion using the internal mathematical model and the following sensors:

- GNSS with differential satellite corrections for positions and Speed Over Ground;
- IMUs for measuring roll, pitch and heave;
- gyrocompasses or Transmitting Heading Devices for accurate Heading measurements;
- ultrasound or conventional anemometers.

The reliability of the estimation depends on the mathematical model, as well as on the accuracy of the ship sensors that feed the extended Kálmán filter. However IMO[56] classifies DP systems as DP1, DP2 and DP3 mainly on the basis of their redundancy (table II–25).

DP Class	Loss of position keeping capability due to the malfunction of a single component	Redundancy
DP1	Acceptable	Not required
DP2	Not acceptable (not even for human error)	Required for all of DP system's active components (two independent workstations and three sensors for each parameter)
DP3	Not acceptable (not even for human error)	Required for all of DP system's active components, with physical separation between them (two independent workstations and three sensors for each parameter measured).

table II–25 : Classification of Dynamic Positioning Systems

While the actual tendency of the off-shore sector is to equip vessels with DP2, in shipping DP1 is considered sufficient. Above all because the automatic control of DP is not used for manoeuvring ships at low speeds.

In fact, automatic control of thrusters on passenger ships only takes place typically at cruise speed via:

- DP (control of Heading and Speed Over Ground); or
- the Track Control System (control of Heading, Course Over Ground, Cross Track Distance and Speed Over Ground according to the chosen operating mode).

At low speeds, namely during berthing and unberthing manoeuvres, thruster orientation and revolutions/pitch are controlled manually.

---

56 "Guidelines for Vessels with Dynamic Positioning Systems". IMO - MSC Circular n.645 (1994).

After having described systems for automatic control of route and manoeuvring, we can affirm that their effective use require not only the understanding of their potential and limitations, but also a knowledge of a ship's manoeuvring characteristics. These are regulated by IMO[57] through the specification of minimum manoeuvring ability for vessels longer than 100 metres and for all chemical/gas tankers regardless of their Length Over All.

The manoeuvring ability must be empirically evaluated by specific sea trials not only upon delivery of a new ship, but also after any significant structural modifications. During these trials ships must perform:

- *turning circle* manoeuvres to both starboard and port with a 35 degree rudder angle;
- a *zig zag test* by performing alternate turns with Heading variations of 10 and 20 degrees;
- a crash stop by performing a full astern stopping test.

For ships that are equipped with non-conventional propulsion systems (such as azimuth thrusters), the Flag State may allow the use of similar rudder angles.

The speed (denominated "V") at which these trials are performed must be at least 90% of the ship's speed, corresponding to 85% of the engine's maximum output and must be expressed in metres per second.

The length (denominated "L") of the ship is considered as that between the perpendiculars when fully loaded and must be expressed in metres.

The parameters that are measured during a turning circle are the following (figure II–49):

- *advance*: the distance travelled by the ship's midpoint in the direction of the original Heading, from the position where the rudder is applied, to the position at which the Heading is at 90 degrees from its original value;
- *tactical diameter*: the distance travelled by the ship's midpoint in a perpendicular direction from the original Heading, from the position where the rudder is applied, to the position at which the Heading has changed 180 degrees from its original value.

---

57 Resolution MSC.137(76) adopted 1 December 2002. "Standards for ship manoeuvrability".

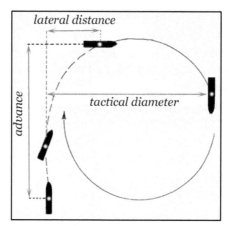

figure II–49: Manoeuvrability parameters during 360 degree turns

On the margin of the manoeuvrability diagram the conditions of the trial must be specified: deep and open waters, absence of wind and current, fully loaded condition (*summer load line draught, even keel*) and a pre-established speed when initiating the turn. The turning circle test is considered satisfactory if the advance and the tactical diameter do not exceed the length between the ship's perpendiculars by 4.5 and 5 times respectively.

Another test to perform is the zig zag test, which includes a series of turns from side to side (figure II–50). This is conducted first with a 10 degree rudder angle, followed by a 20 degree one. Counter rudder must be applied once the Heading has changed by 10 and 20 degrees respectively.

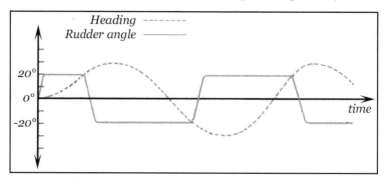

figure II–50 : Example of a "20/20" zig zag test

Heading deviations in excess of the 10 and 20 degrees are known as *overshoot angles.*

The minimum standards stipulated by IMO are conveyed in terms of:

- *initial turning ability*: the distance between the position at which the application of 10 degree rudder angle (to port or to starboard) and the position where the heading has changed by 10 degrees should not exceed 4.5 times the ship's length between the perpendiculars;
- *yaw-checking* and *course-keeping abilities*.
  During the "10/10" test the first overshoot angle must not exceed:
  - $10°$, if $L/V < 10$ sec
  - $20°$, if $L/V \geq 30$ sec
  - $[5 + \frac{1}{2}(L/V)]°$, if 10 sec $\leq (L/V) \leq 30$ sec
  During the "10/10" test the second overshoot angle must not exceed:
  - $25°$, if $L/V < 10$ sec
  - $40°$, if $L/V \geq 30$ sec
  - $[17,5 + 0,75 \, (L/V)]°$, if 10 sec $\leq (L/V) \leq 30$ sec
  During the "20/20" test the first overshoot angle must not exceed $25°$.

The final test carried out during sea trials aims to assess the stopping distance with engines full astern, initiating from the test speed "V". The distance to test is that travelled by the ship's midpoint once the engines are set to full astern until the ship comes to a complete halt. The maximum stopping distance allowed by IMO is 15 ship lengths. For ships of large displacement, Flag States may modify this limit up to 20 ship lengths.

Finally, IMO recommends that the manoeuvring parameters should be displayed on bridges as a poster so that deck officers and maritime pilots can clearly see it. Pilots will have difficulty in being able to read the poster in the limited time at his/her disposal from the boarding place. Realistically, the only way for pilots to review the information from the poster would therefore be to make it available to them beforehand, in due time for the planning of the manoeuvre.

Being fully aware of a ship's manoeuvrability also requires understanding of the effect of forces that are applied to its hull.

These forces can generally be divided into four categories:

- the ship's own propulsion forces (shaft and/or thruster power);
- tugboats' bollard pulls;
- forces from external agents on the hull (wind and currents);
- forces coming from interaction with other ships, the seabed and with port infrastructures.

Knowledge regarding the effect of these forces should be both quantitative and qualitative. Although rigorous quantitative evaluations can only be made at the planning stage, we shouldn't forget that quantitative knowledge of operational limits – even though approximate – could be crucial during manoeuvring. An example of this could be a quantitative assessment of the current's forces varying with Under-Keel Clearances expected throughout the manoeuvre. The different forces of the current (F_C) are expressed in tonnes[58] and can be calculated using the following formula:

$$F_C = K \times f \times L_{PP} \times d \times V^2$$

where:

- K = 0.033 (constant for deep waters)
- L_{PP} = length between the perpendiculars
- d = draft
- V = the current's speed (in metres per second)
- f = an additional factor for shallow waters that varies with the change in the ratio between depth "D" and draft "d" (figure II–51).

As a result of the factor "f", the force of the current applied to a ship's hull increases considerably with the reduction of the Under-Keel Clearance.

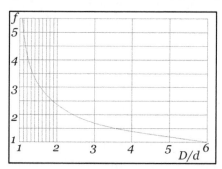

figure II–51 : Additional factor for calculating the current in shallow waters

For example, the force of a current at 1 knot (0.5 metres per second) upon the beam of a ship 200 metres long with 8 metres of draft would be:

- 13 t in deep water, that is when the depth is equal to 6 times the draft (UKC 40 m);
- 26 t in areas where water depth is 2.5 times the draft (UKC 12 m);
- 39 t in areas where water depth is 1.5 times the draft (UKC 4 m);
- 53 t in areas where water depth is 1.2 times the draft (UKC 1.6m);
- 66 t in areas where water depth is 1.1 times the draft (UKC 0.8m).

---

58 All forces involved are generally expressed in tonnes. The equivalent values between tonne-force, power in kilowatts (KW) and power in horsepower (hp) is: 0.74KW = 1hp   74KW = 100hp
1 tonne = 74KW   1 tonne = 100hp

The progression of the forces shows an exponential growth of the current's force as the Under-Keel Clearance reduces.

The same approach can be applied to the effect of wind by using this formula:

$$F_V = K \times A \times V^2$$

where:

- F_V is the force applied by the wind on the ship (in tonnes)
- K is a constant that depends on both the ship's aerodynamic resistance and the wind direction. It is calculated as follows:
  $K = 0.6 \times C_X \times 10^{-4}$ with head wind[59];
  $K = 0.6 \times C_Y \times 10^{-4}$ with beam wind.
- A is the ship's surface exposed to the wind (in square metres).
- V is the wind speed (in metres per second).

When dealing with the forces that derive from interaction with other ships, with the seabed and with port structures, quantitative calculations become less intuitive. Their impact during operations can however be considered in a qualitative manner, provided that evaluations are based on a solid knowledge of hydrodynamics as well as on experience.

Systems for Manual Control of the Route and Manoeuvring

There are two different types of systems for manual control of route and manoeuvring: *Non-Follow-Up* (NFU) and *Follow-Up* (FU).

NFU systems are tillers or buttons that act on the steering pumps for the entire time that the operator keeps them activated. The rudder rests in the position where it arrived as soon as the action on the tillers/buttons ceases. NFU tillers can also have an *override* function, which enables an instantaneous takeover from automatic control systems (such as TCS and DP) to manual control. Given their reliability, NFU systems are mainly used as backup in the case of primary system malfunction.

Follow-up (FU) systems vary rudder angles according to the position of the helm or azimuth handles. The rudder/thruster motion continues until its position coincides with that of the bridge settings.

---

[59] "Cx" and Cy are the drag coefficients of the ship in the wind's airflow. The higher they are, the greater is the resistance of the ship in the wind.

184

From the operator's point of view a potential limitation of manual control systems (both Non-Follow-Up and Follow-Up) derives sometimes from poor ergonomics.

Bridge Alert Management Systems (BAMS)

The aim of a Bridge Alert Management System is to support operators in the identification and the management of emergencies and abnormal situations. A BAMS centralises not only alert signals from all navigation systems, but also a selection of those relating to the ship's general safety.

IMO classifies alerts into *emergency alarms, alarms, warnings* and *cautions*. The classification is based on priority, the type of reaction required and the type of indication that the operator receives (table II–26).

Description	Reaction Required	Type of Indication	Examples
Emergency Alarms			
Indicates that immediate danger to human life or to the ship and its machinery exists	Immediate action	Audio and visual. Audio indication can be silenced, while the visual indication remains until resolution	• General emergency • Use of fire fighting systems • Closure of watertight doors
Alarms			
Indicates a hazardous situation for operational safety	Immediate attention and action	Audio and visual. Audio indication can be silenced, while the visual indication remains until resolution	• Navigation sensor failure • Anomalies to navigation and propulsion systems • Fire detection
Warnings			
Indicates a condition which is not immediately hazardous, but may become so	Immediate attention for precautionary reasons	Audio and visual. Audio indication can be silenced, while the visual indication remains until resolution	• Performance loss of navigation sensors • Approach to Wheel Over Point
Cautions			
Indicates an abnormal situation, not necessarily hazardous	More attention than ordinary consideration of the situation	Only visual. Visual indication remains until resolution	• ENC overscale indication

table II–26 : Classification of alert signals based on their priority

If navigation system alert signals are delegated completely to BAMS, it is crucial to have a BAMS backup in the event that one of the two become unavailable.

Global Maritime Distress Safety Systems (GMDSS)

Before the advent of GMDSS in 1992, distress signals from ships in difficulty were broadcast through on board radio systems in the hope that another ship or coast guard station was within the range of the transmission.

GMDSS[60] is comprised of several types of transmission and data exchange between ships and coast guard stations.

A complete GMDSS should be capable of:

- transmitting ship-to-shore Distress Alerts through at least two separate and independent means of communication;
- receiving shore-to-ship Distress Alerts;
- transmitting and receiving ship-to-ship Distress Alerts;
- transmitting and receiving radio-communication for Search And Rescue (SAR) coordination;
- transmitting and receiving locating signals;
- receiving Maritime Safety Information (MSI) relating to the area in question;
- transmitting and receiving general radio-communication for ship management and operations;
- transmitting and receiving a range of Bridge-to-Bridge communications.

There are essentially three GMDSS transmission modes:

- Radio Telephony (RT): for voice communication on VHF, MF and HF bands;
- Narrow Band Direct Printing (NBDP): for the transmission of telex messages;
- Digital Selective Call (DSC): for automatic transmission/reception of alert messages. VHF DSC systems ensure a transmission speed (1200 bits per second) that is much greater than MF and HF DSC (100 bits per second).

---

60 The information in this section is taken from the GMDSS handbook, published by the Australian Maritime Safety Authority (2013 edition). The document is available online from www.amsa.gov.au

Distress communications often begin in DSC mode before passing to radio telephony and NBDP messages.

If the distress signal is also transmitted via an INMARSAT satellite, the Rescue Coordination Centre (RCC) comes into play and relays the signal to coastal radio stations and nearby ships.

Compared to the past, the carriage requirement for radio equipment on board no longer depends on the ship's dimensions, but on the area in which the ship operates.

For this reason the oceans are divided into the following GMDSS areas:

- A1

  Within the VHF range of at least one coastal radio station that guarantees continuous Radio Telephony (RT) and Digital Selective Call (DSC) service;

- A2

  Within the MF range of at least one coastal radio station that guarantees continuous Radio Telephony (RT) and Digital Selective Call (DSC) service beyond area A1;

- A3

  Within coverage of an INMARSAT geostationary satellite that guarantees a continuous monitoring of distress alerts beyond areas A1 and A2, between 70 degrees of latitude North and 70 degrees South;

- A4

  The polar regions, that is beyond areas A1, A2 and A3.

A bridge's GMDSS installation varies according to the geographical areas mentioned. The minimum IMO carriage requirement for SOLAS ships of over 300 Gross Tonnage is that of A1. However if the ship operates outside area A1 then additional elements are also needed (table II–27).

The Flag State may also require redundancy of some apparatus to enhance ship's GMDSS availability.

Typically the redundancy of VHF, SART and INMARSAT installations is required. For the area A3, for example, the following equipment may be required:

- Two complete two-way VHF transceivers (DSC);
- Two complete INMARSAT-C apparatus, or one complete INMARSAT-C and one complete MF/HF apparatus (DSC and NBDP).

Area	GMDSS Carriage Requirements for SOLAS Ships over 300GT
A1	• a VHF DSC transceiver on channel 70 and RT on channels 16, 13 and 6 • a transponder for Search And Rescue (two per ship > 500 GT) • a NAVTEX receiver if sailing in areas where this service exists • an INMARSAT receiver with Enhanced Group Call (EGC)[61] capabilities where the MSI transmission is not guaranteed by NAVTEX or HF NBDP • an EPIRB at 406MHz or a VHF DSC EPIRB
A2	In addition to those for area A1, navigation in area A2 requires: • a MF DSC transceiver (2187.5 KHz) with RT (2182 KHz) capability • a DSC receiver for continuous watch on the frequency 2187.5 KHz • in alternative to the EPIRB 406 MHz, a VHF DSC EPIRB, MF-HF DSC apparatus or an INMARSAT (Fleet77, INMARSAT-C)[62]
A3	In addition to those for areas A1 and A2, navigation in area A3 requires: • an INMARSAT-C Ship-Earth-Station installation • a MF DSC transceiver (2187.5KHz) with RT (2182KHz) capability • a DSC receiver for continuous watch on the frequency 2187.5 KHz • an EPIRB at 406 MHz, or a HF DSC system or • a MF/HF transceiver for all distress frequencies within the band 1605÷4000 KHz and 4000÷27500 KHz, operating in the three modes RT, DSC and NBDP. It can also be used for routine communications in RT • a DSC receiver for continuous watch on 2187.5 KHz and 8414.5 KHz. In addition, DSC continuous watch must be possible on at least one of the DSC frequencies 4207.5 KHz, 6312 KHz, 12577 KHz, 16804.5 KHz • an EPIRB 406 MHz or an INMARSAT (Fleet77, INMARSAT-C) apparatus
A4	In additions to those for area A1, navigation in all areas requires: • a MF/HF transceiver for all distress frequencies within 1605÷4000 KHz and 4000÷27500 KHz, operating in the three modes RT, DSC and NBDP. The same installation can also be used for routine communication in RT or NBDP • a DSC receiver for continuous watch on the frequencies 2187.5 KHz and 8414.5 KHz. In addition to these two, DSC continuous watch must be possible on at least one of the DSC distress frequencies 4207.5 KHz, 6312 KHz, 12577 KHz, 16804.5 KHz • an EPIRB at 406 MHz

table II–27 : GMDSS equipment on board SOLAS ships

---

61 The INMARSAT system supplies the Enhanced Group Call (ECG) service that allows land-based organisations (information providers) to transmit messages to a group of selected ships in a certain area. The ECG service is considered by IMO as one of the primary systems for receiving and transmitting Maritime Safety Information (MSI).

62 The INMARSAT-C service allows transmission of data or messages at a rate of 600 bits per second. Fleet 77 allows the reception and transmission of data packages that are compatible with the internet protocol at a velocity of 128Kbit per second. Compared to INMARSAT-C, Fleet 77 allows verbal communication, but not telex.

188

Usually the GMDSS apparatus mentioned above are installed on the ship's bridge without much thought to their accessibility during navigation. Only the VHF equipment is in the vicinity of the other navigation systems (ARPA, ECDIS, AIS, engine telegraphs, etc.), even though IMO requires continuous monitoring of a series of GMDSS components (not just VHF).

Continuous GMDSS monitoring must be carried out (according to the area requirements) on:

- VHF DSC channel 70;
- VHF RT channel 16;
- the MF DSC frequency 2187.5 KHz;
- the HF DSC frequency 8 MHz and at least one of the other HF DSC frequencies (4, 6, 12, 16 MHz);
- the INMARSAT terminal for the reception of distress signals from land-based stations;
- equipment for the reception of Maritime Safety Information (e.g. Navtex).

The priority level of GMDSS communication follows International Telecommunication Union (ITU)[63] classification:

- *distress*: for signalling imminent danger to life that requires immediate assistance (using the prefix *mayday* for radiotelephonic transmissions);
- *urgency*: for signalling urgencies regarding the safety of ships or persons (using the prefix *pan pan*);
- *safety*: for communicating important navigational or meteorological warnings (using the prefix *sécurité*);
- *routine*: for receiving and transmitting routine communication between persons on board and those ashore through public telecommunication networks (email, fax, telephone calls, telex).

Distress alerts are automatically generated by a ship in danger by DSC VHF-MF-HF equipment and also using EPIRB and INMARSAT. The possible combinations depend on the specific GMDSS area as follows:

- Area A1: ship-to-ship and ship-to-shore transmissions on channel 70 (VHF) using the VHF DSC apparatus or VHF EPIRB DSC.
- Area A2: ship-to-ship and ship-to-shore transmissions on MF DSC frequencies with satellite EPIRB in addition.

63 Ref. art.58 "Radio Regulations" by the International Telecommunication Union (ITU).

- Area A3: ship-to-ship VHF/MF DSC transmissions and ship-to-shore transmissions via INMARSAT-C (or a combination of HF DSC and satellite EPIRB).
- Area A4: ship-to-ship VHF/MF DSC transmissions and ship-to-shore using one of the higher HF DSC frequencies (8-12-16 MHz) and additionally via EPIRB COSPAS-SARSAT.

Coastal Stations within the range of VHF, MF and HF DSC transmissions are responsible for relaying the distress alerts received to the nearest Rescue Coordination Centre (RCC).

Distress alerts relayed via satellite (INMARSAT or COSPAS-SARSAT) are not directly received by nearby ships, but by the nearest Rescue Coordination Centre (RCC). The RCCs themselves then forward this message to nearby ships through INMARSAT Land Earth Stations (LES)[64].

Figure II–52 demonstrates the possible communication flow of a GMDSS distress alert.

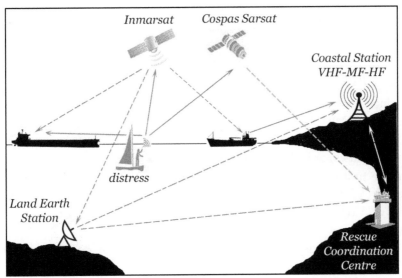

figure II–52 : Relaying a distress alert within the GMDSS system

---

64 Every ocean region that the INMARSAT system is divided into (Pacific, Indian, East and West Atlantic) is controlled by a certain number of Land Earth Stations (LES) that act as an interface between the ship and the various communication networks (public or private) used by the system. LESs are connected between themselves so that they can share information relating to different ocean regions within the INMARSAT system.

The ITU has reserved various frequency bands for GMDSS communication. Frequencies within the VHF and MF bands for distress, urgency and safety communications are all *simplex* (figure II–53).

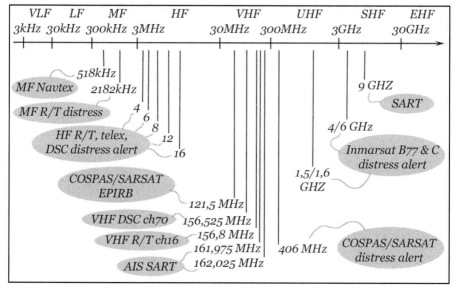

figure II–53 : ITU frequency bands for GMDSS communication

In most cases the radio waves are transmitted by means of omnidirectional antennae. INMARSAT satellite communications however are directive.

Once transmitted, radio waves propagate either along the earth's surface (*ground waves*) or by ionospheric refraction (*sky waves*).

In the first case the range depends on the radio wave frequency: several thousand kilometres for VLF waves and a few kilometres for UHF waves. The range of VHF ground waves depends on the height and the gain of the antennae.

When using ionospheric waves (*sky waves*) the range depends upon both the frequency and the time of transmission. For example, during daytime the lowest level of the ionosphere (50-90km) absorbs radio waves at 2 MHz, whilst at night the lower layers of the ionosphere soften their effect, making transmissions at 2 MHz more efficient.

GMDSS transmissions in MF and HF use both types of propagation with the possibility of selecting a series of frequencies along different bands: such as 2182 KHz in the band of 2 MHz, 4125 KHz in the band of 4 MHz and 12290 KHz in the band of 12 MHz.

A general rule of thumb for the selection of transmission frequencies can be as follows:

- 2 MHz band for communicating with stations that are between 50 and 150 nautical miles away, both during the day and during the night;
- 4 MHz band for communicating during the day with stations that are further than 60 nautical miles away and at night if 2 MHz band is not effective;
- 6 MHz bands for daylight communications when the 4 MHz band is not effective and at night when 2 MHz and 4 MHz bands are not effective;
- 8, 12, 16, 22 MHz bands for progressively greater distances.

~

With the description of the most modern navigation and communication systems concluded, we are now ready to discuss the BRM operational concept.

BRIDGE RESOURCE MANAGEMENT

> *"...given the amount of navigational information*
> *on radar displays, there was the need*
> *to discuss it with someone else..."*
> *Kari Larjo*

Captain Larjo

Great changes are often the result of the talent and courage of just one person. A good example for the maritime world is the Finnish Captain Kari Larjo. We owe him a debt of gratitude not only for the first integrated navigation system, but also for developing and implementing the Bridge Resource Management (BRM)[65] concept. It was indeed Captain Larjo who sensed that new integrated navigation techniques, which were introduced to cope with difficult conditions in the Baltic Sea, needed more effective teamwork compared to what was used in the past.

We meet Captain Larjo on a grey day in August at Turku, Finland. It is raining and he takes us into his office. There are bookcases full of volumes about navigation, geopolitics, history, fiction, or linked to his long seafaring career, which began in 1952 when he decided he wanted to be the first of his family to go to sea.

Despite having being awarded the Gold Medal from the Royal Institute of Navigation, Captain Larjo is reserved and averse to praise, in essence a man of few words. He gives just a simple shake of his head when we ask if he is used to giving interviews. Yet there are few people that can claim to have changed the practices of maritime navigation as much as he has done, with a mixture of insight and tenacity. This he has all done of his own accord without any salary bonuses and very few official acknowledgements.

"When you try to change things, you find yourself arguing with everybody", he says, through a wry chuckle and a hint of irony. "Just think, the Finnish Officers' Trade Union wanted to throw me out. And that would have been a big problem considering that at the time you couldn't work on the country's ships if you weren't a member."

---

65 In civil aviation, BRM's equivalent operational concept – known as Cockpit Resource Management (CRM) – was adopted during the end of the 1970s in the wake of one of the most tragic accidents in the history of civil aviation, that which occurred on 27th March 1977 at Tenerife Airport in the Canary Isles. Two Boeing 747s collided on Los Rodeos Airport's runway, killing 583 people.

Those who have worked with him in the Baltic region still regard him as a role model, a living legend. Elsewhere his name is less known and very few are aware that he is the forefather of the concept of both integrated navigation and Bridge Resource Management. Armed with vast experience gained in the demanding archipelagos of the Baltic Sea, this man pushed for the introduction of these concepts on board ships, working with manufacturers and asking them to develop modern integrated navigation systems.

"It was a lot of fun", he recalls now. His office still contains the first prototype of an autopilot capable of performing turns at a constant radius. It is a small piece of equipment with little buttons for selecting the desired Rate of Turn.

It all started when Larjo became a ship's Captain in the 1960s and he realised that with vessels getting bigger and safety margins smaller, traditional navigation techniques were no longer enough.

One of the main issues was the poor performance of available instruments. For example, in those days gyrocompasses could drift up to two and a half degrees during and after turns. Something that is excessive for navigation in Baltic Archipelagos.

The bridge design was also too dispersive: instruments were positioned so far away from each other that it needed two people just to watch the radar. What was worse however, was that officers relied too much on pilots without being able to manoeuvre the ship on their own.

This was also the reason there were many accidents in the area, one in particular cost the lives of six people in 1968[66]. Larjo was convinced that there was an urgent need to integrate radar and autopilot into one system, capable of conducting a ship with more precision than mere visual navigation. With this in mind, beginning in the 1970s he pushed for the installation of more sophisticated navigational sensors on ferries of the *Silja Line*, the company he worked for. Firstly he obtained a rate of turn sensor (rate gyro), followed by a dual axis Doppler speed log to measure speed and drift angles.

"*Silja Line* was very much in favour of developing new instruments. The company had experienced several incidents during the 1960s and 1970s, small things that with just a pinch more of bad luck could have turned into disasters. For this reason managers decided to invest in the development of

66 On 28th November 1968, the Finnish cruise ship "Ilmatar" collided with the ferry "Botnia" in the waters of the Åland archipelago. The accident claimed the lives of six people aboard the Botnia.

an Integrated Navigation System, even though they had no idea whether or not it would have worked", says Larjo. "It took more than a month to get to the first prototype."

With the first step taken it was already possible to plan turns with a constant radius, but electronic navigational charts that allow route monitoring on radar screens did not yet exist.

During the 1980s, thanks to advances in technology and the widespread use of radars featuring digital displays, it was possible to incorporate the Track Control System designed together with a company called *Atlas*. And so the first version of the modern Integrated Navigation System NACOS (*NAvigation and COmmand System*) was born with three operational modes: "Heading", "Course" and "Track".

"This new system made things easier. I still remember the time when the manager of a Norwegian company came to see how we worked on the bridges of *Silja* ships. He was 85 years old and was a Captain himself. His company wanted to build new vessels and so sent him to see the instruments that we had devised", tells Larjo. "We set sail for Stockholm and I invited him to use NACOS on his own under my supervision. I showed him the more important functions, told him what to do and what the radar screen indications meant. He performed a perfect turn, without ever having piloted that ship before and without ever having used a Track Control System. In the end he ordered systems identical to ours for two of his company's new ships."

The old Norwegian Captain noted how out-dated his idea was of installing the radars on the two bridge wings to dedicate the central part of the bridge to visual navigation only.

"Given the amount of navigational information on radar displays, there was the need to discuss it with someone else in order to avoid possible human errors by those who performed the turns", states Captain Larjo.

The development of the Integrated Navigation System was accompanied by big changes to the layout of the entire bridge, with all instrumentation concentrated in a cockpit that was immediately accessible to officers and maritime pilots. Finally radars were no longer so distant from each other, hidden behind curtains. They were visible and easily accessible to everyone.

"With this bridge layout the job can even be done by just two people, provided they have the same level of skill and are able to communicate with each other well, notwithstanding their rank", explains Larjo with conviction. In fact he trusted ship navigation to just two officers as far back as the 1970s.

Moreover one of his firm beliefs has always been that officers and captains must plan the entire voyage from berth to berth, without having to put so much faith into port pilots.

"With this proposal, if I had any friends amongst captains at that time, I lost them all instantly", he remembers with an air of amusement.

Captain Larjo had quickly developed an interest in piloting techniques when he was still a Third Officer, thanks to a story that he enjoys telling.

"I was on board the Swedish merchant vessel *Uddeholm* that sailed between Canada, Cuba and Mexico. It was 1959", he says. "One day, while we were arriving in Tampico, we called for a pilot to assist us, but nobody came. The Captain realised that we had gone too far to turn back and that we had to cope on our own. He asked me to bring him the charts and he began studying one of them whilst conning the ship. We got into Tampico without any problems, but that evening the Captain called all his officers saying that he did not want to be in the same sort of situation ever again. From that moment on, the Second and Third Officers always planned the route for every port approach", he recalls.

"I was the Third Officer, so the task became mine. I began planning routes and the Captain corrected my work, helping me improve. I can say that I learnt how to become a pilot on board that Swedish ship, and also in the years that followed I continued to prepare routes for all port approaches." He pauses for a moment and smiles amusedly. "I learnt very quickly though to keep this a secret as it would not have been taken too well. It was something that was considered a job for maritime pilots, and not for a deck officer."

Placed on the bookcases of his office, the folders with his bridge design work from the 1970s sit together with those that contain nautical charts used to plan routes through the archipelagos of the Baltic Sea.

The walls are full of pictures that show the various ships that Captain Larjo has worked on, as well as images from the cockpit of the ferry *Silja Serenade*, which was revolutionised according to his ideas. Even family photos are present, such as a few of his father, an aviator who died during World War II. One particular photo taken from the wing of his aircraft cost him several days in prison.

Captain Larjo was born in Northern Finland in an area known for its knives "and for how the locals use them". Today he is a pensioner after retiring from seafaring at 60, "so as not to get in the way of my First Officer's career development", and after fifteen years working in maritime accident investigation.

They say that the Finnish people speak only when necessary. He on the other hand is relatively talkative because he has many things to say. But he always does so to the point, with calmness and a subtle trace of irony. He loves talking about his system as well as problems that still need to be resolved, but less so about his own success and the awards he has received.

He is not very much at home being the centre of attention.

"When I travelled, in hotels they often asked me what my job was. In the beginning I said I was a ship's Captain and as a result everyone tried to talk to me. So I began writing that I was a simple seaman and finally everyone left me in peace", he says.

Bridge Operational Functions

The fundamentals expressed by Captain Larjo can be converted into a set of company policies, operating procedures and practices that, as a whole, allow the implementation of Bridge Resource Management (BRM).

From a practical point of view BRM must be taken as an organisational model aimed at an effective management of both the human and technical resources available on a ship's bridge. Managing resources effectively requires the awareness of the potential and the limitations of both people and navigation systems already discussed in the previous two chapters.

Therefore BRM is not just a set of behavioural rules (of a non-technical nature) that promotes efficient teamwork. The roles of bridge operators must be well defined, bearing in mind their interaction with navigation and communication systems. It is for this reason that it is essential to establish which operational functions (of a technical nature) should be disciplined in BRM organisation. These can be grouped into two broad categories: *Voyage Planning* and *Voyage Execution* (table II–28 and table II–29).

Voyage Planning	
Operational Functions	*Description*
Manoeuvre Planning	*Planning of berthing/anchoring and unberthing manoeuvres. Operational limits for normal, abnormal and emergency conditions are established for:* • *swinging circles* • *speed (both longitudinal and transversal)* • *Heading and Rate of Turn* • *Under-Keel Clearance* • *forces under control (propulsion, tugs, anchors and lines)* • *environmental forces (wind, current and interactions)*
Route Planning	*Planning of routes from the conclusion of an unberthing manoeuvre to initiation of the next berthing/anchoring one. Operational limits for normal, abnormal and emergency conditions are established for each track leg and each turn in terms of:* • *Speed Over Ground and/or Speed Through Water* • *Turn Radius and Rate of Turn* • *Cross Track Distance and Parallel Indexes* • *Under-Keel Clearance* • *drift angle*

table II–28 : Operational functions for voyage planning

Voyage Execution	
Operational Functions	**Description**
Manoeuvre Control	Control of position, orientation and speed based on planned limits. This can be performed through: • manual control systems for steering and propulsion • dynamic positioning systems • tugs and mooring lines
Manoeuvre Monitoring	Observation of a selection of navigational parameters that are critical to keep the limits planned for a specific manoeuvre
Route Control	Control of position, orientation, speed and attitude based on planned limits. Can be performed through: • manual control systems for steering and propulsion • Track Control System
Route Monitoring	Observation of a selection of navigational parameters that are critical to keep the limits planned for a specific route: • Cross Track Distance and Parallel Indexes • Under-Keel Clearance • Heading, Course Over Ground and drift angle • Rate of Turn • Speed Over Ground and Speed Through Water
Collision Avoidance Control	Control of aspect, speed and distance from other ships according to international regulations to prevent collisions at sea and with ARPA-AIS information
Monitoring of Ship Safety and Environmental Protection	Collection of information necessary to verify that: • stability parameters are within planned limits • the status of watertight and firescreen doors follows the plan • the status of all outboard discharges meets local and international pollution prevention regulations
Ship External Radio Communication	Ship-to-ship, ship-to-shore and shore-to-ship communications regarding: • control of route and manoeuvre • collision avoidance control • search and rescue
Ship Internal Communication	Internal communications relating to: • ship safety (with the engine control room); • manoeuvre control (with mooring stations or anchor party).
Control of abnormal and/or emergency situations	Identification of abnormal and/or emergency situations and successive response by applying procedures for abnormal and/or emergency operations, or by improvising if procedures are absent or inadequate

table II–29 : Operational functions for voyage execution

The description of operational functions highlights the importance of *operational limits*, which are determined by:

- a range of values that represents the normality of operations;
- extreme values, which should not be exceeded unless forced to do so in cases of emergency.

All values outside the "normal" range that are still within the extreme ones of an emergency situation make up the *safety margin*. This margin can be used in abnormal situations, i.e. when unforeseen elements make it reasonable to deviate from normal conditions.

In order to clarify this concept, let's take into consideration the example in figure II–54.

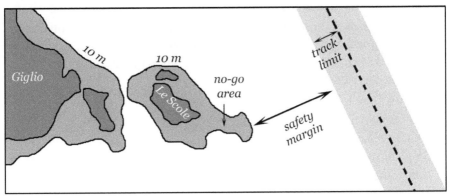

figure II–54 : Operational limits for normal, abnormal and emergency situations

The Track Limit defines half the range of the corridor in which a ship should navigate in, under normal conditions. Whereas the safety margin at a given point along the route is represented by the distance between the corridor's boundary and the *no-go area*. This is based on a ship's maximum draft and – where relevant – also on the height of tide. The entire white area can be used in abnormal situations. Out of these, the most typical is represented by the need to deviate from the corridor in order to perform a collision avoidance manoeuvre. However an abnormal situation can also be generated by an error in controlling the route. In these cases the safety margin consists of the room that is allowed for human error.

Safety margins are not only of a spatial nature. In fact, value ranges and extreme limits can also be defined for speed, Under-Keel Clearance, Rate of Turn and ship orientation. For example, the Rate of Turn can be defined by a range of normal values and by an extreme value, which – once exceeded – causes unacceptable list for cruise ships such as the Costa Concordia. All Rate of Turn values outside the normal range and still within the extreme ones make up a safety margin to use only under abnormal conditions.

From this, it is easy to understand how all operational limits (associated to each single navigational parameter) are interdependent.

In order to accomplish operational functions effectively, good teamwork is needed between all deck officers and also with external pilots – when present. Good teamwork presumes the use of verbal communication techniques and the division of workloads for each operator under normal, abnormal and emergency situations.

As a whole, working effectively as a team means:

- cooperating without being conditioned by hierarchical barriers;
- focussing on operational functions;
- recognising limitations and taking advantage of the potential of technical and human resources available.

It should also be noted that a bridge's operational functions can be essentially described by using four verbs:

- *to plan;*
- *to control;*
- *to monitor;*
- *to communicate.*

Controlling and *monitoring* are two different concepts that must not be confused with each other. Whilst controlling implicates *actions* and/or *decisions* by operators, monitoring implies the *observation* of critical navigational parameters. This observation is not only aimed to ascertain that actions and decisions bring desired results, but also to ensure readiness to respond in the presence of an abnormal situation (i.e. when one or more parameters go beyond their normal limits).

It is also important to clarify the difference between *direct control* and *indirect control* of routes, of manoeuvres and of collision avoidance actions. Direct control is when an operator has both "strategic" responsibility for the use of the safety margin in abnormal situations and "tactical" responsibility for setting each single navigational parameter. Indirect control is obtained when tactical decisions are delegated to another operator.

In extreme synthesis a "functional" BRM organisation establishes why, how and when activities must be done for planning, controlling, monitoring and communicating, together with operator roles to perform them. First of all though, operational procedures on which BRM organisation is founded must be established, keeping account of a bridge's physical structure.

Therefore we will begin from this very point by describing an ideal bridge layout for a functional BRM model.

An Ideal Bridge Layout for BRM

D esigning a ship's bridge can be considered under three different perspectives: technical, regulatory and operational.

That which is purely technical is entrusted to engineers called to resolve issues in assembling navigation systems chosen by shipowners. This choice is made more or less in the following way: the shipyard proposes various options for each navigation system and the shipowner (or its representative) decides which one to install. Regardless of the equipment's quality, the risk is that the assembly is done whilst not referring to the company's operational procedures.

The second perspective, the regulatory one, entails the involvement of organisations responsible for classifying and certifying ships. These organisations refer to minimum equipment requirements and various international standards. However the tests they conduct do not cover the compatibility between operating procedures and the layout of navigation systems.

Lastly, the operational perspective relates to all those who work on the bridge. If the bridge has not been fitted out by taking company procedures into consideration, incompatibilities could arise between operational functions and the disposition of navigational instruments. This inconsistency can become an obstacle when attempting to effectively manage all available resources (technical and human).

In this chapter we will try to describe an ideal bridge for BRM procedures from an operational perspective. In order to do this we will take into consideration some of the more advanced navigation systems available, but above all we will take inspiration from the work and ideas of Captain Larjo.

~

Before beginning we need to take a step back, to 1990 to be precise, when the first real *cockpit* was installed on board the ferry *Silja Serenade.* It was the result of the efforts of Captain Larjo, who as far back as the early 1980s had already understood the need to integrate all navigation systems on a ship's bridge similar to an aircraft's *cockpit.*

A black and white photograph of this bridge stands out among the many others in his office in Turku, Finland (figure II–55).

figure II–55 : The first cockpit aboard the ferry Silja Serenade, 1990

Larjo recalls how bridges were before his revolution.

"On the old merchant ships the radar was often located in the chart room, a place that only the Captain had the key to. It was absolute madness", he says. "Sometimes it was even hidden behind curtains to protect it from sunlight. As a result of this there was someone who controlled the route, someone else who looked after communications and speed, and another two who watched the radar from behind the curtains." Larjo shakes his head. "In 1968 on the Finnish archipelago a collision between two passenger ships cost the lives of six people[67]. The Captain of one of the ships involved admitted not having ever looked at the radar", he tells us.

The situation only improved between the end of the 1970s and the beginning of the 1980s when new technologies were made available for radar systems. The digital screen could even be used next to the window and the reduction in costs allowed ships to install two radars. "A solution along the lines of an aircraft became possible, with two workstations and a control panel in between them", explains Larjo. "Nevertheless this system required two operators on the bridge with the same level of skill and experience: one to control navigation and the other to monitor that all goes according to plan."

His company Silja Lines had already begun discussing bridge roles after the accident in 1968.

---

[67] As already mentioned previously, on 28th November 1968, the Finnish cruise ship "Ilmatar" collided with the ferry "Botnia" in the waters of the Åland archipelago. The accident claimed the lives of six people aboard the Botnia.

Captain Larjo smiles. "I proposed that both officers and captains took pilot licenses."

His proposal involved leaving the ship's bridge with just two operators able to navigate even in the most difficult conditions, just like a maritime pilot.

This first BRM concept was based on two fundamental assumptions: the two operators must have the same level of skill and they must have the same navigation systems (integrated into a *cockpit*) at their disposal (individually).

It was – and still is – a decidedly innovative solution, in spite of the fact that it never took off in the maritime industry apart from a few exceptions (it was adopted on ferries in the Baltic Sea and by some cruise line companies).

We would like to propose this system, adapted to the most advanced technology available today, as a starting point for a bridge layout that is ideal for BRM.

Let's imagine it.

~

Our bridge is composed of a *central cockpit* and two *lateral cockpits*. All three must protrude from the ship's superstructure and its broadsides (figure II–56) so that they:

- allow a horizontal visual field of 225 degrees for operators in the *central cockpit*;
- make the entire ship's broadside visible to the operators in the *lateral cockpits*.

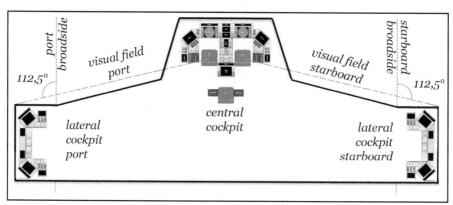

figure II–56 : Central and lateral bridge cockpits

The central cockpit must guarantee the following operational functions:

- planning, control and monitoring of routes;

- planning, control and monitoring of manoeuvres;
- collision avoidance control;
- monitoring of ship safety and environmental protection;
- ship external radio communications;
- ship internal communications;
- control of abnormal and/or emergency situations;

The two lateral cockpits must be mirrored and guarantee the following operational functions:

- control and monitoring of manoeuvres;
- control of abnormal and emergency situations;
- external radio communications;
- internal communications.

All three cockpits must be designed to enhance teamwork.

From an ergonomic point of view, the *central cockpit* (figure II–57) must ensure:

- access to all navigation and communication systems without having to leave workstations;
- the possibility of taking control of navigation from each of the front seats, both in manual and automatic mode;
- a central seat for external pilots (port or coastal), or for a third officer supporting his two colleagues in the front positions. The central seat must be higher than the two ahead and be equipped with a multi-functional display that allows the monitoring of different navigation systems. All this without the possibility of directly manipulating steering and propulsion control systems;
- a reduced distance between the three seats in order to ease teamwork;
- a compact arrangement of all navigation systems, designed to favour the observation of critical parameters through an active monitoring technique based upon cyclic visual scanning.

Always with ergonomics in mind, the *lateral cockpits* (figure II–58) must integrate navigation and communication systems so that the two operators in front can access them whilst standing, with more freedom of movement than that given to the *central cockpit*.

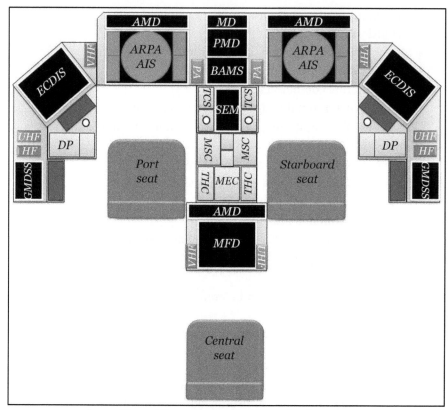

figure II–57 : The central cockpit's navigation systems

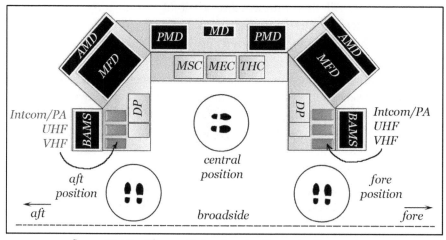

figure II–58 : The port lateral cockpit's navigation systems

Table II–30 shows the ideal combination of navigation and communication systems able to guarantee the operational functions of the three cockpits of our bridge.

Navigation and Communication Systems	Abbrev.	Operative Functions	Quantity Central Cockpit	Quantity Lateral Cockpits
Electronic Chart Display Information System	ECDIS	Route planning Manoeuvre planning Route monitoring Manoeuvre monitoring	2	--
Track control system	TCS	Route control	2	--
Automatic Radar Plotting Aid	ARPA	Route monitoring Collision avoidance control	2	--
Automatic Identification System	AIS	Collision avoidance control	2	--
Active Monitoring Display	AMD	Route monitoring Manoeuvre monitoring	3	2
Mode Display	MD	Route control		
Multi-Function Display	MFD	Route monitoring Manoeuvre monitoring Collision avoidance control	1	2
Dynamic Positioning System	DP	Manoeuvre control	1	1
Manual Steering Control	MSC	Manoeuvre control Route control	2	1
Main Engine Control	MEC	Manoeuvre control Route control	1	1
Thruster Control	THC	Manoeuvre control	2	1
Bridge Alert Management System	BAMS	Control of abnormal and emergency situations	1	2
Global Maritime Distress Safety System	GMDSS	Ship external radio communications	2	Only VHF
Intcom - Public Address - UHF	Intcom PA-UHF	Ship internal communications	2	1
Safety and Environmental Monitoring (SEM)	SEM	Monitoring of ship safety and environmental protection	1	--

table II–30 : Bridge navigation and communication systems

This bridge (figure II–57, figure II–58 and table II–30) includes two innovative elements that are extremely important for human-technology integration: the *Active Monitoring Display* (AMD) and the *Mode Display* (MD). The first is designed to allow the observation of critical parameters for the conduct of navigation (figure II–59). The second highlights both the settings and the actual mode for controlling routes/manoeuvres and the ship's speed (figure II–60).

figure II–59 : Active Monitoring Display (AMD)

figure II–60 : Mode Display (MD)

The Active Monitoring Display is inspired by the grouping of the primary flight instruments in the cockpit of an aircraft. Pilots are taught that actively monitoring instruments means performing cyclic visual scans of these parameters. Active monitoring contributes to maintaining so-called *situation awareness* and its development through time. In particular the projection of the situation in the immediate future is done thanks to the integration of the visual perception of the outside world, together with that derived from the *curved heading line* and the *predictor*. These tools are operated through the Track Control System and/or the Dynamic Positioning System.

The Mode Display must ensure a defence against so-called *mode-errors*, that occur when an operator believes to be in a control mode that is different to the one actually being used. A typical example is the confusion between Heading and Course Mode when using the Track Control System, despite them being considerably different: in the first mode the system does not correct the effect of the wind and the current as it does in the second.

The different automation levels indicated by the Mode Display must be subdivided for controlling routes and manoeuvres, as well as for speed control. For routes and manoeuvres the Mode Display must give a clear indication of:

- *Manual Steering Control: Follow-Up, Non Follow-Up*;
- *Track Control System: Heading, Course, Track modes*;

- *Dynamic Positioning: Position, Heading, Track modes.*

With regards to the various speed control modes, the Mode Display should indicate:

- *Manual Speed Control: Main engine control;*
- *Track Control System: RPM/pitch, Speed Over Ground, Arrival Speed modes;*
- *Dynamic Positioning System: Position, Track modes.*

The Track Control System and Dynamic Positioning System settings are no less important. These in fact are critical for the correct functioning of the selected level of automation.

In both the central and lateral cockpits of our bridge we have planned for the presence of a *Multi-Functional Display* (MFD). This allows the visualisation of either ECDIS or ARPA, to be used by the operator in the central seat or by those who control the manoeuvre from the lateral cockpits. ARPA integrates AIS and must be stabilised with respect to the seabed through the Heading and Speed Over Ground sensors being used (figure II–61).

The choice of *Head-Up* view is based on studies which show that *North-Up* representations require more cognitive effort. This is due to the mental rotation necessary to realign the radar image with the visual image of the outside world.

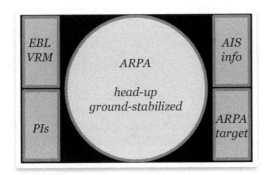

figure II–61 : Radar ARPA-AIS

On the other hand however, Head-Up displays do not guarantee the overview that is typical of a nautical chart. To compensate for this, the two ECDIS used by the officers in the front seats of our bridge would exclusively display North-Up views.

To avoid overloads of information, parameters that are already present on the Active Monitoring Display should not appear on ARPA and ECDIS screens. The basic principle is that screens dedicated to radar and electronic charts must be minimal and with a reduced number of options for operators.

As already mentioned the ECDIS screen should be North-Up orientated, differently from the ARPA screen. In this way operators can access a complete overview of the area they are sailing in. At the same time they don't have to put too much mental effort into identifying any eventual *Maritime Safety Information* (MSI) received from external sources.

Furthermore ECDIS mustn't display navigational parameters already visible on the AMD. As a result we obtain a double advantage:

- the operator does not lose focus on ARPA and AMD[68];
- the ECDIS screen is maximised for electronic charts.

Only a portion of the ECDIS screen should be dedicated to information and telematic services specific to certain geographical areas (figure II–62). A good example would be the Dynamic Under-Keel Clearance service, which is able to calculate the minimum clearance for each point along a ship's planned route.

The ECDIS screen can also be used for controlling manoeuvres by means of DP. This is done by maintaining the background of an electronic chart and showing all information needed to operate DP in the screen's lateral pane.

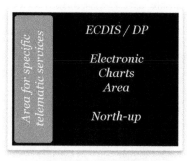

figure II–62 : ECDIS

There is just one final consideration to be made regarding the navigation sensors discussed in the previous chapters. The basic principle is that their data must be integrated and compared upstream from the navigation systems that they are being directed to. In this way the actual sensors are

---

68 As already mentioned, the central Head-Up view makes the comparison between the outside world and the radar image much easier.

physically invisible to the operators, who only receive the information that is derived from them. The automatic identification and resolution of possible drops in sensor accuracy is communicated to the operators exclusively through the *Bridge Alert Management System* (BAMS). As occurs with AMD navigational parameters, all alerts should be centralised by the BAMS without being duplicated on any other display.

The combination of available navigation sensors on our bridge is summarised in table II–31.

Navigation Sensor	Data
• One X band radar scanner • One S band radar scanner	Radar bearings and distances
Two PNT multi-receivers, both capable of: • using different GNSS constellations (GPS/GLONASS) • operating in differential mode with SBAS corrections (for route control and route monitoring) • operating in relative mode with RTK corrections (for controlling and monitoring manoeuvres) • processing radio-electric positions (e.g. E-LORAN) • using Doppler speed technology for the calculation of Speed Over Ground at low speeds • integrating GNSS data with inertial sensors (tactical level IMUs) to improve positioning accuracy at low speeds • ensuring autonomous inertial positioning in the case of temporary absence of external GNSS/radio-electric signals	Positioning (satellite, radio-electric and autonomous inertial) - Orientation (Course Over Ground) - Speed (Speed Over Ground)
• One satellite Transmitting Heading Device (THD) based on a dual antenna GNSS system • Two mechanical gyrocompasses • One fibre optic gyroscope for rate of turn	Orientation (Heading and Rate of Turn)
One dual axis Doppler speed log	Speed (Speed Over Ground & Through Water)
Four ultrasonic anemometers (bow, stern, and the superstructure, one to port and one to starboard)	Wind (direction & speed)
Two echosounders with two transceivers each: • frequency 200 KHz (fore sectors) • frequency 50 KHz (aft sectors)	Depth (Under-Keel Clearance)
Two tactical level IMUs integrated with GNSS in order to: • improve positioning accuracy • ensure autonomous inertial positioning in the case of GNSS/radio-electric signals outage	Attitude (Roll-Pitch-Heave) autonomous inertial positioning

table II–31 : The navigation sensors on our bridge

To engineer a ship's bridge like the one we have proposed needs more than just assembling systems and sensors that exist on today's market.

What is needed is that every single hardware and software component be designed in an integrated manner to minimise spaces and thus allow operators to sit (or stand) close to each other. As already mentioned, this is something that is essential for effective teamwork.

Finally, the information available on the navigation system screens should be arranged in relation to both the operational functions and operator roles. In particular the latter will be discussed within the next chapter.

BRM Roles and Responsibilities

The operator roles on a bridge ideal for BRM vary according to the different level of navigational risk, which is associated to two distinct *manning levels*.

Under *green manning*, that is when there are large safety margins and/or good visibility, our bridge requires the presence of two officers. At least one of these must hold a deck qualification as Chief Mate, whereas for the other a qualification as Mate is sufficient. Both however must have been educated to understand the potential and limitations of available resources, as well as trained in the use of all specific navigation systems present in the cockpit.

Under *red manning*, which is when safety margins and/or visibility conditions are reduced or when navigating in congested waters, our bridge requires the presence of the Master, the Chief Mate and another operator in the role of *Pilot*. If not part of the ship's crew, the Pilot must have been trained to use all the navigation systems necessary for controlling and monitoring routes, manoeuvres and collision avoidance (Track Control System, Dynamic Positioning System and Multi-Function Display).

The Master can assume the Pilot's role in harbour or coastal waters where piloting is not mandatory or when he holds a specific exemption.

The threshold that determines whether a safety margin is "large" or "reduced" cannot be established in an absolute manner as it depends on ship dimensions and loading conditions, as well as on specific risk factors for the area concerned.

The operational functions performed by the operators on our bridge in green and red manning are summarised in table II–32 and table II–33.

Role	Operational Functions
Navigator	• *route control* • *route monitoring* • *collision avoidance control* • *control of abnormal and/or emergency situations*
Co-navigator	• *route monitoring* • *monitoring of ship safety and environmental protection* • *ship external radio communications* • *ship internal communications* • *general supervision of all operational functions* • *overall responsibility for the control of navigation according to planned operational limits*

table II–32 : Bridge roles under green manning

Role	Operational Functions
Navigator	• *control of routes and manoeuvres* • *monitoring of routes and manoeuvres* • *collision avoidance control* • *control of abnormal and/or emergency situations*
Co-navigator	• *monitoring of routes and manoeuvres* • *monitoring of ship safety and environmental protection* • *ship external radio communications* • *internal communications* • *general supervision of all operational functions*
Pilot	• *control of routes and manoeuvres* • *monitoring of routes and manoeuvres* • *collision avoidance control* • *control of abnormal and/or emergency situations* • *overall responsibility for the control of navigation according to planned operational limits*

table II–33 : Bridge roles under red manning

Under red manning the Navigator sits to port, the Co-navigator to starboard and the Pilot in the middle (figure II–63). Given the cockpit's symmetry, the functions of Navigator and Co-navigator can also be inverted if the situation requires. When operations are conducted from the bridge wing, the Navigator remains standing in the central position, the Co-navigator is in the aft place and the pilot in the fore position (figure II–64).

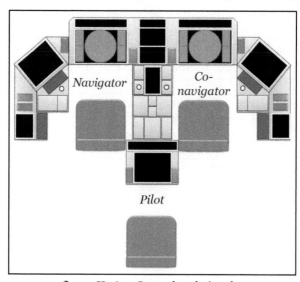

figure II–63 : Central cockpit roles

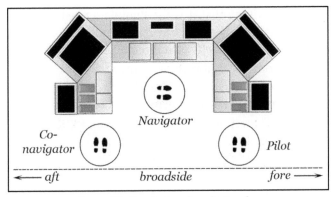

figure II–64 : Lateral cockpit roles

The roles described can be divided between mates, masters and maritime pilots. Ideally, the combinations that ensure more effective teamwork should be those shown in table II–34.

	NAVIGATOR	CO-NAVIGATOR	PILOT
Green manning	Deck officer qualified as Mate	Deck officer qualified as Chief Mate	--
Red manning with no external pilot on board or where external pilot is not responsible for the control of navigation	Deck officer qualified as Mate	Deck officer qualified as Chief Mate	Master
Red manning with external pilot on board who is responsible for the control of navigation	Deck officer qualified as Chief Mate	Master	Coastal/Port Pilot

table II–34 : Ideal division of roles between bridge operators

It is difficult to universally define the operational relationship between Navigator and Pilot because pilotage laws change from nation to nation.

Some states require that ships take a pilot on board, without the pilot being obliged to assume any type of control over the route or manoeuvring[69]. In this case the Captain himself can decide to assume the role of pilot in the cockpit's central seat, with the pilot remaining at his side to give any eventual advice.

---

69 A pilot's role as advisor comes from continental Europe traditional legislation. Article 92 of the Italian Code of Navigation, for example, gives the pilot the obligation of suggesting routes and assisting the Captain in determining the necessary manoeuvres to perform.

Other countries envisage that it is the Pilot who must directly assume the "conduct of navigation"[70], therefore having control of manoeuvres, route and collision avoidance, either directly or indirectly.

The decision to opt for a direct or indirect type of control affects the relationship between the role of Pilot and that of Navigator. In the first case, if the Pilot takes direct control of navigation he must:

- give "tactical" level orders (on Heading, speed, Rate of Turn, etc.) to the Navigator, establishing also the method of execution (through manual or automatic control systems);
- make "strategic" level decisions for the eventual use of safety margins under abnormal conditions.

In the second case, if the Pilot takes indirect control he must:

- delegate "tactical" level decisions and actions to the Navigator who will operate the available systems in order to conduct the ship within planned operational limits or agreed deviations;
- retain "strategic" decisional power on the eventual use of safety margins in abnormal situations.

When the Navigator is fully capable of controlling the ship, an indirect type of control will ensure an optimal condition for the Pilot to carry out his strategic role.

However, it is fundamental to realise that an effective cooperation between the Pilot and the Navigator is the basis of both types of control. Cooperation can be enhanced by two communication techniques: *thinking aloud* and *closed loop*. The first is based on verbalising the intention, its expected outcome and the motivation behind an action before its execution. In this way the elements are given for either confirmation or for an eventual challenge from other team members.

An example of *thinking aloud* is:

- Intention: "I intend to reduce speed from 16 to 10 knots and, at 2.5 miles from the Island of Giglio, begin a starboard turn with a Rate of Turn of 10 degrees per minute."
- Expected outcome: "The turn will end with a Heading of 334° and a distance of no less than 0.5 nautical miles from the rocks."
- Reason: "The reduction in speed from 16 to 10 knots is needed to prevent excessive heeling during the turn."

---

70 The legal obligation to "conduct navigation", i.e. to control routes and manoeuvres, is linked to British and North American tradition.

The second communication technique, *closed loop*, is used to ensure that orders are received correctly. It foresees that once an order is given, the operator who receives it repeats and awaits final confirmation before executing it. Here is an example:

- The Pilot orders: "Starboard ten."
- The Navigator repeats: "Starboard ten."
- The Pilot confirms: "Yes."

Only after the final confirmation should the Navigator turn the helm ten degrees to starboard using the Manual Steering Control.

Closed loop must be used for all orders given by the Pilot to the Navigator and also to mitigate the risk of misunderstandings on the type of control being used. Every variation from direct to indirect control and vice versa must be verbalised by whoever has assumed the Pilot's role during red manning (under green manning the Navigator always has direct control).

Before concluding there is one last element to keep in mind. Despite the differences in pilotage laws from country to country, the responsibility of command – and therefore of navigation safety – always lies with the Master. This is true even when it is the external Pilot that actually controls the route, the manoeuvre and collision avoidance. It is also generally recognised that the Master has the right to remove the Pilot from navigation control in the case of manifested incompetence or imminent danger. Even under these circumstances though, the Master may only have the option of conducting the ship to a safe position and requesting another Pilot from the competent authority. In this he would not be able to continue navigating alone in waters subject to compulsory pilotage.

At present, confusion regarding the Pilot's role on a bridge is fed not only by differing existing legislation but also by issues of civil liability for accidents in waters subject to compulsory pilotage[71]. In any case it is the shipowner that must compensate for economic losses, even when the accident is caused by Pilot error. This is a convenient arrangement due to shipping company interests in containing pilotage costs. In fact if Pilots and the organisations they are part of were to be considered liable from a civil point of view, they would have to sustain higher insurance premiums that would inevitably be added to their fees.

---

71 George A. Quick (2010). "Master-Pilot Relationship, The Role of the Pilot in Risk Management." Article published on the website (www.impahq.org) of the International Maritime Pilots' Association (IMPA).

From what has been mentioned above, we can confirm that it is not possible to understand the Master-Pilot relationship without making reference to national laws and the interpretation of courts in the case of accidents. And it is for this reason that operational functions and our bridge layout have been thought out to guarantee the flexibility required in adapting to the many different pilotage laws.

The definition of operator roles and responsibilities therefore represents an indispensable link between bridge layout and operational procedures, which we will discuss in the chapter that follows.

The 4Ps: Principles, Policies, Procedures and Practices

A ship's bridge is a socio-technical system characterised by a complex interaction between man and technology. In order to effectively manage this interaction, we propose a BRM model based on the so-called "4Ps"[72]:

- Operational Principles;
- Company Policies;
- Operating Procedures;
- Specific Practices.

Let's take an example starting from the principle according to which good planning requires the definition of operational limits. This should translate into a company policy that establishes responsibilities and generic methods for determining these limits. The procedure should then go into technical details describing how and when to carry them out, and who is responsible for them. Finally there are the practices that are in themselves a specific or even alternative method to perform this task correctly.

Nowadays on board ships, operational procedures often consist of a list of "do's and don'ts" for operators, accompanied by generic recommendations that use the same language as international regulations or that simply refer to *good seamanship*. Furthermore, ship captains receive new procedures from management without being involved in their development and without understanding the full meaning or the motivations behind them. As a result they treat them with scepticism and an open mistrust, even more so when the "do's and don'ts" are worlds apart from the actual situations officers are called to manage to ensure navigation safety. In effect such procedures are seen more as a way of shifting responsibility, rather than useful operating instructions. To make things worse, the lack of "how" is also an issue. In fact, low quality procedures are those that impose certain actions without specifying the methods that should be used.

The 4P model that we propose has been primarily conceived to reduce the ambiguity mentioned. In particular with regards to procedures, we propose the definition of the following elements for each task associated to an operational function:

72 Asaf Degani (1994). "On the Design of Flight Deck Procedures". NASA Ames Research Centre. Even though the study is based on observing flight operations, the author does not prevent the application of the 4P model to other complex man-technology systems characterised by high-risk operations.

- when;
- who (identifying responsibility);
- how (including the sequence of actions);

In order to guarantee the balance between procedures and operator discretion, the 4P model also leaves ample space to practices. These are in effect an alternative method to the "how" of a procedure in performing a certain task. When they are widely accepted and routine, they can also be elevated to the same status as a procedure through time, provided that they remain coherent with company policy.

An essential tool in facilitating the correct application of procedures is the checklist. According to veteran pilot Daniel Boorman of Boeing in Seattle[73], a good checklist should be brief, efficient, straight to the point and easy to use even in the most difficult situations. It can't list all possibilities or substitute the judgement of an expert. It should be considered as a reminder for the more critical elements, those that anyone could forget. In the most delicate of situations checklists can help in selecting correct priorities and working as a team, but alone – emphasises Boorman – they cannot fly a plane. Contrary to operational procedures, checklists are not actually a guide on how to do things.

There are many different types of checklist, but we will deal with two in particular: *"do-confirm"* and *"read-do"*.

With a *do-confirm checklist* operators complete their tasks using memory and experience. It is only in a second moment that they pause and take out the checklist to confirm that they have completed all that was necessary to do. With a *read-do checklist*, operators use the list as a recipe, acting in sequence by following the listed items.

Choosing between these two types depends on the situation where they should be applied. However in both cases checklists only work if they are created by people that know the operational context very well. Once the type of checklist has been chosen, we need to select its elements. Their number depends on the time available to perform the task, but should never exceed half a dozen.

"A checklist must be brief", suggests Boorman, "otherwise it will just become a distraction and operators will start to look for shortcuts."

A golden rule for checklists is to include the so-called *killer items*, which are the critical elements more at risk of being forgotten by operators. Even

---

73 The American surgeon Atul Guwande reports Boorman's ideas on checklists in his 2010 book "Checklist Manifesto" (Profile Books Ltd).

the format is very important. A checklist should not exceed one page and should be essential, i.e. without titles, logos or anything else that can be considered as not strictly necessary.

Nevertheless, the actual test for checklists is in the real world where things inevitably become more complex than what we imagined. Boorman warns that however well a checklist is made, first drafts may fail miserably. Therefore it is always recommended to test them first in a simulator before putting them into practice in the real world.

Checklists are considered as a valuable tool in aviation, yet their level of acceptance on board ships is still very low. How could that be?

Certainly maritime training does not stress the fallacy of memory and judgement as much as it does for an aviator. In addition, checklists available on board ships are usually too long, too detailed and too distant from officers' needs. They are often seen as a threat, a constraint that limits discretion and individual professionalism. On the contrary, checklists should be considered as a means for aiding experts in performing mundane and routine tasks by freeing their mind for important decisions and by mitigating the risk of forgetting elements that may compromise their judgement.

In a nutshell, not only checklists but also the entire 4P model serves this: to reduce improvisation and to discipline bridge operations, whilst leaving operators with discretion for the management of abnormal and emergency situations that are not covered by procedures.

Discipline is in fact fundamental for an effective implementation of BRM, even though its importance is not adequately emphasised outside civil aviation[74]. But what exactly do we mean by discipline?

Above all it is a positive attitude towards teamwork and operational procedures. An attitude that has become essential for mates, masters and maritime pilots to face increasingly complex and dynamic operational scenarios. Bridge operators must learn to delegate and to establish priorities, possibly without omitting the evaluation of critical elements. They must be aware of their own vulnerability as human beings and to trust in procedures and practices (including checklists) to prevent consequences from possible errors.

Having said this, we can now define our bridge's 4Ps. We will concentrate particularly on two groups of operational functions: voyage planning and

---

74 Discipline is a dimension of professionalism that only belongs to the world of aviation. In fact, codes of conduct in other professions only include expectations of selflessness (in the case of a conflict of interest), of the quest for excellence (within their own skills and available knowledge), and of trustworthiness (toward responsibility in the role they perform).

222

execution. First we will establish the principles, which are the assertions to make based on the potential and limitations of both the operators and the navigation systems. We will then use the template shown in table II–35 to develop company policies, operating procedures and specific practices for each of the bridge's operational functions.

Operational Function		
Policy 1 Policy 2 ... Policy n		
Task 1	Procedure 1	Practice
Task 2	Procedure 2	Practice
...	...	...
Task n	Procedure n	Practice

table II–35 : 4P model for normal situations

Voyage Planning

The principles of voyage planning can be expressed through the following assertions:

- planning the voyage implies identifying specific risks and the measures necessary for mitigating them in a proactive manner;
- voyage planning is based on the definition of operational limits that are capable of outlining the normality, abnormality or emergency level of a situation;
- planning operational limits for normal situations is based on all foreseeable conditions before departure;
- planning operational limits for abnormal situations (not foreseeable before departure) aims to highlight available safety margins for necessary deviations;
- quantifying and discussing operational limits before departure increases the possibility of identifying and correcting eventual planning errors.

Manoeuvre Planning			
• Specific risks must be identified and assessed based on company experience and that of pilot organisations. They should also be identified based on accidents that have occurred over time, both to the company itself and to others operating in a similar context.			
• Operational limits must be established by the shipping company based on high fidelity simulations. In waters where pilotage is compulsory, operational limits should be agreed upon with the local pilotage provider.			
• A ship's master has the right to modify operational limits before departure, provided that they have been mutually agreed with the company and pilotage organisations.			
• Planning of manoeuvres must clarify the pilot's role on the bridge according to specific legislation regarding compulsory pilotage.			
Definition of operational limits	Who	Shipping company	Practices -- Data analysis techniques for high fidelity simulations
	When	Before issuing voyage orders	
	How	Operational limits for normal, abnormal and emergency situations should be established for: • swinging circles • distances off dangers • speed (longitudinal and transversal) • Heading and Rate of Turn • Under-Keel Clearance • forces under control (propulsion, tugs, anchors and mooring lines) • environmental forces (wind, current and interactions)	
Identification of specific risks	Who	Shipping company	Practices -- Guidelines for the setting up of working groups
	When	Before issuing voyage orders	
	How	By analysing accident and incident reports that have occurred in the waters where the manoeuvre will be performed, as well as by analysing local experts' practices	
Verification of planned manoeuvre	Who	Master	Practices -- Forms for notifying changes to the manoeuvring plan
	When	Before departure	
	How	Through consideration of specific risks identified during the planning stage. Any variations deemed necessary must be communicated to the company by the Master upon an agreement reached with the local pilotage provider	

table II–36 : Policies, procedures and practices for manoeuvre planning tasks

Route Planning			
• Planning of the route must be performed on the basis of operational limits established through simulation (in waters subject to compulsory pilotage) and through the analysis of data relating to previous voyages. • In waters subject to compulsory pilotage, the established limits must be agreed upon with the competent local authorities. The ship's master has the right to modify operational limits before departure by agreement with the company and the local pilotage provider. • Route planning must clarify the pilot's role on the bridge according to specific legislation regarding compulsory pilotage.			
Definition of operational limits	Who	Shipping company	Practices -- Data analysis techniques for high fidelity simulations
	When	Before issuing voyage orders	
	How	Operational limits for normal, abnormal and emergency situations are established for each track leg and each turn in terms of: • Speed Over Ground and/or Speed Through Water • Turn Radius and Rate of Turn • Cross Track Distance and Parallel Indexes • Under-Keel Clearance • Drift angle	
Identification of specific risks	Who	Shipping company	Practices -- Guidelines for the setting up of working groups
	When	Before issuing voyage orders	
	How	By analysing accident and incident reports that occurred in the waters where the route will be followed, as well as by analysing local experts' practices	
Verification of planned route	Who	Master	Practices -- Forms for notifying changes to the route plan
	When	Before departure	
	How	Through automatic ECDIS function for checking operational limits and through confirmation of specific risks identified during planning. Any variations deemed necessary for the emergence of risks or other unexpected operational needs must be communicated to the company by the Master upon an agreement reached with the local pilotage provider	

table II–37 : Policies, procedures and practices for route planning tasks

Voyage Execution

The principles of voyage execution can be expressed through the following assertions:

- a safe and efficient voyage execution under normal conditions is based on controlling routes and manoeuvres within planned operational limits.
- Operational limits for normal situations are not a constraint for operator discretion. They can be exceeded by using available safety margins if the abnormality of the situation requires.
- Safety margins are aimed at being used when necessary and reasonable to do so. The evaluation of this need is a responsibility of those who exercise control of routes and manoeuvres.
- Monitoring voyage execution is enhanced by the *active monitoring* of navigation systems. This monitoring is based on the sequential and cyclic observation of parameters that are considered critical for a specific navigational phase. *Active monitoring* represents the heart of the integration between man and technology on a bridge and the basis for achieving, maintaining and recovering *situation awareness*.
- Full *situation awareness* can be maintained through the comparison between visual perception of the external world and the image of this created by the *active monitoring* of navigation systems.
- Operator improvisation during abnormal or emergency situations not covered by operating procedures and specific practices is also essential to the safety of the ship.
- Human error is inevitable. This renders the doctrine of *error management* indispensable for bridge operations. Strategies for limiting errors are accompanied by those for limiting their potential consequences. These strategies translate into communication and coordination techniques aimed at enhancing teamwork.
- Quantifying and sharing operational limits between team members increases the possibility of identifying and correcting eventual errors committed by those who exercise control of manoeuvre and routes.
- The effectiveness of communication and coordination techniques that lie at the base of good teamwork is only ensured if all team members have comparable skills and experience.

Manoeuvre control			
• Operational limits for normal situations must not be considered a constraint for operators. They can be exceeded by using available safety margins if the abnormality of a particular situation requires. The extreme limits of a safety margin can be exceeded only in emergency situations.			
• Operator discretion is guaranteed in choosing the method of control: manual or Dynamic Positioning System. When there are doubts regarding the correct functioning of the Dynamic Positioning System, manual control is recommended.			
• The manoeuvre during red manning must always be performed under control of the operator that assumes the role of the Pilot.			
Pre-departure preparation	Who	Navigator	Practices -- Pre-departure checklist
	When	One hour before assuming red manning	
	How	By performing checks on navigation systems, by verifying ship stability, and the status of the watertight doors	
Pre-arrival preparation	Who	Navigator	Practices -- Pre-arrival checklist
	When	One hour before assuming red manning	
	How	By performing checks on navigation systems, by verifying ship stability, and the status of the watertight doors	
Team briefing	Who	Conducted by the Pilot for the bridge team, for those responsible at mooring stations, and for the Chief Engineer	Practices -- Team-briefing checklist
	When	Immediately after assuming red manning and with external Pilot on board	
	How	By briefly summarising the idea of the manoeuvre, highlighting eventual changes to planned operational limits, and stating the specific risks identified	
Control of planned operational limits	Who	Pilot	Practices --
	When	During manoeuvre execution	
	How	Either through manual control systems or by using the Dynamic Positioning System	
Cooperation	Who	Navigator and Pilot	Practices -- Standard phraseology
	When	During manoeuvre execution	
	How	By sharing intentions through "thinking aloud", and by communicating using "closed loop"	
Changeover between central and lateral cockpits	Who	Entire team	Practices --
	When	At Pilot's discretion	
	How	Co-navigator joins Navigator and Pilot only after receiving positive confirmation	

table II–38 : Policies, procedures and practices for manoeuvre control tasks

Manoeuvre monitoring			
• Manoeuvre monitoring must always be conducted integrating visual information from the outside world with that derived from the navigation systems, not only when facing restricted visibility. • The identification of abnormal situations and the eventual challenge in the case of unnecessary deviation is a responsibility of all team members.			
Active monitoring of parameters critical for the manoeuvre	*Who*	*All three team members*	*Practices* -- *Scanning pattern of critical parameters to monitor (specific to manoeuvre)*
	When	*During manoeuvre execution*	
	How	*Through cyclic visual scanning of parameters available on the Active Monitoring Display (AMD), with particular attention to those associated with the risks mentioned during team briefing.* *In the case of deviation from normal limits without any apparent reason, the challenge should be carried out in two stages:* • *Verbalise the value of the parameter that has exceeded its normal limit* • *Suggest returning within normal limits if the operator in control does not give a reasonable explanation for using the safety margin*	
Team de-briefing	*Who*	*Conducted by the Master for the bridge team, those responsible at mooring stations, and the Chief Engineer*	*Practices* -- *Debriefing checklist* -- *Report on "learning event" or "near miss"*
	When	*Immediately after completing the manoeuvre and as soon as green manning is assumed*	
	How	*By including all participants and asking (from youngest to oldest) to highlight positive and negative events of the manoeuvre.* *The Master must be ready to take responsibility for the team's overall performance, closing the de-briefing on a positive note.* *In the case of significant events that have affected safety, the manoeuvre should be discussed in depth at a later stage, in order to write a report to the shipping company (learning event or near miss)*	

table II–39 : Policies, procedures and practices for manoeuvre monitoring tasks

Route control			
• Operational limits for normal situations must not be considered as a constraint for operators. They can be exceeded – if the abnormality of a particular situation requires – by using available safety margins. The extreme limits of a safety margin can be exceeded only in emergency situations.			
• Operators discretion is guaranteed in choosing the most appropriate method of control for the various phases of the voyage. When there are doubts regarding the correct functioning of the Track Control System, the operator in control must consider selecting a lower level of automation.			
Track keeping within planned operational limits	Who	Navigator and Pilot	Practices -- TCS operational guidelines
	When	During navigation along planned routes	
	How	Through manual control systems or by means of the Track Control System (TCS). Before engaging the TCS, the Navigator must state the level of automation he/she intends to use or that agreed with the Pilot.	
Cooperation	Who	Navigator and Pilot	Practices -- Standard phraseology
	When	During navigation along planned routes	
	How	By sharing intentions through "thinking aloud", and by communicating using "closed loop	
Takeover of the watch	Who	Conduct by incoming Co-navigator	Practices -- Takeover checklist
	When	Before every change of the watch during green manning or when passing to red manning. At night, incoming operators must arrive on the bridge at least 20 minutes before beginning watch duties.	
	How	The incoming Co-navigator initiates the takeover procedure by requesting information from the actual Co-navigator according to the specific checklist. This is done only after obtaining authorisation from the Navigator who remains focused on route control	
Master-Pilot exchange	Who	Pilot and Master	Practices -- Master-Pilot Exchange checklist
	When	When the external Pilot comes on board	
	How	The Pilot asks the Master for confirmation of the agreed plan, informing him/her of eventual last minute changes and of the type of control to assume (direct or indirect).	

table II–40 : Policies, procedures and practices for route control tasks

Route monitoring			
• Monitoring of manoeuvres must always be conducted integrating visual information from the outside world with that derived from the navigation systems, not only when facing reduced visibility. • The identification of abnormal situations is a responsibility of the entire bridge team. • Data from the navigation systems, the power management system and those relating to fuel consumption must be recorded and transferred in real-time to the shipping company's control centre. • Data collection must be automated and aimed at optimising safety and efficiency of navigation. However, if the data analysis reveals repeated use of safety margins without any apparent reasons, the company reserves the right to investigate events to identify latent conditions and/or responsibilities.			
Active monitoring of critical parameters	Who	All team members	Practices -- Scanning pattern of critical parameters to monitor (specific to the phase of voyage)
	When	During navigation along the route	
	How	Through cyclic visual scanning of parameters available on the Active Monitoring Display (AMD), with particular attention to those associated with the risks identified during voyage planning. In the case of deviation from normal limits without any apparent reason, the challenge should be carried out in two stages: • Verbalise the value of the parameter that has exceeded its normal limit • Suggest returning within normal limits if the operator in control does not give a reasonable explanation for using the safety margin	
Remote monitoring of the route	Who	Shipping company's operational centre	Practices -- Specific thresholds for "significant" deviations
	When	In real-time	
	How	Through data collection from navigation systems and comparison with planned operational limits. In the case of "significant" and prolonged deviations from the limits of normal operations, the ship should be contacted by the company's control centre using all available means of communication.	

table II–41 : Policies, procedures and practices for monitoring the route

Collision avoidance control			
• Control of ship aspect, speed and positioning must meet international collision regulations (COLREGs). • When navigating in restricted waters characterised by high density traffic, the risk of collision must be prevented by adopting "defensive navigation". • If necessary, the collision avoidance manoeuvre can be outside of normal operational limits by using the available safety margin.			
Defensive navigation	Who	Navigator and Pilot	Practices -- Established minimum distances for specific high density traffic areas
	When	Navigating in restricted waters characterised by high density traffic	
	How	By maintaining minimum distance from all targets, whether or not there is a risk of collision. The defensive manoeuvres must be performed presuming worst case scenarios and by ensuring other close vessels are aware of intended changes of course and/or speed (application of the concept of "see and be seen"). Use of VHF must be considered for preventing potentially dangerous situations, especially when dealing with high relative speeds.	
Assessment of the risk of collision	Who	Navigator and Pilot	Practices -- Guidelines on the combined use of ARPA and AIS tracking features
	When	In all phases of the voyage	
	How	Through the integration of visual and instrumental information from ARPA and AIS relative vectors. During red manning the Navigator filters targets of interest for the Pilot's benefit, who is responsible for controlling collision avoidance manoeuvres.	
Collision avoidance manoeuvre	Who	Navigator during green manning Pilot during red manning	Practices -- Guidelines on the use of ARPA's trial manoeuvre feature
	When	In all phases of the voyage	
	How	The intention to carry out a collision avoidance manoeuvre must be shared between Navigator and Co-navigator (during green manning) and between Navigator and Pilot (during red manning), by stating the desired outcome in terms of CPA and distance from the route. Only after positive confirmation can the Navigator or the Pilot initiate the manoeuvre.	

table II–42 : Policies, procedures and practices for collision avoidance control tasks

Monitoring of ship safety and environmental protection			
• The monitoring of ship safety and environmental protection systems is a responsibility of the Co-navigator.			
• Direct control of ship safety and environmental protection systems is a responsibility of the Engine Control Room.			
Stability monitoring	Who	Co-navigator	Practices
	When	In all phases of the voyage	--
	How	Co-navigator must monitor the limits established before departure by means of the SEM system	Guidelines for stability calculations
Monitoring of watertight doors and fire screen doors	Who	Co-navigator	Practices
	When	Before departure and during navigation	--
	How	Through visualisation of SEM system's dedicated pages. In the event of violations of any planned statuses, the Co-navigator must inform the engine control room via INT-COM	Pre-departure checklist
Monitoring status of discharges	Who	Co-navigator	Practices
	When	At specified distances from nearest land for the discharge of liquid substances in the sea	--
	How	Through visualisation of SEM system's dedicated pages. The Co-navigator must give authorisation to the Engine Control Room via INT-COM for the discharge of liquid substances in the sea.	

table II–43 : Policies, procedures and practices for ship safety and environmental protection monitoring tasks

Ship External Radio Communications			
• The Co-navigator is responsible for external communications regarding Search And Rescue, as well as control of manoeuvres, routes and collision avoidance			
Communications regarding control of manoeuvres and routes	Who	Co-navigator	Practices
	When	As required by Navigator or Pilot	--
	How	Via VHF Radio telephony	Standard phraseology
Collision avoidance communications	Who	Co-navigator	Practices
	When	As required by Navigator or Pilot	--
	How	Via VHF Radio telephony or AIS msg	
Search And Rescue Communications	Who	Co-navigator	Practices
	When	Upon receiving distress signals	--
	How	Through GMDSS	

table II–44 : Policies, procedures and practices for external radio communications

Internal Ship Communications			
• The Co-navigator is responsible for shipboard communications between the bridge and the Engine Control Room, and for the Public Address network			
Communications with the Engine Control Room	Who	Co-navigator	Practices --
	When	When assuming and ceasing red manning, and for changes to the status of propulsion, watertight doors, fire screen doors and outboard discharges	
	How	Through INT-COM speaker during green manning. During red manning the Co-navigator must communicate with the Engine Control Room using hands-free headphones and relaying relevant information to the Navigator and Pilot	
Communications with mooring stations	Who	Co-navigator	Practices --
	When	During manoeuvres	
	How	Through UHF hands-free headphones, using the "closed loop" technique and relaying relevant information to the Navigator and Pilot	
Public Address network communications	Who	Co-navigator	Practices -- Special codes for crew alert
	When	In the event of announcements for crew/passengers or general emergency	
	How	Using the Public Address network	

table II–45 : Policies, procedures and practices for internal communications

Control of Abnormal and Emergency Situations
• The control of abnormal and emergency situations is based on a series of checklists designed to facilitate an initial response and to supply a series of optional measures that depend upon the situation itself.
• The checklists should cover the most common abnormal/emergency situations:

- Adverse weather conditions
- Restricted visibility
- Engineering failures (steering gear, main engines, electrical black-out)
- Ship at anchor with dragging or drifting anchor
- Man overboard
- Fire or explosion on board
- Flooding of watertight compartments

• Abnormal and emergency situations not covered by checklists must be tackled by establishing priorities within the team and by reallocating tasks as deemed necessary.

table II–46 : Policies for abnormal and emergency situations

Operational functions, bridge layout, operator roles, and not least the 4P model all emphasise the complexity of the Bridge Resource Management concept. This complexity, which is dictated by ever increasing production drives and by the on-going reduction of safety margins, requires a cultural revolution within the entire maritime industry.

Tradition and seamanship – so dear to many ship captains – are no longer enough. Mitigating emerging navigation risks in the digital age requires a more sophisticated approach to safety that goes beyond the mere technical ability to manoeuvre a ship. There are many organisational processes to analyse should a company be genuinely committed to making navigation safety the primary defence against large scale accidents.

And it is precisely these principles and organisational processes for an effective implementation of BRM that we will go on to discuss in the third part of this book.

PART III   IMPLEMENTATION

I n this third part we will discuss conditions for implementing the operational concept of Bridge Resource Management, both at an organisational and a regulatory level.

The first chapter will trace the history and evolution of BRM on cruise ships through the stories of some of the key players in its development. Understanding the context in which BRM has been applied up until now will take us to the next step: the adaptation of safety management systems to the risks emerging from human-technology integration. In short, we will review the organisational processes more strictly linked to navigation safety and to an effective implementation of BRM.

In the second chapter we will talk about the international maritime scene to analyse the regulatory context into which BRM must be situated.

The underlining idea is that in order to implement BRM, and more generally to integrate new technologies on ship bridges, it is necessary to lift the level of education and training of seafarers. With this in mind the criteria of minimum standards will be put up for discussion regarding both the competency and working conditions of those who go to sea.

FROM THE SHIP TO THE BOARD OF DIRECTORS

*"Few organisations understand
the true nature of the safety war...
a long guerilla struggle
with no final conclusive victory"*
James Reason

"What is a man that can be expressed as a number?"
E. M. Dougherty

The History of BRM on Cruise Ships

"You think that safety costs a lot? Try an accident!". We can see that David Christie has used this line many times. He smiles and sips his coffee. He is *Carnival Corporation's Senior Vice President for Marine Quality Assurance* and is always very busy, so much so that we have managed to squeeze in an interview during the half hour dedicated to breakfast. We are in Almere, in the Netherlands. Christie arrived only the night before from the United States to see the site where the Corporation's new training centre will be built, and seems satisfied with the new venture that awaits him.

Everything began for him at the age of thirteen when he was sent to a nautical school by his father. Just three years later he embarked as a cadet officer with *P&O*. From that point he worked his way up to become a ship's captain in 1992 with *Princess Cruises,* before being called up in 2002 to assume a management role within the same company.

"During that time, from taking command of a ship to coming ashore, was when I first realised the problems we had", he says.

For him the creation of a safety management system for a corporation as large as Carnival needs to go through many steps: consistent procedures for everyone, the involvement of ship captains, the use of available technologies and in particular, a lot of training. The latter is one of the elements that he believes in most, given that he was the person who advocated for the construction of the largest maritime training centre in the world.

Firstly, we asked when he realised the need to improve officer training.

"It was when I took command of the brand-new *Sea Princess*. I got there when the ship was still in Fincantieri's yards, four days before delivery. The Captain's cabin didn't have a bed or carpet fitted yet, but there was a big cardboard box full of operating manuals. One of my officers took me to see the brand new instruments on the bridge. Nobody had trained me and four days later I signed for the ship and took her out. I spent the next two weeks studying all the manuals, but they weren't very easy to read. I read everything and studied as much as I could manage on my own but I felt that it wasn't enough. And I swore that one day I'd have launched some kind of training initiative for the whole company."

When did the occasion present itself to keep that promise to yourself?

"Beginning in 2006. There had just been two accidents, one of which, the Queen Mary II, had cost 40 million dollars. That's a lot of money for a shipping company. My boss at the time, the CEO of *Princess Cruises*, asked me to investigate what happened and to find a way of preventing such events. It didn't matter how much it cost or how we did it – we had to stop it. I flew to Australia to meet Ravi Nijjer, a world expert on Bridge Resource Management. I asked him how we could prevent navigation accidents and Ravi responded without mincing his words: «how serious are you about safety? If you are serious you must be patient and consistently work at improving safety for an extended period of time».

When I returned home I selected four consultants, including Ravi Nijjer, and sent them on board our ships. In the report of one of them [Hans Hederström – actual Managing Director of *Carnival Corporation*'s Training Centre – Ed.], one paragraph in particular struck me: «the company's operations are very professional in a traditional sense, but the human factors component has to be strengthened. This must be addressed, it is necessary».

Ravi Nijjer and Hans Hederström convinced me to go to Singapore to see how Star Cruises worked [one of the cruise companies more renowned for its safety management – Ed.]. I watched a captain and his officers really putting BRM into practice. It was spectacular. I went straight back to my boss and told him we had to build a training centre similar to Star Cruises with selected instructors and equipped with the same navigation systems as our ships. You cannot depend on nautical schools for this level of training. As recommended by Ravi Nijjer – based on his experience in implementing BRM in Australia – I also told him we had to follow up BRM training with on board guidance by suitable persons.

During that period there was another accident and my boss was convinced that it was necessary to do something as soon as possible. He gave me the green light and as a result CSMART[75] was born here in the Netherlands."

---

[75] Centre for Maritime Simulator Training. www.csmartalmere.com

Why is officer training so necessary today?

"In the past officers learned their trade on board through years and years of experience. The younger members of the crew respected the older ones that had been at sea longer and who knew all there was needed to know. The transfer of knowledge went on with time, observing and learning on the job from the experts. Then when the cruise industry exploded, all of a sudden many officers were promoted very quickly without having gained much experience and without having ever received the training necessary. At the same time the bridges of new ships became more and more sophisticated, with navigation systems integrated into a central cockpit. [Given the gap between officer training and the growing complexity of instruments – Ed.] it's no surprise that still today there is some resistance in using the technology available."

Do you think that nautical schools today really prepare officers to operate modern navigation systems?

"Not always. Take medicine for example, when you want to learn something you go to a hospital where they actually operate and have state-of-the-art equipment. Whereas in maritime schools you rarely see the actual navigation systems you will use on board."

The enhancement of officer training is only one of the elements you have worked on to improve P&O/Princess's safety management. What have been the other measures?

"First and foremost we wrote some formal procedures [BTCC: Bridge Team Command and Control – Ed.] that clearly established officer roles on the bridge. Not only did this introduce the roles of Navigator, Co-navigator and Operations Director, but also closed-loop communication. Then we tried to get the captains on our side, as recommended by Ravi Nijjer. This was a fundamental factor for changing management processes, otherwise it would all have been a waste of time. With their consensus, we built our own training centre where officers could practice on the very navigation systems installed on their ships. In exchange we asked that they also did what we proposed, and a year later [following *Star Cruises'* example – Ed.] we introduced the position of "fleet captain" able both to coach officers on board and to establish a constructive professional relationship with ship captains. From that moment – touch wood – we have not had any more big accidents within the *P&O/Princess* group and our insurance premiums have fallen."

Up to now we have talked about the P&O/Princess group. Do any other companies within the Corporation follow the same safety management processes?

On the bridges of *Carnival Corporation* ships there is now [after the Costa Concordia accident – Ed.] one unique system of BRM procedures that is valid for all the companies: from *Cunard* to *Costa*, from *Princess* to *P&O*, from *Holland America* to *Seaborne*, from *Carnival Cruise Lines* to *Aida* and *Ibero Cruseiro*. We also want the safety management system to be the same for all of the Corporation's ships, which are more than 100. It isn't easy though. Every month we sit down to streamline new policies and procedures that we want to implement. Each company has a long history and it is understandable that it will take some time to embrace the change.

Once we have succeeded in balancing the standards within the Corporation, we will be in a better position to have a positive influence on the rest of the cruise industry."

~

David Christie is yet another example of how a single individual can have a determining role in kick-starting big changes. Another of these is Hans Hederström, ex-Director of *Star Cruises'* training centre and actual Managing Director of CSMART, *Carnival Corporation's* training facility.

240

An Afternoon in Gothenburg

We interview Hans Hederström on a bright summer's day at his house in Gothenburg, Sweden. This is the place where his roots and family are, even if his time and thoughts are increasingly absorbed by the city of Almere, in The Netherlands.

Almere is where CSMART – *Carnival Corporation*'s training centre – has been active since 2009, with Hans Hederström as Managing Director. After all he himself has been saying for years that the maritime world is in dire need of change, of higher training standards and procedures in order to improve teamwork and implement Bridge Resource Management.

Hans has a calm voice and a gentlemanly manner, yet he has always been a revolutionary in his own way. He began his career in the Swedish Merchant Navy, and he was a pilot for the Port of Gothenburg before being appointed Director of the *Star Cruises'* training centre in Malaysia.

His present challenge is in building the new CSMART, a 50 million dollar project that will give life to the largest maritime training centre in the world. An ambitious project for a corporation whose officers (coming from many companies that have been absorbed through the years) are still missing a uniform level of competence. Nevertheless Hans Hederström – who has been committed to professional development right from his early piloting days – has a very clear idea of the problems existing in the maritime world and of possible solutions to improve them.

We asked him why the number of navigation accidents has increased over the last few years.

"I think the answer lies in the fact that navigation is not taken seriously enough: there is not enough preparation, communication is not as effective as it should be and all available resources are not managed properly."

At this present moment, what are the priorities to address that would make bridge operations safer?

"Above all it's the planning, which affects everything else when inadequate. When it is good however, we need to pass on to the next level: to share the plan with all persons involved, or at least be certain that they understand it. It's an important step because it puts the entire team in the situation of being able to intervene if something happens. In fact planning must include clear operational limits, which should be emphasised during briefings. So if limits are exceeded, any officer is ready to speak up without reserve. On the other hand if limits are not clear, a third officer wouldn't dare contradict a captain. Moreover, route and manoeuvre planning should be agreed upon with pilot organisations. The differences between planning by the ship's crew and that done by an external Pilot cannot be resolved in the short time frame he/she is on board."

Do you believe that there is a key to preventing accidents?

"We need to aim towards better planning that is shared by all officers and the Pilot. Furthermore the tasks and roles on a bridge must be more clearly defined. The leader should guide the others and not operate directly. I think this is the key to preventing navigational accidents at an operational level. Obviously good company management processes are needed to support this."

The clear definition of roles on a bridge is one of the fundamental aspects of Bridge Resource Management. As far back as 1993, you launched the first training course on this operational concept. How would you define BRM and can you tell us about how it was conceived?

"BRM is the correct use of all available resources on a ship's bridge, both technical and non-technical. It was conceived in the early 1990s when I was still a pilot for the Port of Gothenburg. I understood its importance in 1990 when I was invited to attend a *Cockpit Resource Management* (CRM) course at the Scandinavian Airlines' (SAS) Flight Academy by Eric Wahren. At the time Wahren was working at the Academy and he was trying to interest the maritime industry in CRM. Eventually he managed to gather seven maritime organisations to sponsor the transfer of that knowledge. He formed a working group which I became member of together with eight other mariners, including Captain Kari Larjo. Our task was to convert the CRM course into a course fit for deck officer's needs. The first BRM programme was launched in May 1993 and attracted a lot of interest from many parts of the world. In 1995, after an invitation from Ravi Nijjer on behalf of the Australian shipping industry, I also travelled to Melbourne, Sydney and Brisbane to conduct three BRM seminars and six courses. At the time we really thought that Bridge Resource Management would have been the solution for all the problems that we had."

What are the limitations of BRM?

"I think that BRM cannot be put into practice without looking at the whole picture. It must be integrated with management processes and operating procedures. I also believe that a BRM course has a limited impact if what has been learnt is not then applied on board by coaching the Captains for its implementation."

Do you remember any episode during the early times of BRM?

"Yes, one in particular. Once a shipping company heard about the course and sent us their most difficult man. He was an old captain, profoundly autocratic and anchored to tradition, who had quite a serious accident when his ship ran aground. On the second day when we talked about short-term strategies to improve the decision-making process, the captain burst out, red in the face. «This is all absolute nonsense», he said. «When I have a problem, I make a plan and I put it forward to my officers asking what they think. Why should I ask them before coming up with my plan?» He just couldn't understand it. It took me twenty minutes to explain it to him, but I'm not sure that I convinced him in the end."

How can a company implement BRM if it has never done so before?

"Firstly there is the need to observe and analyse bridge operations, and verify existing procedures. In most cases these procedures need to be rewritten together with a group of captains in order to make them part of the process. These captains, either before or after the review, must receive specific training on all aspects of BRM. Ideally it would be good to gather all captains to discuss the changes and gain consensus. Experts must comprehend and agree upon the need for change, otherwise in the end new procedures will not be successful."

Are captains usually in favour of changes?

"Normally only a minority are in favour, because they are already aware of the need to change. We call them "champions". The majority of captains sit and wait, whilst only a minority is evidently against it. In these cases we need to select those in favour and help them convince and influence the undecided. So if you succeed in getting the majority on your side, the more hostile will also surrender in the end."

What needs to be done once captains are convinced and the procedures have been rewritten?

"At that point we need to consolidate training with follow-ups on board ships. In the beginning the instructors are those who monitor that all proceeds as it should, but in the long-term this activity must be carried out by a captain, perhaps one chosen from those that were initially in favour of changes. This particular captain must then receive special training to learn how to teach, coach and supervise the others. When ready, he must then visit all the other captains at least once a year to help them apply the new procedures. You can experience a lot of realism in simulators, but real learning occurs on board a ship under the supervision of an expert. Even more so, the ideal aim would be to transform all captains into mentors, experts able to inspire his or her own officers and make them develop professionally."

This approach nevertheless, has not been followed by many companies. Is it true that BRM often only exists on paper?

"It's true yes, companies often send officers on BRM courses, but afterwards they don't worry about implementing it on board. There are also positive cases, though. For example *Star Cruises* was one of the first companies to really understand BRM and put it into practice, thanks also to a series of visionary captains."

Are there any economic advantages that could encourage a company to adopt BRM?

"It is impossible to quantify the impact of accidents that have not occurred. What you can do is to look for trends over a ten year period and compare them with those of other companies operating in the same sector."

If we talk instead about deck officers on board ships, what is their general level of competence?

"It varies a lot, even between officers that come from the same country. Their most common limit however is in the use of bridge equipment. Also some gaps exist in the ability to fit into the team, which for example can arise in too low assertiveness towards a superior. In the *Star Cruises* simulator we tried to change this behaviour through training. I do remember one episode in particular with an officer who was especially submissive. We gave him the position of navigator and we put a captain next to him as co-navigator. During the exercise we got to a point where he didn't turn when he should have. «Did you not know that you should have turned?», we asked. «Yes», he replied. «So why didn't you?». «Because the Captain didn't say anything», he retorted. We had to repeat the same exercise three times before he understood, but in the end he managed it. This demonstrates that behavioural problems can be corrected with training."

Nowadays officer training is very different from the past. When you began sailing, what did your training consist of?

"I had my first command in 1978 and I also began my career as pilot in the same year. Training was only on the job, not in simulators."

Lately there is much talk about training and assessment, and whether the two things go together or whether they should be considered separate entities as is done in aviation. What is your opinion on this?

"I think that in combining them both, the fear of making errors and maybe even losing a job would compromise the training's effectiveness. Of course we need some sort of evaluation during training, but it should only be on course objectives and not on the overall competence of an officer. The overall assessment must be done separately with dedicated sessions in different scenarios, possibly with an examiner different to the instructor."

How is it possible to demonstrate the effectiveness of training for the purpose of improving safety?

"It must be understood that safety is affected by the interaction between human, technical and organisational elements. Therefore officers must have a thorough understanding of bridge equipment as well as human performance and limitations. There must be also an effective bridge organisation that promotes teamwork. Once these three elements are firmly established, it is possible to achieve higher levels of safety. This can be demonstrated in a simulator when trained officers manage to cope with abnormal and emergency scenarios successfully."

At the moment Carnival Corporation is building a new training centre. What is your vision?

"First of all I want to continue to provide top quality maritime training for all deck and engineering officers. We should also aim to increase the amount of time officers spend training together with maritime pilots. For instance, when planning a call to a challenging port for the first time, the bridge team and the pilots should spend a few days together in a Full Mission Bridge Simulator to determine operational limits. At CSMART we already do this over weekends, but I would like to see more of it when we have more capacity in the new facility. I believe that this kind of familiarisation – combined with feasibility studies – can bring about a significant positive impact on the safety of bridge operations under pilotage."

For the third time you are involved in starting up a new maritime simulator. What are the most important aspects to be taken into account?

Building a successful simulator training facility is not only a matter of money. You need the right people. I would say that there are two critical factors to be taken into account. First of all you must have instructors that are passionate about helping other people to develop their skills. An inadequate instructor can ruin a course and damage the reputation of the most sophisticated training centre. Secondly, you need skilled technicians in order to minimise training downtime and to keep the simulator equipment up to date.

Can a corporation like Carnival also play a role in lifting the competency level of officers in other sectors of the maritime industry?

"Yes, a large corporation like Carnival can certainly pave the way. A little like what happened to us in the beginning, when we applied our experience from *Star Cruises*. When large companies change, others are going to look in the same direction. And let's hope that this contributes to a general decrease in the number of navigational accidents, and above all, to the prevention of catastrophic ones."

The Safety Management System

"**T**he main aim of a safety management system is to reduce the risk of a large-scale accident". This statement comes from Ravi Nijjer, who, apart from being one of the most accomplished experts of BRM, is also a leading figure for maritime pilotage in Australia. He is convinced that the international code for maritime safety management, known as the *ISM Code,* has limited application on a moving ship operating in a dynamic environment. He says that maritime transport accidents are of the *Low Probability/High Consequence* type[76] which makes it very difficult to acquire safety information at operational level.

To overcome the deficiencies in the ISM code approach, Ravi Nijjer developed safety management systems for pilotage from first principles after extensive research, which was validated by the *Australian Maritime Safety Authority* and the *Australian Transport Safety Bureau.*

The ISM Code, conceived during the 1990s in response to a series of tragic accidents[77] is based on an approach typical to industrial quality management systems. These are mainly oriented towards the prevention of workplace injuries, rather than to mitigating the risk of large scale accidents in an operational environment that is as varied and uncertain as a navigating ship.

According to Ravi Nijjer, managing the dynamic risks of marine navigation requires the understanding of the safety principles devised for high-risk industrial plants, such as nuclear or chemical facilities. He says that the concept of *proactive safety management* was actually introduced in the 1950s as a direct response to the needs of the first nuclear power plants. Given the little experience that competent authorities had in overseeing the safety of this new sector, the principle of self-regulation was introduced. This was very different from prescriptive safety legislation that was imposed in other industries at the time. Following catastrophic accidents in the 1970s and 1980s, this principle was also extended to include the chemical and off-shore industry[78].

---

76 Quoting a 2012 report from the Australian Transport Safety Bureau (ATSB) on the effectiveness of Safety Management Systems, Ravi Nijjer illustrates that managing the risks of workplace injuries (typical of industrial production plants) presents very different challenges from those faced to mitigate the risks of Low Probability High Consequence accidents.

77 On 6th March 1987, the ferry "Herald of Free Enterprise" capsized and sank in the North Sea, causing the death of 193 passengers and crew. Three years later, on 7th April 1990, a fire broke out on the passenger liner "Scandinavian Star", killing 158 people.

78 On 10th July 1976 an explosion occurred in a chemical manufacturing plant located in Seveso, north of Milan (Italy). More than 100,000 people were exposed to a massive toxic cloud. As a

Adopting self-regulating Safety Management Systems forced significant changes not only within organisations, but also within the regulating bodies. These authorities were transformed from mere inspectors who checked compliance with prescriptive safety legislation, into assessors for the effectiveness of the specific Safety Management System created by the organisation.

This type of assessment is not an easy task and it is not carried out in the maritime industry, which is characterised by a compliance culture. Authorities often limit themselves to controlling the existence of procedures required by the ISM Code, without thoroughly evaluating their quality and effectiveness. It was actually the Costa Concordia accident that brought the limits of this approach to light: the ship was operating under a Safety Management System which was formally compliant to international requirements, but inadequate for the prevention of a large scale accident.

However, accidents such as those occurred to the Titanic and the Costa Concordia happen once in a hundred years. Nevertheless, how can we evaluate the effectiveness of a Safety Management System in the context of marine navigation, which is characterised by an extreme variability and by low probability/high consequences events?

The key is a proactive approach, rather than a mere reactive one. James Reason[79] believes that the error committed by most organisations is adopting safety measures in the wake of past accidents, or even to consider systemic defences as sufficient when no accidents have occurred.

We can just imagine every company coming to grips with safety management as if it were enclosed in a so-called *safety space*. This imaginary area has two extremes: one represents the zone of maximum resistance and the other that of greater vulnerability to the risk of accidents. The position within the safety space that an organisation assumes over time is determined by the ability (or inability) to identify and mitigate specific operational risks. This ability is also a way to build resilience into the system. It is not easy however to understand where this position is, especially in operational environments characterised by a low frequency of accidents and by high variability.

---

consequence of the disaster the European Union issued the Seveso Directive, a new system of industrial safety regulation. Twelve years later, on 6th July 1988, the off-shore platform Piper Alpha, in the North Sea oil field, was engulfed in a fire that cost the lives of 167 people. A public enquiry chaired by the Scottish judge William Cullen included several recommendations that led to the adoption of the Offshore Installations (Safety Case) Regulations 1992.

79 James Reason (1997): "Managing the Risks of Organizational Accidents". Ashgate.

Reason explains that the concept of absolute safety does not exist: as long as there are natural dangers, human fallibility and latent conditions, even the most resistant of companies could suffer a catastrophic accident. Nevertheless it is the organisation's responsibility to do all that is possible – within the limits of available resources – to manage safety by applying available knowledge in the field of risk management.

In the wake of a serious accident a company usually increases its investments in safety, under pressure from internal forces, public opinion and the competent authorities. Using the safety space metaphor, we can see this company "navigating" towards the extreme of maximum resistance. Management shifts its attention temporarily from production to protection. But as time goes on, bolstered by the absence of significant accidents for prolonged periods, initiatives and programmes aimed at improving safety are scaled down and lose their vigour. Management once again shift their focus on production and the company slowly drifts towards the vulnerability zone of the safety space.

So effective safety management means not only reaching the zone of maximum resistance, but above all maintaining this level through time. In order to do this it is necessary to adopt:

- reactive safety measures, based on errors and latent conditions that emerge from the analysis of accidents;
- proactive measures, based on data collected regularly within the organisation and through independent reviews. Information regarding "near miss" events is particularly valuable for this purpose.

Safety managers should therefore collect information regularly both on what happens on ship bridges and on the organisational processes that have a greater impact on the safety of navigation. Some of these processes are listed in table III–1.

Bridge operations	*Identification and assessment of specific risks*
	Definition of operating procedures and good practices
	Monitoring of operating procedures and good practices
	Remote monitoring of voyage execution
Human Resource Management	*Recruitment*
	Training
	Competency assessment
	Professional development

table III–1 : Organisational processes linked to navigational safety

The basis of all these processes must be a *safety culture*[80], which according to Reason stems from the following elements:

- participation of personnel at an operational level in controlling the Safety Management System, reporting near misses and other significant events;
- definition of a clear dividing line between acceptable and unacceptable behaviours;
- achievement of a balance between operator discretion and operational standardisation;
- continuous improvement of the Safety Management System on the basis of information reported by operators and on lessons learnt from accidents and/or near misses.

A safety culture is one where information is reported without fear of being blamed, where there is flexibility, fairness and continuous learning. Although it seems utopian to aspire towards a totally "just culture" within a company, we can at least aim towards a situation where the majority of personnel believe a certain level of fairness is usually guaranteed. To achieve this though, we need to establish the two fundamental points of a just culture:

- it is unacceptable to punish errors without taking into account the latent conditions and the circumstances under which they are committed;
- it is equally unacceptable to guarantee immunity to errors caused by negligence that could produce or have already produced negative consequences.

These fundamental points are an invitation to caution, a warning to not point the finger at operators before having verified the circumstances and the latent conditions that may have induced their errors. And still, especially after a large scale accident, we often slide into the culture of blame, as demonstrated by the statement issued by the CEO of *Costa Crociere* on 16th January 2012, just a few days after the disaster[81].

"[...] We cannot, unfortunately, deny human error [...]. The company cannot be associated with this behaviour. The Captain took a decision on his own which is contrary to our written and certified rules [...]. This route was set correctly upon departure from Civitavecchia. The fact [that the ship

---

80 The concept of safety culture was first introduced following the Chernobyl nuclear disaster in 1986.

81 This declaration can be heard on the Telegraph.co.uk's YouTube Channel under the title: "Costa Concordia owner blames Captain for capsizing."

deviated from this route – Ed.] is solely due to a non-approved and unauthorised manoeuvre and which Costa Crociere was not made aware of. The procedures implemented after the ship hit the rock did not respect in any way the strict rules, procedures and training we have given our officers."

In 1984, the sociologist Charles Perrow[82] already asserted that in an error-inducing system the tendency to blame operators is particularly prominent. The maritime industry is one of these systems and to get past the blame culture it should target a systemic reconfiguration and not limit itself to acting exclusively on single elements.

Perrow also highlights that the responsibility of maritime accidents is primarily attributed to low status, unorganised seamen. Up until a few years ago investigations were seldom conducted to uncover the latent conditions associated with the causes of an accident.

During the last decade though, things have also changed from a legal perspective due to a public opinion that is less and less inclined to accept the consequences of catastrophic accidents. As a result the concept of *due diligence*[83] – that makes organisations accountable for putting all the protective measures that are reasonably possible into place – is becoming more widespread. Predominantly in the event of pollution and the loss of human life, the shipping company must demonstrate its *due diligence* through a Safety Management System that is:

- founded on available knowledge in the field of safety, navigational techniques and human factors;
- aimed at both the reactive and proactive mitigation of the most critical risks;
- relevant not only to bridge operations, but to all organisational processes more directly linked to navigational safety (table III–1).

If all legal courts were to adopt this approach, minimum compliance with international legislation established by IMO would not be enough to limit the liability of a shipping company in the aftermath of a catastrophic accident. In a scenario such as this, the company would find itself having to demonstrate not only the effectiveness of its operating procedures, but also of the organisational processes linked to navigational safety.

---

82 Charles Perrow (1984): "Normal Accidents. Living with High-Risk Technologies". Princeton University Press.

83 The expression "due diligence" comes from the Latin term "debita diligentia", which means "with the diligence necessary for the specific case".

Organisational Processes

Identification and Assessment of Specific Risks

At the root of a maritime Safety Management System lies the analysis of the specific risks associated with the conduct of navigation. In itself it is a delicate process: risks change according to the context and because of their extreme variability in space and time they need to be specifically assessed for every operational scenario.

The word "risk" comes from the medieval Latin *riscus* which literally means *rock or cliff above the sea's surface,* hence the figurative sense of "hazard" for ships. Its concept became more complex and articulated during the era of great geographical exploration, when vast profits from the global shipping business had to be balanced by potential losses caused by pirates or navigational accidents. It is not by chance then that the first modern insurance company was founded in 1688 by merchants, shipowners and financiers at the historic *Lloyd's Coffee Shop* in London in response to the growing demand of protection against the dangers of maritime navigation. During the last few decades the world of finance has changed the concept of risk by including not only possible negative oscillations of returns compared to expectations, but positive ones as well.

Since some form of risk is present in all human activity, it is no surprise that there are multiple definitions of the term, each one depending on the context that is being analysed.

In the field of industrial or transport safety, the concept of risk is commonly associated with the potential that an action, a decision or an event causes losses or undesirable situations. In this light the level of risk is often defined as the product between the probability that an undesirable event will occur and the severity of the losses that could derive from it.

Nowadays the perception that the level of risk is quantifiable (in as much as any other productive process) is widespread, but the belief of being able to measure it is a mere illusion. With this in mind, a Safety Management System should be based primarily on the identification and assessment of risks perceived as critical for preventing large scale accidents. If we take cruise ships as an example, large scale accidents should be associated with the risk of fires on board, as well as with the risk of navigational accidents such as collisions, groundings and excessive heeling.

However the discipline in the conduct of navigation is not always perceived by the board of directors as the primary defence against large scale accidents. To this end, Peter Listrup remembers the positive example of *Star Cruises* during the years in which he directed the company's training centre. He says that the management considered the conduct of navigation as the most important defence against large scale accidents.

We can therefore assert that the identification and assessment of specific navigational risks requires an awareness from the board of directors regarding the importance that this holds for the true effectiveness of a Safety Management System.

Secondly, according to Ravi Nijjer, it is necessary:

- to listen to experts' opinions in the specific operating environment (e.g. port pilots, captains with experience on the type of ship, local authorities, etc.);
- to analyse accidents and near misses that have occurred not only to the company itself, but also companies in similar operational contexts to that being evaluated. This is a remedy for compensating the lack of a representative sample of events for assessing risks of a specific operational scenario;
- to consider emerging good practices from outside the company itself;
- to observe normal (everyday) operations in order to identify both latent conditions associated with the most frequent human errors and emerging good practices devised by bridge teams.

This last point also constitutes a foundation for the process of defining and monitoring operating procedures.

Defining Operating Procedures and Practices

In the chapter dedicated to Bridge Resource Management we have already described the so-called 4Ps: principles, policies, procedures and practices. We will now discuss what we need to do when a company's procedures and operating practices need to be defined or reviewed.

First of all from an organisational point of view, it is essential that we understand the importance of letting captains and officers actively participate in the process.

As Hans Hederström already mentioned in his interview, firstly we need to select the "champions", a restricted number of captains that know company operations very well and are convinced of the need for better procedures. This elite must be updated on the latest developments in the field of safety management at both organisational and operational levels.

Ship captains are in fact the key link between principles and policies established by management and bridge operations. They have a critical role in the correct transmission of the principles and policies which operating procedures and practices are based on.

The champions must also be trained as instructors, or more appropriately, as mentors. A mentor is capable not only of transferring knowledge and experience, but also of inspiring and preparing younger officers to assume ever increasing responsibilities. These abilities are innate in some captains, but it is a good idea to validate and improve them with specific courses given by specialists in the field.

Once trained, these champions should be sent on board to observe bridge operations on a substantial number of company ships. The significance of their reports depends not only on the number of ships visited, but also on the quantity and variety of operational scenarios observed.

Reports written by the task force during this cycle of initial observations must list:

- evident inconsistencies between existing procedures and informal practices;
- informal practices considered incorrect;
- informal practices considered correct, to be evaluated for possible conversion into procedures.

Once this first phase has terminated, the reports written by the champions must be analysed in the presence of company managers. The aim of this analysis is to produce an initial draft of new operating procedures and practices.

If necessary, policies and principles can also be reviewed. The draft must be tested both on board a sample ship and in a simulator.

After completing all required revisions of the initial draft, the company can issue the first consolidated version of BRM procedures and practices to be rolled out on board. Motivations and results from the experimental phase must be presented to all captains, who in turn will explain them to their officers.

Nevertheless, if BRM is a totally new concept for the company, the actual implementation of procedures must be preceded by an intensive training programme in a simulator for all deck officers.

Monitoring of Operating Procedures and Specific Practices

Once new procedures are implemented there is a need to focus on their monitoring.

In 2012 *Carnival Corporation*, in cooperation with the *Australian Maritime College*, experimented with a methodology for the systematic observation of normal operations on a ship's bridge.

This approach, named MOSA (*Maritime Operation Safety Analysis*) after civil aviation's LOSA[84] (*Line Operation Safety Audit*) aims to monitor the so-called *practical drift*[85]. This consists of the gap between informal practices (what is actually done aboard) and operating procedures (what the company believes ought to be done).

The company must recognise the possibility that informal practices are the result of various factors such as:

- the failure of formal procedures and practices to respond to the real needs of deck officers engaged in managing the inevitable conflict between productivity (take the ship to its destination in the allotted time) and protection (managing the specific risks of dynamic environments);
- officers' growing faith in informal practices as a result of their proven experience and effectiveness over time. This faith appeals to the innate tendency of human beings to create future expectations on the basis of past events, without considering extreme cases able to disprove practices that have guaranteed a long series of successes;
- negligence due to lack of motivation or loose behavioural patterns that are not ideal for an operational environment such as a ship's bridge, which requires discipline.

The company must always be ready to admit the need to modify procedures if they are inadequate to actual operational needs. At the same time it must also rectify informal practices considered incorrect with regards to the assessment of specific risks.

Once an informal practice has been verified as correct, we also need to be certain that it is efficient from an operational standpoint. This is an important aspect given that the main objective of a shipping company, just like that of an industrial chemical plant, is not as much its safety as its capability to generate profit.

---

84 ICAO (2002): "Line Operations Safety Audit". Document 9803.
85 Sydney Dekker (2010): "The Field Guide to Understanding Human Error". Ashgate.

It is fundamental officers understand that the observation of normal operations is not aimed at assessing their performance, but at analysing the adequacy of procedures and of emerging informal practices.

Therefore they must not change their usual behaviour in any way whatsoever. The validity of the information collected would actually be compromised by so-called "angel behaviour", i.e. adhering to formal procedures and practices during the observation period only. For this reason officers must be reassured that some of their informal practices could be considered safe and efficient.

To minimise angel behaviour, the supervisors of a MOSA programme at organisational level must work to build a relationship of reciprocal trust with bridge teams.

The arrival of MOSA observers on board must be announced beforehand by senior management through a letter that guarantees anonymity of the information collected.

MOSA observers must be captains or instructors from the same company, trained especially for acquiring this information on board. Furthermore MOSA observations must be standardised in order to make it possible to analyse information collected by different observers consistently.

Table III–2 and table III–3 show an example of a MOSA form based on our BRM's operational functions (tables II-28 and II-29) and the evaluation of operator tasks according to a scale of four values:

- "A": correct execution, fully compliant with formal procedures and practices;
- "B": correct execution, in the absence of (or in partial accordance with) formal procedures and practices;
- "C": incorrect execution, in the absence of (or in partial accordance with) formal procedures and practices;
- "D": incorrect execution that does not comply with formal procedures and/or practices.

| Observer: |
| Location: |
| Phase of Voyage: |

The execution of a task is considered correct when it respects BRM policies and demonstrates an appropriate risk assessment by the operator

Operating Function	Task	Operator roles	Manning level Green	Red
Manoeuvre planning	Verification of planned manoeuvre	Master		
Route planning	Verification of planned route	Master		
Manoeuvre control	Pre-departure preparation	Navigator		N/A
	Pre-arrival preparation	Navigator		N/A
	Team briefing	Pilot	N/A	
	Control of operational limits	Pilot	N/A	
	Cooperation	Pilot		
	Changeover between cockpits	Pilot	N/A	
Manoeuvre monitoring	Active monitoring and challenge deviations from planned limits	All team members	N/A	
	Team de-briefing	Captain		N/A
Route control	Control of operational limits	Nav & Pilot	N/A	
	Takeover of the watch	Co-navigator		
	Master-Pilot exchange	Pilot		
Route monitoring	Active monitoring and challenge deviations from planned limits	All team members		
Collision avoidance control	Defensive navigation	Nav & Pilot		
	Collision risk assessment	Nav & Pilot		
	Collision avoidance manoeuvre	Nav or Pilot		
Monitoring of ship safety and environmental protection	Stability monitoring	Co-navigator		
	Monitoring of watertight doors and fire screen doors	Co-navigator		
	Monitoring status of discharges	Co-navigator		
External ship radio communications	Communications regarding route and manoeuvres	Co-navigator		
	Collision avoidance communications	Co-navigator		
	SAR communications	Co-navigator		
Internal ship communications	Communication with the Engine Control Room	Co-navigator		
	Communication with mooring stations	Co-navigator		
	Public Address network communications	Co-navigator		

table III–2 : MOSA form for routine operations (FRONT)

mosA MARITIME OPERATION SAFETY ANALYSIS	*Observer:* *Location:* *Phase of voyage:*		
Narrative *(state the circumstances that led to exceeding operational limits and the use of safety margins)*		*Manning level*	
		Green	*Red*
Conclusions *(summarise positive elements and opportunities for improvement)*			

table III–3 : MOSA form for abnormal and emergency situations (BACK)

Observers must be trained in using the same criteria during evaluation so that their observations are comparable. This uniformity can be obtained by means of a simulated scenario, during which many evaluations of the same bridge team are compared and eventual differences in judgement are discussed with the help of a moderator. Training can only be considered complete when observer evaluations become similar.

At this stage data collection on board should begin. Observers ought to stay on each vessel for at least five days, of which the first two must be spent building a relationship of trust with officers and not used to fill in any MOSA form at all. It has actually been noted that officers behave in a natural way only once they become accustomed to the presence of an observer on the bridge. From the third day onwards official observations can commence, distributed between arrivals, departures and navigation in green manning.

The observation's narrative is particularly important for the data analysis that follows. The analysis involves preliminary quality control of data collected on board. This stage falls under the responsibility of a coordinator nominated by the company for the entire duration of the MOSA programme. The coordinator and the observers meet to review and discuss all of the forms.

Once this has been completed the coordinator can initiate the data analysis stage, which is aimed at highlighting peaks in correct performances (rated as "B") and those incorrect (rated as "C" and "D"). Each of these peaks can be associated to possible provisions such as:

- the creation or revision of operating procedures and/or specific practices;
- the introduction of operational scenarios in training programmes for tackling the most critical incorrect performances.

Lastly, the final report must be discussed with those responsible for operating procedures and training, who must evaluate suggested recommendations. If approved, the provisions resulting from the MOSA programme must be communicated to all of the company's captains and officers.

In extreme synthesis, the stages of a MOSA programme are as follows:

- selection of observers;
- training of observers;
- information campaign regarding the objectives of the MOSA programme for all captains and officers;

- data collection on a significant number of vessels and operational scenarios;
- quality control of the data collected by the observers;
- data analysis and drafting of the final report with recommendations on the possible revision of procedures and/or training programmes;
- evaluation and implementation of provisions at organisational level;
- information campaign on new provisions adopted upon the MOSA programme's completion.

For a shipping company, starting up a MOSA programme is a little like taking a medical examination capable of:

- identifying problems that are otherwise invisible,
- and tackling them to prevent their negative effects.

For this reason it is a good idea to undertake regular "check-ups" and to repeat the MOSA programme through time. The frequency depends on many different factors and not only on the eventual absence of accidents. Essentially it shouldn't be forgotten that an effective Safety Management System must be proactive. The absence of visible symptoms (accidents and near misses) is not always an indication of good health.

Remote Monitoring of Voyage Execution

As well as navigation techniques, technological progress is also modifying the way in which we analyse information relating to safety management.

David Christie knows what this means. He gives the example of the remote monitoring of Carnival's cruise ships by means of data collected from their navigation systems.

"It's actually an electronic monitoring of navigational data inspired by civil aviation's FOQA [*Flight Operation Quality Assurance* – Ed.]", he explains. "It consists of the real-time acquisition of navigational data from each of the fleet's ships. The idea is that when a vessel exceeds the planned operational limits, it triggers an alert directed to a dedicated control centre and to those responsible for navigation safety at organisational level."

Systems such as these make it so that a ship can be monitored constantly from land. Yet Christie underlines the fact that the programme has not been set up to spy on officers, but rather to help them.

"First impressions of trials carried out on *Princess Cruises* ships seem to have been positive, even though there is still a lot of work to be done. I myself have received an alert message at three in the morning and I couldn't get back to sleep until the following morning, when I contacted the ship to discuss what had happened. I hate the word *audit*, but officers must understand that operational criticalities should not be hidden anymore. In civil aviation the FOQA is accepted by pilots because companies have been using it for thirty years. For the most part of the maritime world though, it's a complete novelty."

The analysis of data acquired by a remote monitoring system could also contribute in optimising fuel consumption, which isn't a result that should be taken lightly. Fuel prices can represent double any other ship cost, including staff salaries, port services and insurance.

"Fuel consumption is directly proportional to the speed cubed. If most of our fleet's ships slowed down their average speed without ever going over 17 knots, we'd save hundreds of millions", says David Christie. "We're talking about huge sums of money: fuel costs just for *Princess Cruises* are hundreds of millions dollars a year. Besides, if ships went slower navigation safety would certainly benefit from it."

In spite of the unquestionable advantages mentioned by David Christie, the adoption of a remote monitoring system does not go without risks. The greatest one is that triggering alert signals for exceeding operational limits can influence the effectiveness of decisions made on a ship's bridge. For example, a decision made in order to avoid a collision may be delayed as it implies exceeding the planned Track Limit. The same could happen with a speed variation that is not economical on fuel, yet effective from a safety point of view.

So how can we avoid the problem of officers perceiving a remote monitoring system as a threat to operational flexibility, something which is so often needed to guarantee navigation safety?

One possible way could be a campaign of awareness and a training programme on two of BRM's fundamental principles:

- the discipline of controlling a ship within planned operational limits in normal situations;
- the flexibility in using safety margins when abnormal or emergency situations require.

It should be clear to all, both on the bridge and in the control centre ashore, that exceeding "normal limits" is not always a marker of negative performance. On the contrary, it is for this exact reason – the ability to make decisions in volatile situations – that humans are still present on a ship's bridge or in an aircraft's cockpit. Therefore it's desirable that officers act with discretion in using safety margins as soon as they deem it necessary, without any external influence. It is important that whoever decides to do so shares his intentions and reasons with the other members of the team.

In conclusion, establishing thresholds for the generation of alert signals without considering different perceptions that exist at various company levels, could actually render a remote monitoring system counter-productive for navigational safety.

Recruitment

The criteria for recruiting ship's crew are traditionally based on the qualifications required by IMO's STCW Convention. Only a handful of companies – such as *Star Cruises* and a few within the *Carnival Corporation* – subject candidates to psychometric tests calibrated for profiles that are specific to the responsibilities of the roles in question.

The selection of candidates can be done in many different ways, with levels of quality and associated costs being very variable. In some cases it is advisable to perform a preliminary selection with much more generic criteria.

Usually a psychometric test aims to shed light on a candidate's attitude, mindset, organisational skills, intellectual level, motivation and not least the ability to cope in stressful situations. Resistance to stress in itself can be the theme of a specific test to assess adaptability and self-control that can limit the number of errors committed under pressure.

A universal psychological profile for each BRM role does not exist and the same goes for an ideal captain. Therefore there is a need to establish a specific profile adapted to the principles, the policies, the traditions and the nationality of each company. Qualities that are perceived as important in one company can in fact be irrelevant in another.

Examples of specific criteria used for the selection of candidates in the role of Master[86] is shown below. The main categories concern:

- *personality features linked to safety*: the ideal candidate must possess a fair perception of his/her own capabilities and limits, a good balance between caution and risk exposure, rooted within a marked critical thinking. Furthermore it is necessary to have a high

---

86 Bengt Schager (1997). "Advantages of Psychological Assessment Prior to Employment and Promotion". Marine Profile ab.

tolerance to stress and emotional stability both in normal conditions and under pressure;

- *leadership*: the ideal candidate must possess outstanding communication skills together with a willingness to share experiences with others. A master must be able to evaluate the potential and limitations of colleagues demonstrating impartiality and approachability, whilst at the same time asserting his/her role. A master must be loyal in accepting responsibility, capable of inspiring others and genuinely enthusiastic to spend energy on tasks as well as people;
- other personality features: good intellectual capacity, creativity and flexibility together with a distinct aptitude for his/her own professional development.

Selecting candidates whose profiles meet the criteria mentioned above can prove very difficult. However it is equally difficult to change the attitudes of officers with many years of experience.

One solution that meets the needs of a constant flow of personnel coherent to company values is the creation of a "breeding ground" for deck cadets. The concept comes from the world of football and in Spain it finds its finest application. The word *cantera* – literally meaning "quarry" in Spanish – is used to describe out-and-out youth academies where teenagers receive a regular school education and play football.

At the moment one of the most famous of these is Barcelona's. The children are taught to play with the same tactics and formation as the first team, so that when one of the youngsters makes it through the ranks the adaptation required is minimal. Greats such as Andrès Iniesta and Lionel Messi are both products of the Catalan *Cantera*.

Creating a breeding ground for deck cadets could be a long-term solution to form officers who are able to adapt to company BRM principles with little effort. In doing so these principles would be embedded within basic nautical training. In concrete terms, a training centre for young cadets should be developed in tandem with that used for officers already working on board.

Certainly it would require a considerable investment that only large companies and corporations like *Carnival* can afford. Nevertheless such a long term solution could turn into a driving force and a source of inspiration for the rest of the maritime industry, even in the mid-term.

Training

"There is no school for becoming a captain, it just happens", says Captain Larjo with a pinch of bitterness when commenting on the industry's traditional approach towards training.

The job of a seafarer is something that is learnt in the field, hoping that errors committed do not cause accidents. Once, the margin of error for learning was ample. Nowadays this is no longer the case due to ships ever increasing in size. A bridge organised according to BRM principles is now essential but it requires much more operator training than the minimum requirements set out by the STCW International Convention.

The first thing to do is to abandon the idea that attending a course is enough to become competent. Realistically a course is just the starting point for developing the experience required for the role to cover once on board. After a certain period of time necessary to consolidate the practices learnt, a competency assessment independent from training would then be needed.

Nowadays experience can be gained on board as well as in simulation centres that are becoming ever closer to reality. Time has passed since the first maritime simulators were introduced, when trainees had just a radar image to use and the rest was left to the imagination.

From that time technology has developed so much that we are now able to create environments that really do resemble the bridges of a number of ships. The image projected on the screen can reproduce ports and fairways down to minute details, atmospheric conditions and tidal streams together with various unforeseen events.

These simulation centres are the place where today's seafarers could acquire both the technical and non-technical skills necessary to apply the BRM concept discussed in this book.

The industry has only just begun to understand the importance of simulation. In fact shipping companies and pilotage organisations know that in the event of accidents with loss of life and/or pollution involved, they could be accused of not having done as much as was reasonably possible to train their own personnel. The courts could in fact deem that simply meeting STCW standards is not enough for the mitigation of specific operational risks.

To this end it is useful to remember that the STCW Code, despite the important Manila Amendments agreed upon in 2010, reduces BRM to the understanding of principles that only concern teamwork[87]. Whereas our BRM model is based on the integration between technical and non-technical competences needed for the correct execution of tasks associated to each operational function on a ship's bridge.

Simulation centres are ideal learning environments for exercising these skills, provided that training is given by instructors that possess both seagoing and educational experience.

The instructor is actually the director of the simulated scene and must be capable of being able to apply specific training techniques. His/her direction consists in creating different situations and controlling external events to facilitate the achievement of each exercise's training objectives. These objectives must be communicated before the exercise is started. If trainees do not achieve them the instructor must intervene and pause the simulation. The intervention must be aimed at avoiding so-called *false learning*, i.e. the consolidation of an incorrect practice that contributes to success in the simulation exercise. False learning makes it very difficult for the trainee to remove the incorrect practice from his/her mind.

Whilst keeping the simulation paused, the instructor must ask the operators to describe the situation and the actions that caused the interruption, in order to make them consider the possibility of acting in the correct manner. Once the issues have been clarified, the scenario can be resumed.

A more detailed discussion must then be undertaken upon termination of the exercise. De-briefing should include the summing up of correct and incorrect performance with the instructor as moderator, whose only aim is that training objectives have been achieved and consolidated.

In order for this simulator training technique to be effective, officers must not fear evaluation. In addition to this instructors must be aware that acknowledging a small improvement can be better than highlighting all errors committed.

Eventual actions against substandard performances should be taken only when assessing competence, which is a process that follows principles, methods and times that are different from learning.

One last consideration regards the role of *e-learning* to reinforce the theoretical knowledge that is at the basis of BRM before simulator training. Nowadays in fact, thanks to IT platforms known as *Learning Management*

---

87 The term "resource" in the STCW seems to refer implicitly only to human resources on a ship's bridge.

Systems, a company can remotely control the diffusion of theoretical knowledge, which gives the following advantages:

- optimisation of time spent in a simulation centre;
- reduction of costs compared to traditional training courses in classrooms;
- increase in the effectiveness of the learning process of theoretical notions;
- standardisation of theoretical knowledge.

The notions acquired autonomously by an officer should make up the basis of a classroom discussion with simulator instructors. These instructors then have the delicate task of creating a link between acquired theoretical knowledge and practice.

Whoever works in training knows how complex the relationship between theory and practice actually is. Almost a century ago, the British philosopher Alfred North Whitehead[88] had already highlighted the crucial role of this relationship for education in general, arguing that without the connection between theory and practice there is a risk of generating "inert knowledge", i.e. concepts that are acknowledged by students without ever being applied or tested in the real world.

Making an effective connection between theory and practice depends on many different factors such as intellectual level, motivation and the knowledge base of officers, but also on the operational contexts they work in and on the professional culture within a company. For this reason also BRM expert Ravi Nijjer always reminds us how the most important thing for instructors and educators is to understand what level their students are at.

In conclusion we can assert that laying down detailed training programs risks limiting the instructor's potential in the evaluation of the highly dynamic balance necessary for linking theory with practice.

Staffan Persson, Director of Training Courses for CSMART, is working towards developing a Learning Management System for all *Carnival Corporation* officers. His source of inspiration is not Whitehead, but rather the *Khan Academy*[89], an organisation that aims at spreading education on a digital platform through remote access to resources. Its founder and mastermind Salman Khan proposes an educational process divided into two phases:

---

88 Alfred North Whitehead (1929). "The Aims of Education". The Free Press.
89 www.khanacademy.org

- active and autonomous learning of theoretical knowledge through an e-learning platform;
- consolidation of knowledge acquired independently through interaction with instructors.

Khan suggests a training approach able to take advantage of digital age technologies, whilst at the same time founded on the solid, old principles of the psychology of learning. The basic principle is that students have different learning paces, something that is not usually taken into consideration by schools where students passively follow lessons given by teachers.

Getting back to the maritime industry, a Learning Management System could change the role of instructors, whose main responsibility would be to consolidate the theoretical knowledge autonomously acquired by bridge officers and maritime pilots.

The time in classrooms would be greatly reduced, but also enhanced by a more critical interaction between instructor and trainees. These could make the most of the time spent in a high fidelity simulator, which is an exceptional tool for connecting theoretical knowledge and practical experience.

~

Peter Listrup is the Director of the training centre *Smartship Australia* in Brisbane. Here port pilots and deck officers attend courses for their professional development and for practicing instrumental navigation. Their interests are also in testing possible port developments and their associated operational limits through high fidelity simulations. Listrup is Swedish and was called to Australia in 2010 after having directed the *Star Cruises* training centre in Malaysia for years.

We ask him what types of simulator exist nowadays.

"The majority of simulators are managed by schools or colleges for basic nautical training or for issuing generic STCW qualifications, whilst a minority have been developed with more specific aims in mind. Our own simulator is amongst one of the latter ones as it was built for advanced pilot training and for testing the development of port infrastructure. There is also the one built by *Carnival Corporation* to train cruise ship officers well beyond STCW minimum standards. Some school simulators are halfway between these two types and try to offer more advanced and specific training, but they do have limits to what they can do because of the equipment at their disposal. In fact they cannot afford all that is required for high fidelity simulation - it would cost far too much."

What role do school simulators play in the training of seafarers?

"They allow mates and cadets the opportunity of facing situations that they would maybe not see for 10 or 15 years on board. In the real world you could sit on the bridge of an oil tanker or a bulk carrier for two months without ever finding yourself in a challenging situation from a navigational point of view. Whereas in simulators there is a lot more action and you can experience operational scenarios completely different from one another in a short time frame. You learn a lot and you can use and treasure what you have experimented in the real world."

And what is the role of simulators such as Smartship Australia?

"Here maritime pilots try to understand what the operational limits of their routes and manoeuvres are, from boarding place to berth. For example, before the arrival of a new ship of large dimensions they can try out new manoeuvres in different wind and current conditions. In the past safety margins were so ample that a particularly precise navigation or specific procedures was not a must. Since then, port structures have remained the same while ships continue to grow in size, and there is no longer that much room for errors."

This tendency to reduce safety margins for manoeuvres in confined waters requires a more rigorous approach compared with the past. Can you work on this in simulators?

"Of course. In our simulator for example, we often have maritime pilots, tug masters, deck officers and ship captains training all together, so that they can discuss operational limits and optimal manoeuvres for conducting a ship in harbour waters. The fact is that procedures which should specify operational limits of manoeuvres under pilotage are not always well defined. Arrival and departure manoeuvres in harbour waters are a critical phase of the voyage, often characterised by small safety margins. This is where the risk of incompatibility between shipboard and piloting procedures becomes critical in preventing large scale accidents. However, sometimes these inconsistencies can even lead to contrasts due to large differences between the two systems. A solution could be to define procedures and operational limits that are agreed upon by both parties. Joint training in a simulator can definitely help because it lets each player understand the problems of the others. The advantage with respect to the real world is that a simulation can be paused in order to discuss a critical phase and analyse it together before carrying on. Moreover, in a simulation centre such as ours, pilots, tug masters, ship captains and officers need only to walk across the corridor to go from one ship to another and see how the others work."

What are the advantages and limits of training in a simulation centre?

"Simulators such as ours can create scenarios that are very close to reality. Their limit though is that they cannot replace the experience matured on board a ship. It's true that navigating in open sea for a week will not give you as much experience as a week of simulation, however it is important all the same. In fact, gaining experience on board doesn't only mean standing watch on the bridge and conducting the ship from one port to another. There is much more to it, from cargo management to ship safety and stability. We can say that navigation is just a fraction of what is done on board and this part can be taught in bridge simulators."

What is the relationship between training on board and in simulators?

"They should be linked. If we think of maritime pilots for example, training should be carried out in ports on actual ships, before following up in simulators where they learn how to manage extreme situations. In this way pilots would know what to do if they ever found themselves facing real world problems similar to those experienced in the simulator."

Does it cost a lot to build and manage a simulation centre?

"It depends on the dimensions, the scope and the bridge equipment. On average though, just to have a simulator that is able to offer STCW training we are already talking of sums in excess of a million dollars – without counting the structure's fixed costs, instructors and all the rest. In order to reduce costs and meet the demands of nautical schools, simulator providers try to simplify hardware and software by supplying only generic bridge equipment with a computer that acts as an interface. It's when you buy real navigation systems and more advanced visualisation systems that costs begin to rise."

What is the life cycle of a simulator?

"Probably from 10 to 15 years. At a certain point though, maintenance becomes so expensive that it is no longer convenient to run it. And then you start having problems in finding spare parts, a bit like trying to fix a ten year old computer. Our simulation centre for example is only four years old, and yet we have already done several updates. It's a continuous process until you arrive at a point where the simulators would need investments that are too substantial to keep them going."

Is simulator training actually worth all these investments?

"What's the alternative? Not doing anything and having more accidents, loss of life, pollution, public outrage, increases in insurance premiums? I hope that in the future simulators will become more affordable, which will give large shipping companies the opportunity to set up their own and have complete control over training of their personnel. In such a way it would be easier to maintain a consistent level of competence, which would also fit to mitigate specific operational risks."

Are there ways of evaluating the effectiveness of simulators in improving navigation safety?

"Of course there are, and the experience of *Star Cruises* is a good example of this. It was one of the first companies to build its own training centre and from that moment on it has not had any significant accident. The insurance companies take it as a model to show how training investments can translate into fewer accidents."

And yet the use of simulation is not the only method used by Star Cruises to improve safety...

"No, for sure, but it makes up an important part, together with the use of a sophisticated system of operating procedures. *Star Cruises* has adopted an approach to safety similar to that of civil aviation, whereas other shipping companies don't do more than what is absolutely required. They would actually need a long-term vision on training, based on continuous professional development."

~

In conclusion, it appears that simulation can positively influence the industry's traditional reluctance for quality training. A change of mindset that is undeniably necessary for an effective implementation of BRM.

Assessment of Performance

In the future simulators could also play an important role for assessing BRM performance.

"Some companies are trying to take steps in this direction, but we are only at the beginning and simulators have a lot of potential that is yet to be explored", explains Peter Listrup.

Assessments of performance based on simulations could be useful for the purposes of recruitment and promotion as well as for periodic competency checks.

According to Listrup many aspects of human performance can only be evaluated in a simulator, rather than in the real world.

"Nowadays pilots already undergo periodic competency checks, mostly conducted by a senior pilot who observes colleagues on board with the task of judging their performance", he tells us. "There could be potential weaknesses in this approach. First of all the fact that objectively judging the performance of a colleague can be difficult. In addition to this, it's impossible to have control of environmental conditions during the check on board. In simulation centres, we can also assess a pilot's performance in adverse weather conditions such as with reduced visibility or with strong winds. And we can also make it so that all pilots are assessed using exactly the same weather conditions, something that is obviously impossible to do in the real world."

Modern simulators guarantee the possibility of recording all navigation data. If we were to use this data to assess operator performance we would need to establish a series of indicators and criteria for the analysis of collected information.

Evaluating human performance is not such a simple task: not only do we require a delicate methodological balance between qualitative and quantitative observations, but also a balance between the subjectivity and objectivity of whoever is called upon to express a judgement.

The Danish psychologist Erik Hollnagel expresses his perplexities regarding the quantification of human performance in complex operational systems[90]. According to him there is the need to evaluate people acting within their own operational context.

In our case, the activities examined could be the tasks associated with each BRM function, whilst the whole context could be recreated in a high fidelity simulator.

However Hollnagel warns that the complete objectivity of collected data is nothing more than an illusion[91], regardless of the robustness of the devised qualitative model and the validity of evaluation criteria.

On the objectivity of performance assessment, the psychologist Daniel Kahneman has also expressed his concerns on both possible errors of judgement (derived from the innate trust in our intuition) and the unnecessary complexity of the statistical algorithms used in the field of social and behavioural sciences.

Kahneman asserts that a simple formula based on the unweighted combination of a reduced number of performance indicators can guarantee

---

90 Erik Hollnagel (1993). "Human Reliability Analysis. Context and Control". Academic Press.

91 On this subject, Hollnagel also quotes an article called "What is a man that can be expressed as a number?", in which the author (Dougherty) criticises the excessive emphasis on the quantification of human performance in studies that have been conducted since the beginning of the 1980s.

better results than one generated from complex algorithms based on multiple regression[92].

According to him therefore, the reliability of an assessment depends above all on an intelligent choice of performance indicators and on devising a formula that combines them in a simple and effective manner.

A good example of this approach is the evaluation of a newborn baby's state of health, which is performed on the basis of just five indicators: heartbeat, breathing, reflexes, muscle tone and colouring[93]. To each of these indicators the doctor gives a value from zero to two and then adds them together. If the sum is higher than eight, the baby is in perfect condition. If it is less than four, it means that immediate intervention is required. It is a very simple assessment scheme, however it is recognised globally for its contribution to reducing infant mortality.

Applying the principles of Hollnagel and Kahneman to our bridge (for the purpose of BRM performance assessment) requires:

- the definition of an operational scenario in a high fidelity simulator;
- the identification of the most significant BRM performance indicators;
- devising a formula for evaluating each operator.

Let's imagine that we have to assess the performance of an operator in the role of Pilot who is engaged in controlling and monitoring a normal manoeuvre. In order to evaluate his/her actions within a realistic operational context, we should include the presence of a Navigator and Co-navigator that can assist in executing the manoeuvre.

The Pilot's performance in controlling and monitoring a planned manoeuvre could be evaluated – for example – using the following indicators (each one associated to a specific task of the two operational functions under examination):

- team briefing;
- cooperation;
- control of planned operational limits;
- active monitoring of critical parameters for the manoeuvre.

---

92 An algorithm of multiple regression aims to define a formula that optimises a weighted combination of independent variables.

93 The so-called "Apgar Score" was developed in the 1960s by Dr Virginia Apgar. Examinations are performed during the very first minutes of a new-born baby's life and repeated until its condition stabilises.

A rating from 1 to 4 should be assigned for each of these indicators. Rating criteria (table III–4) should be qualitative for the first two indicators and quantitative for the other two.

Indicator	Criteria
Team briefing	4: correct execution, fully compliant with formal procedures and practices
Cooperation	3: correct execution, in the absence of (or in partial accordance with) formal procedures and practices 2: incorrect execution, in the absence of (or in partial accordance with) formal procedures and practices 1: incorrect execution that does not comply with formal procedures and/or practices
Control of planned operational limits	4: manoeuvre is "always" within the limits of normal operations 3: "partial" use of safety margin 2: "extensive" use of safety margin 1: safety margin exceeded
Active monitoring of critical parameters for the manoeuvre	4: cyclic visual scanning of all AMD parameters 3: cyclic visual scanning of some AMD parameters 2: sporadic observation of some AMD parameters 1: little observation of AMD parameters

table III–4 : Evaluation criteria for controlling and monitoring a manoeuvre

The quantitative assessment of controlling operational limits can be carried out automatically by the simulator software. Ratings from 1 to 4 should be calculated on the basis of the correspondence between the adjectives "partial" and "extensive", together with the amount of time spent beyond the normal operational limits.

The quantitative assessment of active monitoring could be automated on the basis of data collected by *eye-tracking devices*. The rating from 1 to 4 would then be established by software able to process the degree of thoroughness of visual scanning patterns. Alternatively, the evaluation could be performed in a qualitative manner on the basis of the Pilot's verbalisation of observed parameters at pre-arranged stages of the manoeuvre.

Once ratings have been assigned to all four indicators, we need to add them up and establish performance ranges such as:

- from 16 to 14: fully competent;
- from 13 to 11: competent;
- from 10 to 4: not yet competent.

From what has been discussed it is evident that a modern assessment process for officers or pilots should be based on a solid BRM functional model, which is characterised by:

- well defined operational functions, roles and tasks;
- consolidated operating procedures and practices;
- a standardised bridge layout.

With all this guaranteed, we still need to define the regularity of assessments for each BRM role, along with thresholds for maintaining competency and for promotion to a higher level of responsibility.

As Peter Listrup observed, there is still a long way to go.

Professional Development

An officer or pilot's professional development shouldn't stop once they have reached the level of competency required for their role on the bridge.

Nevertheless professional development is only possible if the organisation creates the opportunity for its staff to grow and if the staff themselves are motivated to improve.

The first condition is relatively simple to create from an organisational point of view, while it can be arduous to keep deck officers motivated. To do so it is necessary to:

- guarantee a level of financial satisfaction and work conditions that are consistent with expectations;
- guarantee career prospects through transparent and meritocratic mechanisms;
- promote professional development as a founding value of the organisation's culture.

The last point is certainly the most difficult because there aren't any recipes to implement it and indicators to measure it. At the same time though it is also the most important, especially considering that nowadays managing navigation safety entails considering emerging solutions to face dynamic risks.

Ravi Nijjer has understood this for a long time. It is no coincidence that he has been involved in the professional development of Australian maritime pilots for nearly two decades through a course conducted in a workshop environment on law, regulations, technology, human factors, safety management, new techniques and emerging good practices. To facilitate the professional development experts selected by Ravi Nijjer are invited to make presentations and lead discussions on the different topics with the aim of providing pilots with the knowledge that enables them to have an informed viewpoint on the latest trends in the maritime industry and the ability to identify and track lines of development affecting their profession. To further enhance learning, care is taken to include in every course group pilots from different jurisdictions to promote sharing and interchange of knowledge, ideas etc. for mutual enrichment.

Unfortunately at this stage opportunities of this sort are still very rare for seafarers. And yet with the digital age's rapidly growing complexity, a continuous professional development is no longer an option, but rather a necessity.

THE INTERNATIONAL SCENARIO

"Each generation of vessels brings new challenges,
but accidents still occur and
safety must be taken into a new era"
Koji Sekimizu

E-navigation

T he principles and techniques developed by Captain Larjo eventually arrived at IMO. "This is how the debate on *e-navigation* began", he comments.

In fact, since 2005 IMO has begun developing the concept of e-navigation, which is a regulatory framework for the harmonisation of new technology both on a ship's bridge and in shore-based control centres. At the time the international maritime community agreed upon the need to coordinate the development of new navigation technologies in the name of higher safety levels.

After two years of international debate, IMO members finalised the following definition[94]:

"E-navigation is the harmonized collection, integration, exchange, presentation and analysis of marine information on board and ashore by electronic means to enhance berth to berth navigation and related services for safety and security at sea and protection of the marine environment."

Between 2015 and 2019, IMO will coordinate the implementation of five solutions – originating from a decade of discussions – which regard:

- the ergonomics of a ship's bridge and its integrated navigation systems;
- the reliability of navigation and communication systems;
- the standardisation and automation of routine ship-to-shore communications;
- the integration and portrayal of information received via radio on integrated navigation system displays;
- the development and standardisation of maritime services offered by coastal providers.

---

94 IMO MSC 85/26/Add.1, annex 20

One of the principles that was established right from the beginning was that the development of e-navigation would be driven by user needs and not by technology.

However great conceptual innovations can be triggered by technological development and not by detailed considerations of human needs. In other words, great steps forward can occur when technology finally makes it possible. Innovations such as electrical lighting, the automobile, aeroplanes and modern telecommunications were not human necessities before they were invented. Nowadays they are an essential part of our lives and if we do use them, we have to thank technological development for it[95].

This means that great innovations can be conceived outside of the world of research, following non-conventional and unforeseeable paths. It is only when they penetrate our lives that they generate new needs. And it is at this point that studies and research can contribute to the development of the tools that stem from them.

All of this is also probably true for e-navigation: great innovations on a ship's bridge can be driven by technological progress, and for this reason we should limit ourselves to rendering them functional to a BRM model. It is this very model that is in fact based on the balance between the potentials and the limitations of both new technology and the human element.

Having made this distinction, we should try to understand e-navigation's role better, which in effect also covers the exchange of information between vessels and coastal control centres. In this light we could also define e-navigation as a new operational concept aimed at improving the integration between new technology and operators, both on a ship's bridge and in the control room of a coastal station.

There could be a lot to learn from civil aviation, where the integration of man and technology on the flight deck and in air traffic control centres has already been successfully tackled over the last few decades[96]. So far, the maritime industry has debated on this integration by stating its intention to implement regulatory solutions for improving bridge ergonomics. One of these envisages the introduction of guidelines for a *human-centred* design of navigation systems and for the evaluation of their usability. The idea is certainly a valid one and it should be associated to a solid operational

---

[95] This thesis is sustained by Donald Norman, a world famous cognitive scientist who has worked for years in the research of ergonomic solutions for many industrial sectors. The article "Technology First, Needs Last" can be viewed on the website www.jnd.org

[96] Sydney Dekker and David Woods (1999). "Automation and its Impact on Human Cognition", within the book "Coping with Computers in the Cockpit". Ashgate.

concept. Indeed, in order to evaluate bridge ergonomics it is necessary to establish operational functions, roles and responsibilities beforehand.

Captain Larjo designed his first integrated cockpit after having clearly defined the operational concept he wanted to follow. A concept based on cooperation between at least two operators with the same level of skill and with the same navigation systems at their disposal (integrated in a compact way as in aircraft cockpits).

The future role of bridge operators has been discussed within IMO[97] by envisaging two scenarios: the first with operators in direct control of navigation (*navigating navigator*), the second with operators dedicated more to the monitoring of automated navigation systems (*monitoring navigator*).

In the BRM model proposed in the second part of this book, operator roles and responsibilities were tackled introducing the concept of *active monitoring*. Only after having defined the concept was it possible to "integrate it" into the bridge's cockpit under the form of an *Active Monitoring Display*.

Another important debate along e-navigation's development concerned the exchange of planned routes between ships and sea traffic management centres. Also in this case, technical solutions such as the standardisation and automation of ship-to-shore communications would certainly benefit from the definition of a solid conceptual base.

Questions to ask ought to be similar to these: what sort of role will sea traffic management centres actually have? Mere monitoring or active traffic control? What should the limits of access to ship information be? And in the event of active traffic control, what are the limits that these coastal centres will have in order to control navigation?

These questions have been tackled since 2010 as part of the project *Monalisa*, coordinated by the Swedish Maritime Authority and financed by the European Union. Its final aim is to define an operational concept of *Sea Traffic Management* (STM) founded on the following principles:

- the aggregation between onshore and offshore operational functions;
- the adoption of processes and methods inspired by *Air Traffic Management* (ATM) and *Air Traffic Control* (ATC);
- the development of an implementation plan only after defining the operational concept.

97 International Maritime Organization (2010). "Report of the Correspondence Group on e-navigation to the Sub-Committee on Standards of Training and Watchkeeping" (STW42/6).

Some technical solutions have already been put forward on this theme. One of these includes the real-time exchange of voyage related information with all stakeholders right along the transport chain.

Aggregating operational functions is a delicate concept that should not be confused with the static allocation of functions, which has responded to the needs of dividing work between man and machine ever since the times of the industrial revolution.

Scholars as renowned as Erik Hollnagel[98] have warned of the risks of the allocation of functions ("who does what" in a rigid manner) between the various controllers of a complex system such as that of Air Traffic Management. On the contrary, aggregation should ensure an overlap between operational functions assigned to various elements of the system, both human and technological, on board and ashore. The redundancy of some operational functions is actually essential in being able to face the dynamicity of the context. It means that a system component can take control of a function that is partly shared with another element if the situation requires. In order to make this overlap possible, operational functions must be well defined and accompanied by procedures for their dynamic redistribution.

The BRM model proposed in this book also foresees the aggregation of operational functions on a ship's bridge. For example, route and manoeuvre monitoring are distributed to all team members, thanks also to the presence of several *Active Monitoring Displays* (AMD). The rules for this distribution are established for each manning level and for situations with or without an external pilot on board.

The aggregation of BRM functions with STM ones will certainly not be easy. It will have to be designed whilst containing the complexity of ship-shore interaction within the limits of the operator's ability to comprehend. If this limit is surpassed, not even teamwork (both on the bridge and in the control room ashore) would be enough to ensure an effective monitoring of increasingly automated processes.

So what can we do to ease operators' work and to adapt it to the demands of the digital age?

On the one hand there is the need to improve the man-machine interface of navigation systems, on the other it becomes essential to raise the level of professionalism for officers, maritime pilots and sea traffic controllers. We

---

98 Erik Hollnagel (1999). "From Function Allocation to Function Congruence" inserted within the book "Coping with Computers in the Cockpits". Ashgate.

should never forget that an increase of investments in new technology does not allow the reduction of funds allocated to operator training. Often companies are not aware of this because the need of more sophisticated competences, well above those required to meet minimum standards, only emerge on rare occasions.

If "ideal" levels of competence were also established at international level (in line with the most advanced navigation systems), it would be up to the company to demonstrate that its officers are adequately trained in facing the complexity of their operational context. This would imply changes in the philosophy of both compliance audits and accident investigations carried out by the competent authorities.

In conclusion, international initiatives such as e-navigation or the *Monalisa* project should be accompanied by investments aimed at:

- raising the level of competence of operators both on board and ashore;
- designing ship bridges and control rooms ashore that are functional to a new BRM operational concept.

Who will absorb these costs? The relationship between shipping companies, navigation equipment manufacturers, insurance companies, national regulatory bodies and international organisations has always been tenuous and has been further aggravated in the present climate of global financial uncertainty.

The risk is that the different players involved will try to shift the responsibility for necessary investments upstream in the name of potential benefits for the entire maritime system.

To address this issue we should aim to have a global regulatory framework that promotes cooperation and challenges the traditional way of doing business in the maritime industry. Manning and equipping ships that just meet bare minimum standards as well as limiting liability in the case of accidents is no longer deemed acceptable by a public that has zero tolerance for accidents that result in loss of lives and/or environmental pollution.

And lastly and most importantly, until the industry is ready to reconsider the working conditions and the rights of seafarers it will be difficult to motivate and prepare them to face the challenges and complexities of the digital age.

Duties and Rights of Seafarers

I n order to understand just how difficult and precarious living conditions for seafarers are, we need to read between the lines of the Maritime Labour Convention (MLC 2006) by the *International Labour Organisation* (ILO)[99].

Known as "The Seafarers' Bill of Rights" [100], it is considered as the fourth pillar of shipping's international regulatory regime, together with three major IMO treaties: the International Convention for the Safety of Life at Sea (SOLAS), the International Convention on Standards of Training, Certification and Watchkeeping for Seafarers (STCW) and the International Convention for the Prevention of Pollution from Ships (MARPOL).

The maritime world is somewhat peculiar. On the one hand it has always been a globalised and liberalised domain, in that it even allows shipowners to change flags in order to find the most convenient conditions. On the other hand it is the only industrial sector to be regulated by international conventions such as the MLC 2006. Regulations that tend only to establish minimum requirements and that often reveal the profound gap between the working standards of those ashore and those at sea.

Let's examine the new Maritime Labour Convention. It deals with almost every aspect of work and life on board, including the minimum age of seafarers, hours of work and rest, wage conditions, health and safety protection, accommodation, repatriation and access to shore-based welfare facilities. Yet it is immediately noticeable that its aim is simply to define minimum standards at international levels and to prevent ships from operating in conditions of evident exploitation, whilst leaving some of the anomalies still present within the sector untouched.

The MLC 2006 is not an easy read. It is split into three parts (Articles, Regulations and the Code) with each one containing an increasing level of detail[101].

---

99 The International Labour Organization (ILO) is a specialised agency of the United Nations, based in Geneva. It deals with the promotion and defence of rights at work and social justice.

100 The Maritime Labour Convention 2006 applies to all commercial vessels, other than ships engaged in fishing or in similar pursuits. It does not apply to warships or naval auxiliaries. An exemption could also be obtained for vessels of less than 200 gross tonnage that do not proceed on international voyages.

101 The Regulations and the Code cover five general areas, organised under five Titles: Title 1 is about minimum requirements for seafarers to work on a ship; Title 2 deals with conditions of employment; Title 3 relates to accommodation, recreational facilities, food and catering, Title 4 focuses on health protection, medical care, welfare and social security protection; and Title 5 deals with compliance and enforcement.

The Articles and Regulations state both the obligations and fundamental principles, as well as the primary duties of member states that have ratified the convention. The Code gives indications on how to apply the Regulations and it is further divided into mandatory Standards and Guidelines. Guidelines provide recommendations on how to meet the provisions set out in Standards and Regulations but leave the flexibility for each single state to individually take measures, on the condition however that they arrive at the anticipated objectives.

Reading the text with attention, it is evident that many steps are still needed to improve rights and working conditions at sea. According to MLC 2006, seafarers can work more than 72 hours per week for a maximum period of about a year. All this is without shipowners having any obligation to guarantee at least one effective rest day per week or per month: a rest day that is not financially compensated but is used to combat long term fatigue for the benefit of ship safety.

ILO's Director of the International Labour Standards Department, Cleopatra Doumbia-Henry claims she is proud of "her" convention. The daughter of a former Minister of Labour on the Caribbean island of Dominica, she has worked for ILO for almost thirty years. From the very beginning she has been involved in the development of the MLC 2006 and subsequently, in its ratification process.

"It is important to understand that international standards are only the parameters of what is acceptable", she explains in writing, responding to our questions.

"The problem for seafarers on ships that voyage internationally relates in large part to what we now call globalization", she says. "Shipowners are increasingly distanced from the operations and conditions on board ship and responsibility is dissipated among different corporate entities and countries."

According to her the criticality, more so than in the standards themselves, is in the way in which ships put them into practice. It is also for this reason that an entire part of the new Convention envisages a system of certification and controls by Port States: ships that do not respect the standards imposed by ILO may be detained in port and penalised with long delays.

"The MLC 2006 establishes several different approaches for inspectors to use to verify situations", says Doumbia-Henry. And the reporting by seafarers themselves is just one of many instruments used to get around any eventual false declarations regarding actual working hours.

There was a lot of celebrating on 20th August 2013, when the MLC 2006 entered into force among the states that had ratified it the previous year. The convention was wanted by shipowner and seafarer organisations, aware of the fact that in one of the most globalised sectors in the world there were situations that needed to be stopped. Shipowners complained about unfair competition from so-called sub-standard ships, whilst seafarer representatives denounced the existence of openly exploited working conditions. Officially they asked that the chaos ensuing from 66 resolutions and recommendations be put in order and updated into one unique convention. In 2001 they managed to find an agreement in principle, but it took five years to draft the document and for each individual state to approve it, followed by another seven before its practical implementation. At present the convention already covers over 80% of the world's total fleet, including the entire cruise sector. Over the next few years it will near a universal ratification.

Remo di Fiore participated in negotiations for the MLC 2006 as the representative for Italian seafarers in the delegation of the International Transport Federation. He argues that the new convention will not change the lives of around 40,000 Italian seafarers very much, as well as the ones of their colleagues in developed countries. As a matter of fact, in the large part of the Western world working conditions are already much better than the minimum standards established by the MLC 2006.

"This document however makes us stronger because if there were any problems tomorrow, it will not only be the trade unions who claim rights towards correct conditions from shipowners, but also port authorities", he specifies. "The positive aspect from this is that the convention will help in eradicating that form of unfair competition carried along by flags of convenience and sub-standard ships. Therefore it will help serious shipowner competition and will ensure additional protection for seafarers."

Yet living conditions for those who work at sea often remain more oppressive than the ones of those who work ashore. You only need to look at working hours. The convention states that seafarers should have a working day of eight hours, but it then adds that in a week they have either the right to at least 77 hours rest or that they can work for a maximum of 72 hours. It counts as saying that a seafarer can work up to 13 hours per day[102].

---

102 Standard A2.3 on "hours of work and hours of rest" states that "the normal working hours' standard for seafarers, like that for other workers, shall be based on an eight-hour day with one day of rest per week and rest on public holidays". It then established the maximum number of hours of work which shall not be exceeded in a given period of time, or a minimum number of hours of rest which shall be provided in a given period of time as following:

a)   maximum hours of work shall not exceed 72 hours in any seven-day period;

b)   minimum hours of rest shall not be less than 77 hours in any seven-day period.

Remo di Fiore shrugs his shoulders.

"The two formulas [72 hour working week and at least 77 hours resting time – Ed.] were left in at the time because shipowners and unions could not find an agreement. So we said to keep them both to allow each state the choice of which one to apply to their flag. But the result of this was that states left both formulas without selecting one in particular. And logically, shipowners prefer using the calculation based on hours of rest."

His opinion is that such a heavy workload is due to the fact that the ship is an environment in constant movement that cannot afford to have more than one crew at the same time.

"In order to entitle a seafarer to have an eight-hour working day, shipowners would need to employ much more people on board. The costs would be prohibitive", says di Fiore.

"It is a complex situation, especially during the present economic climate. Shipowners are forced to cut costs just to survive and the only variable expense of a ship is that of personnel. For this reason shipowners are very diligent with officer and crew costs and they often transfer their ships under flags that allow the boarding of low-cost labour."

He tells us that in the Sea of Marmara, in the Singapore harbour, or in the Greek port of Piraeus, there are hundreds of ships that have been abandoned by shipowners that are insolvent or even untraceable.

However this does not justify the fact that working hours on board sometimes exceed those envisaged by the ILO Convention.

"What we managed to obtain to contrast eventual exploitation is that a seafarer signs a form which shows the hours he has worked", he adds.

The convention will impose more severe cross-checks to monitor whether what is reported within on board documents corresponds to reality. Di Fiore laughs. "It's becoming more difficult to lie about hours worked. For example, when cruise ships arrive in Miami there are lawyers on the quay hunting down seafarers. They try to persuade them into suing shipowners if they have worked more than they should. There have already been class actions that have cost cruise companies a lot of money", he explains. "And when a class action in the United States is ruled in a seafarer's favour, usually the judge establishes that all those found in the same situation have the right to compensation, even if they did not participate in the case themselves. This means that shipowners now think twice before running the risk. It will certainly take time before this system is fully implemented, but in the future it will be the shipping company itself that gives indications to its personnel to ensure that compliance is ongoing".

For the moment though, work aboard is intense even without lying about the quantity of hours worked. In fact in the name of containing costs, seafarers have a 7-day working week without a single day off. There is not a single ship where the weekly rest day is used for relaxing, sleeping or recovering from fatigue. In the majority of cases it is simply paid as overtime or counted as an additional rest day after landing.

We are not only talking about a few weeks without ever having a break. In fact the convention states a right of repatriation just once a year.

Cleopatra Doumbia-Henry defends "her" document.

"The MLC 2006 sets out minimum standards, it establishes a floor", she says. And this is "less than 12 months", before having the right to repatriation. "In many cases collective agreements are based on 9 months of service [...] and ratifying countries should consider requiring shorter periods", she adds. "However the reality of the industry must also be considered. While some seafarers return to work on the same ship after repatriation and leave, many do not and there may be no certainty of work being available after repatriation."

Di Fiore agrees. He tells us that his union sometimes finds itself having to stop seafarers, especially those from poorer countries. Given the difference in wages between work at sea and work on land, when the time of repatriation comes they request immediate departure on another ship or even to remain on the ship they have just signed off from.

The challenge is that long periods on board without ever having a rest day not only concern lower ranked seafarers, but also cruise ship officers that have the responsibility of thousands of people on their shoulders.

The situation varies a lot from company to company.

Star Cruises officers usually alternate eight weeks on board with an equivalent rest period at home. Whereas for Italian officers the situation is decidedly worse.

"Usually they spend four or six months on board and one or two months at home, depending on the company they work for", says di Fiore. "They all talk of wanting to reduce the period at sea not only for the job's stress, but also for the burden of being away from family", he adds, maintaining however that in many cases the seafarers are reluctant to accept changes. "The officers themselves don't actually want shorter periods because it would reduce their retirement pension fund. It's absurd, but it has happened in the past that the union had held talks with large companies not to shorten the period spent on board, but to keep it as it is."

Is it really possible however to ensure a high level of safety when deck officers work three, four or even six months in a row – including night watches – without a single day of rest?

Di Fiore thinks for a moment before responding.

"As a union we maintain that the major cause of maritime accidents is human error, most commonly induced by fatigue. This is especially clear when ships enter ports and when a series of other responsibilities overlap the conduct of navigation", he says. "But the limits within the MLC 2006 are what they are."

He tells us that it has not been possible to make these limits stricter or more courageous due to opposition from shipowners.

"When we discussed this in Geneva, they said that it was already difficult competing with ships that fly the flags of countries with less stringent rules, where workers are paid much less."

Then there is the question of continuity in labour relations, which concerns less than half of Italian seafarers. It means that after having worked for months without even one day off, they return home and may not be paid at all for the entire period they stay ashore.

"Shipowners don't like continuity in labour relations because it reduces the flexibility they have in distancing or dismissing people when necessary", explains di Fiore. "In alternative they often prefer to give an additional bonus to wages. I believe around 60% of Italian officers have continual labour relations, which increases among ship captains."

He confirms that the situation is particularly dramatic not for officers – that find work quite easily and receive salaries that are higher than contractual minimums – but for common seamen. It is estimated that amongst them there are around 500,000 layoffs, which makes the category exceptionally vulnerable and often forced to pay for training courses out of their own pocket.

According to his views, the new convention was drawn up especially with those in mind.

"Even today there are some flags that allow conditions inferior to those envisaged by the MLC 2006. And the problems are not found in the larger companies but with small shipowners, who when facing financial difficulties attempt to speculate on everything and escape controls. Soon though, their crumbling ships won't be able to sail and call in to ports in countries that have adhered to the convention because they will be halted", he says. "There is no other industrial activity in the world other than shipping that has universal rules for everyone, regardless of their nationality, religion or the colour of their skin. For example I can move a shoe factory to a third world country and exploit child labour without having any international obligations. Whereas in the maritime domain there is still a lot to do, but at least a ten year old kid will never be able to work on board a ship."

Since the convention only defines minimum standards, it should be the responsibility of each individual state to impose stricter rules to protect the wellbeing of seafarers. Maybe they could push towards shorter periods at sea that would ensure not only a defence against long term fatigue but also a better life-work balance. Then seafarers would not be forced to stay away from home for months at a time.

Cleopatra Doumbia-Henry is clear on this point.

"I must emphasize the key role of national law", she says. "In the interest of the well-being of seafarers and especially to avoid the risk of fatigue, one would hope that national laws will, where possible, seek to provide for a day of rest on which work could be performed only in the case of need."

It seems that in order to arrive at a change of this sort, there is still a lot of work to be done.

Navigation Safety in the Digital Age

The need to redesign the maritime system's integration between man, technology and organisation was exposed by the Costa Concordia accident, but it does not just concern *Costa Crociere* or the passenger ship sector. The systemic analysis has highlighted criticalities that are potentially common to the entire maritime industry.

So much so that IMO's Secretary General Koji Sekimizu has openly stated the necessity for a comprehensive review of the International Convention for the Safety of Life at Sea (SOLAS) by 2024, fifty years after the introduction of the one actually in use[103]. Sekimizu argues that navigation safety must enter into a new era, promoting goal-based standards rather than prescriptive regulations. His vision is expressed through the following recommendations to IMO's Maritime Safety Committee[104]:

- improve data collection in order to support monitoring and development of safety regulations;
- improve integration between risk-based methodologies and the latest analysis techniques into the safety regulatory framework to provide a sound scientific and practicable basis for the development of future safety regulations;
- encourage a safety culture beyond mere compliance with regulatory requirements;
- minimise the burden any new or changing regulation(s) place on the seafarers;
- undertake a long-term comprehensive review of the existing safety regulatory framework with a view to ensuring that it will meet the future challenges associated with the application of new technologies, the human element, the needs of the maritime industry and the expectations of society, taking into account the ever-increasing pace of change and technological advancements made since the 1974 SOLAS was adopted.

Within the first two recommendations the intention is clear to count on a more analytical rule-making process based on the collection and study of operational information. This is not a simple task, either for IMO or for any other large organisation committed to managing ever more complex and technologically advanced operations and processes. In fact in the digital era

---

103 Article published on Lloyd's List's website on 11th September 2013.
104 "Statement of the Participants to the IMO Symposium on the Future of Ship Safety" (2013).

useful information needs to be extracted from a mass of data that is constantly growing, making the ability of "extracting the signal from the noise" essential[105]. Sometimes digital technologies can be both the solution and the cause of problems that we find ourselves facing.

IMO also supports the need to adopt the most modern analysis techniques to provide a scientific basis for the development of future safety regulations.

On this point we need to pay close attention and avoid methods based on what the philosopher Nassim Taleb calls *naïve empiricism*[106]. In his book entitled *"The Black Swan"* Taleb argues that, given the amount of digital information we have access to, it is now possible to find confirmation for just about anything. Human beings naturally tend to look for confirmation in order to validate their ideas. However, up until the 1980s the analysis of available data was carried out manually and the effort required for qualitative evaluations cast doubt and uncertainty on the results produced. Whereas with the introduction of computer spread sheets and databases the numbers have gained the upper hand, rendering the production of confirmations even more seductive.

Taleb maintains that the best way for verifying the validity of a theory consists in looking for arguments or in conducting experiments aimed at disproving it and showing its fallacy. According to him a theory should be proved not by looking for confirmations, but by demonstrating that attempts made to disprove it turn out to be ineffective. As experiments go along and fail, the theory becomes stronger and stronger and is "temporarily" included in the encyclopaedia of scientific knowledge.

This type of "negative" empiricism is in contrast with the "positive" one that spread through continental Europe in the first decades of the twentieth century. At that time negative empiricism was strongly opposed by the wider academic community. Just think that Albert Einstein, a follower of negative empiricism, took many years to have his theory of relativity accepted by the academic world. It is said that for his entire life the German-born physicist continued in vain to look for conditions where his theories were not valid.

The forefather of negative empiricism though was the Austrian Karl Popper, one of the twentieth century's greatest philosophers of science. His principles and reflections are relevant for those who battle with the practical

---

105 In the book "The Signal and the Noise" (2012), the author Nate Silver writes that our brain can store three terabytes of information, which represents only a millionth of the information produced each day by the human species.

106 Nassim Taleb (2010). "The Black Swan. The Impact of the Highly Improbable". Penguin Press.

problems of today's operational environments, which are dominated by uncertainty, variability and growing complexity.

According to Popper, the search for confirmation is particularly misleading in the field of social sciences. His advice for studying sociotechnical contexts is to begin with the formulation of "daring conjectures" based on previous observations and experiences. Conjectures formed in this way are not scientific because they haven't yet demonstrated their resistance to experiments aimed at disproving them. A scientist's ability is both in the formulation of the initial conjectures and in the devising of experiments aimed at questioning them. It is only when these experiments repeatedly fail in their intent that the conjectures can be elevated in status to scientific theory.

Such an approach requires more time and effort than a search for confirmation. However it could actually be useful for the comprehensive review of the SOLAS Convention. Social sciences are in fact the basis of both Bridge Resource Management's operational concept and a modern Safety Management System. Conducting research in these fields by adopting the philosophy of negative empiricism could provide the sound scientific basis that is recommended by IMO's Secretary General.

In his *Black Swan*, Taleb provides another reflection that can also be relevant for navigation safety. It is about the risk management of events that are not very probable but could have substantial consequences. Given their rarity, these "black swan" events are cut off from statistical analysis based on so-called normal distributions. When they do occur though, these black swans are able to profoundly modify the balance of complex socio-technical systems.

Let's take the Costa Concordia accident as an example, which is kick-starting the review process of the SOLAS convention. Or maybe the more recent sinking of the South Korean ferry *Sewol* that provoked the dissolution of an entire country's coast guard[107]. Accepting that a black swan is able to upset all our plans is not an easy thing to do. It implicates the admission that we cannot influence the system as much as we would like.

It is often an excessive faith in technology that feeds the illusion of total control on complex socio-technical systems. However, if total control is not

---

107 The ferry "Sewol" capsized on 16th April 2014 in South Korean waters, causing the death of over 300 people, most of whom were secondary school students. In the wake of public shock and criticism of the South Korean government for its management of the emergency, not only did the Prime Minister resign but the entire South Korean coast guard was dissolved.

realistically achievable, how can we at least obtain an economically sustainable level to mitigate the risk of black swans?

As well as recommending specific techniques for data analysis, Taleb also advises taking a leaf out of Mother Nature's book.

Just as she does, we should aim at redundancy, i.e. the type of defence that allows us to survive in the face of adversity thanks to the availability of spare parts. The human body is a perfect example of this: we have two eyes, two kidneys, two lungs... *Defensive redundancy* does have a cost though, which is ensuring the presence of a second component even in normal conditions when it is not strictly necessary. The exact opposite of defensive redundancy is optimisation based on naïve empiricism: the search of confirmation for organisational models that are increasingly efficient in normal conditions, but also more vulnerable to black swans. Taleb warns that in the long-term, naïve optimisation brings about a collapse of a system, simply because it makes it more vulnerable to uncertainty and to the intrinsic unpredictability of a complex operational context.

There is another type of redundancy, which is more sophisticated than the duplication of some of a system's vital components. It is called *functional redundancy*, and entails that a certain function be carried out by two components that are completely independent from one another.

An example of the co-existence of defensive and functional redundancy is on our BRM bridge, where active monitoring of navigation is performed by each operator using different navigation displays (functional redundancy) and also by at least two operators with the same level of skill (defensive redundancy).

As well as the utility of redundancy, Mother Nature also gives us another precious indication: it is better to avoid things that are too big. Nature in fact limits the dimensions of its creatures, contrary to the principle of the economy of scale, where expansion makes the company more efficient and more competitive on the market. When companies become large enough to be listed on the stock exchange they need to optimise their resources in order to satisfy business analysts. In turn these analysts apply pressure until all redundancies that make the system inefficient have been eliminated. Maybe they support their strategies by looking for confirmation from research based on the famous 95% of cases in a normal distribution. And in the long-term this will make the company vulnerable to black swans that can even spell bankruptcy in a large corporation.

In conclusion to what has been discussed in this book, we can assert that a reform of navigation safety requires a change in operational, organisational and regulatory philosophy.

The concept of Bridge Resource Management, in the way in which it has been formulated, represents merely a conjecture to put to the test. Only time will tell if the provisions recommended for its implementation at all levels of the maritime industry will turn out to be effective.

Perhaps the most arduous task awaits IMO, ILO and above all each single flag state: it is the improvement in the working conditions of seafarers. Although some steps have been taken compared to the past, the new convention on seafarers' rights still allows companies to keep officers on board for months, working seven days a week and for more than ten hours per day.

If we really want to manage the risks emerging from the growing complexity of the digital age we need more sophisticated competencies on board ships. Acquiring them is going to be very difficult under the present employment and living conditions of seafarers.

This is the fundamental message from a book dedicated to all those who have lost their lives at sea.

ESSENTIAL BIBLIOGRAPHY

Bibliographical references have been included within the footnotes. The following list contains only the key sources of inspiration that have contributed to shape the principles discussed in all three parts of the book. They are the signal that has been extracted from the noise.

Billings, C. (1996). *Aviation Automation. The Search for a human-centered approach*. CRC Press.

Chialastri, A. (2012). *Human factor. Prestazioni e limitazioni umane*. IBN Editore.

Conrad, J. (1900). *Lord Jim*.

Daniel Maurino, J. R. (1999). *Beyond aviation human factors*. Ashgate.

Degani, A. (1994). *On the design of flight-deck procedures*. NASA Contractor Report 177642.

Dekker, S. (2006). *The field guide to understanding human error*. Ashgate.

Dekker, S., & Hollnagel, E. (1999). *Coping with computers in the cockpit*. Ashgate.

Garin, K. A. (2005). *Devils on the deep blue sea. The dreams, schemes and showdowns that built America's cruiseship empires*. Viking.

Gladwell, M. (2008). *Outliers*. Little, Brown and Company.

Guwande, A. (2011). *Checklist manifesto. How to get things right*. Picador.

Gyldén, S., & Pettersson, B. (1991). *Navigation in fog*.

Hollnagel, E. (1993). *Human reliability analysis. Context and control*. Academic Press.

Kahneman, D. (2011). *Thinking, fast and slow*. Penguin Press.

Kern, T. (1997). *Redefining airmanship*. McGraw-Hill.

Khan, S. (2012). *The one world school house. Education reimagined*. Hodden & Stoughton.

Larjo, K. (2010). *Practices in pilotage. Past, present and future.* Accident investigation board. Finland.

Norman, D. (2002). *The design of everyday things.* Basic Books.

Norman, D. (2010). *Living with complexity.* The MIT Press.

Perrow, C. (1984). *Normal accidents: living with high-risk technologies.* Princeton University Press.

Popper, K. (1934). *La logica della scoperta scientifica.*

Popper, K. (1969). *Scienza e filosofia. Problemi e scopi della scienza.* Einaudi.

Popper, K. (2004). *Il mito della cornice.* Edited by Mark Amadeus Notturno. Il Mulino.

Rasmussen, J. (1982). Human errors: a taxonomy for describing human malfunction in industrial installations. *Journal of occupational accidents n.4*, 311-33.

Rasmussen, J. (1983). Skills, Rules and Knowledge: signals, signs, symbols and other distinctions in human performance models. *IEEE Transactions: Systems, Man and Cybernetics. SMC-13*, 257-67.

Reason, J. (1990). *Human Error.* Cambridge University Press.

Reason, J. (1997). *Managing the risks of organisational accidents.* Ashgate.

Reason, J. (2008). *The human contribution. Unsafe acts, accidents and heroic recoveries.* Ashgate.

Risukhin, V. (2001). *Automation.* McGraw-Hill.

Silver, N. (2013). *The signal and the noise. The art and science of prediction.* Penguin Press.

Taleb, N. (2010). *The Black Swan. The impact of the highly improbable.* Penguin Press.

Thomas, M. (2012). *A Systematic review of the effectiveness of safety management systems.* Australian Transport Safety Bureau.

Whitehead, A. (1929). *The aims of education.* The free press.

Wilson, T. (1993). *Aircraft Human Performance and Limitations.* Civil Aviation Safety Authority Australia.

ACKNOWLEDGEMENTS

There are many years of my life in this book, which summarises and brings together all that I have learnt and understood about navigation safety. It has been a long, non-linear path that has passed through different phases.

It all started a few years ago in Almere at CSMART, *Carnival Corporation*'s training centre. This is where I met my friend and colleague Gabriele Petruzzelli, the instructor of the very first Bridge Resource Management course I had ever attended. I understood that behind all the topics discussed in the classroom and experienced in the simulator, there was a new world that I wanted to know and study in depth.

At CSMART I was welcomed with open arms as in a family. The two founders, Hans Hederström and Staffan Persson, supported my hunger for understanding this new (at least for me) navigational philosophy. Apart from the professional relationships, the entire time I spent in the Netherlands, Hans and his wife Lena treated me just like a son.

It is above all thanks to the trust Hans and Staffan placed in me that the research project conducted in cooperation with the Australian Maritime College was started. The research led to MOSA, a method for analysing the effectiveness of Bridge Resource Management on board cruise ships.

I also owe gratitude to David Christie, who believed in me and despite all his commitments as a senior manager at *Carnival Corporation*, found the time to take me to California to present the results of the research project to Princess Cruise's CEO. The success obtained from the highest levels of management would not have been possible without the precious collaboration of Marco Fortezze and Alistair Clark, two highly regarded captains of the entire Carnival fleet.

I could never thank Nick Lemon and Mahesh Alimchandani from the Australian Maritime Safety Authority enough, both for having supported the research project and for having taken me with them to the IMO meetings in

London. A unique opportunity to comprehend the decisional mechanisms at a regulatory level and to interact with world experts.

In Australia I also met Peter Listrup, Director of the Smartship training centre where I presently work as an instructor. I owe him my more recent professional development and particularly his accounts of Bridge Resource Management at *Star Cruises*.

Whereas it was Hans Hederström and Benny Pettersson who took me to Finland by sea on board one of the Silja Line ferries, to allow me to meet Captain Larjo. In Turku we found ourselves all chatting in a room for hours. I had so many questions I wanted to ask but the time just flew by. After that meeting I never stopped repeating the words of Captain Larjo during my courses in integrated navigation.

I would also like to thank the Australian Maritime Pilots for helping me understand their perspective and the challenges of their job.

Then there is Ravi Nijjer, who has been my mentor and has allowed me to enter into the Australian maritime world. He welcomed me into his study crammed with books, where he transmitted to me the "first principles" – as he calls them – of safety management. I will never forget the evenings spent philosophising on the most disparate topics, from the latest navigation techniques to Lord Jim and the elusiveness of the human condition. He dedicated long hours to review the book with me line by line. I feel like I wrote it on his behalf.

If Ravi Nijjer has been my guide along this path, my friend Francesco made it possible by introducing me to the philosophy of science and in helping me to understand what I was writing: a daring conjecture for the organisation of a modern bridge. Without that afternoon spent discussing Popper, Galileo and Descartes, I would never have managed to get out of the hole I had dug myself into.

And finally Roberta, my travel companion, who conducted the interviews injecting a lighter touch to all three parts of the book. But above all she endured my long absences and my absent-mindedness. I could never have done it without her.

CPSIA information can be obtained
at www.ICGtesting.com
Printed in the USA
LVHW081113090122
707934LV00024B/514